Taking Charge of Change

Also by Douglas K. Smith

The Wisdom of Teams

Fumbling the Future:
How Xerox Invented Then Ignored
the First Personal Computer

Sources of the African Past

METROPO̲

Taking Charge
OF Change

---

10 PRINCIPLES FOR MANAGING
PEOPLE AND PERFORMANCE

Douglas K. Smith

▲▼ *Addison-Wesley Publishing Company*

Reading, Massachusetts   Menlo Park, California   New York
Don Mills, Ontario   Wokingham, England   Amsterdam   Bonn
Sydney   Singapore   Tokyo   Madrid   San Juan
Paris   Seoul   Milan   Mexico City   Taipei

The illustrations appearing on pages 245 and 270 are reprinted from
The Wisdom of Teams, by John R. Katzenbach and Douglas K. Smith © 1993,
by permission of Harvard Business School Press.
Many of the designations used by manufacturers and sellers to distinguish their
products are claimed as trademarks. Where those designations appear in this
book and Addison-Wesley was aware of a trademark claim, the designations
have been printed in initial capital letters.

Library of Congress Cataloging–in–Publication Data
Smith, Douglas K., 1949–
    Taking charge of change : ten principles for managing people and
performance / Douglas K. Smith.
        p.   cm.
    Includes bibliographical references and index.
    ISBN 0-201-48408-0
    1. Organizational change—Management. 2. Personnel management.
3. Performance standards. 4. Work groups. I. Title.
    HD58.8.S637   1996
    658.3—dc20   95-32314
                                                                CIP

Jacket design by Andrew Newman
Text design by Diane Levy
Set in 11-point Century Expanded by Weimer Graphics, Indianapolis, IN

1 2 3 4 5 6 7 8 9-MA-0099989796
First printing, November 1995

Addison-Wesley books are available at special discounts for bulk purchases
by corporations, institutions, and other organizations. For more information,
please contact the Corporate, Government, and Special Sales Department,
Addison-Wesley Publishing Company, One Jacob Way, Reading, MA 01867,
1-800-238-9682.

To Jennifer, Julia, Lynn, Nancy and the Rockport Seven,
for sharing an aspiration

Contents

Acknowledgments

My sincere thanks go to all of the people who have shared with me their struggles and triumphs during periods of fundamental change. Without their collaboration, the management principles, strategies, and visions discussed in this book would not have emerged. All of them were pioneers; all discovered the risks and responsibilities associated with truly taking responsibility for change.

Thanks also go to Bill Patrick, Ellie McCarthy, Tiffany Cobb, and their colleagues at Addison-Wesley for their enthusiasm and support. I am indebted to Susan Thornton Rogers for her invaluable help designing the illustrations. In addition, I would like to thank Carol Amore, Charles Baum, Bill Brennan, Chris Cappy, Obie Charlap, Paul Chung, Megan Cogswell, Paul Cohen, Tom Curren, Steve Dichter, Jan Dillon, Jenna Dorn, Jim Emshoff, Carol Franco, Rita Fritz and The Three Amigos, Ron Gervais, Don Gogel, Joy Harris, Jan Hillier, Jon Katzenbach, Margaret Lera, Jud Linville, Christina Macy, Mark Maletz, Ann Matthews, Bill Morin, Cheryl Ramirez, Nancy Reardon, Rick Rogers, Jim Rosenthal, Kurt Schmoke, Bob Sicina, Bill Taylor, and Jeff Weiss.

Finally, thanks to Alena and Eben, who in their own ways reminded me about the importance of deadlines, and to Jane for her help in meeting them.

Introduction

▶ **Headline:** "Many Companies Try Management Fads, Only to See Them Flop," trumpets the *Wall Street Journal.*

▶ **Caution:** "Most organizations that undertake a reengineering effort do not achieve the dramatic results they intended," write Michael Hammer and James Champy in *Reengineering the Corporation.*

▶ **Statistics:** Studies consistently report that *no more than a fifth to a third* of the reengineering, total quality, core competencies, downsizing, learning organizations, strategies, and other significant new programs monitored achieve their performance aspirations.

This book is dedicated to you and your colleagues who must change your skills, behaviors, and ways of working with one another if you are to continue playing a valuable and meaningful role in your organization. I believe far more of you than ever can meet this challenge successfully. You can learn how to

▶ deliver both team and individual performance within and across both functions and processes

▶ coach others as well as command them

▶ take direction while still managing yourself

- perform while simultaneously changing the skills, behaviors, and working relationships necessary to that performance
- lead hundreds and even thousands of people who must transform the way they provide value to customers, beneficiaries, shareholders, and other critical constituencies.

I believe most of you can succeed because, deep down, you already know that you have no choice. You are only looking for reliable guidance on how to grapple with change yourself and how to lead others through change. Begin by facing up to the headlines and statistics of most fundamental change efforts to date. *Up to 80 percent of those efforts have failed.* Far more people have emerged as losers instead of winners from the storms of change raging inside organizations, disappointing not only themselves but also their families and friends. A tremendous number have joined the ranks of the unemployed and the underemployed without learning new and different ways to add value. And more will follow, possibly including you and your colleagues, unless the required skills, behaviors, and working relationships are mastered.

We must ask "Why?" In my view, and, I suggest, your experience, the blunt answer is that far too many of you fail because you are unsure about *how* to manage through the period of change itself. How, for example, can you hope to change your own skills, behaviors, and working relationships if you delude yourself into believing that someone else, some "they" out there—the head of another function, the board of directors, the middle managers, the sales force, the front-line workers, the suppliers, the CEO—is responsible for *your* behavior change? And, since new behaviors take time to learn, how can you take responsibility for your own change and simultaneously do your job without following some set of principles for managing your purpose, time, and effort?

Moreover, how can you, as a leader of change at any level of the organization, help other people take responsibility for change if you continue to ignore the profound difference between managing *real* performance, *real* work, and the *real* people who must change versus managing—important as they are—*theories* of performance such as strategy, *theories* of work such as organization charts and core competencies, and *theories* of skill and behavior change such as culture? How can you lead others who must both perform and change unless you adhere to a set of principles to sustain the courage to perform and change yourself?

My central purpose in writing this book, then, is to share with you a perspective and set of management principles that will substantially improve your odds of learning new skills and behaviors in organization settings. As you will see, my philosophy arises from a series of unshakable convictions:

▶ *Only* **people** *change skills, behaviors, and relationships, and only in the real work that they do.* Not systems or strategies or structures. Not visions or cultures or processes. People. Shifts in organization direction and design can help people grapple with change, particularly if they articulate models for *how people can work* to deliver value to customers. But new directions and designs help only when the people who must change behaviors engage in understanding and shaping them. Until managers enlist people to perform and change in the context of real work, elements of organization direction and design as well as discussions about them remain, like quicksand, no better than the illusion of change.

▶ *No one—not a boss, not a subordinate, not a supplier, not a customer—can take responsibility for another person's behavior change.* Each of us must choose to act for ourselves. Yes, the vast majority of people—you, me, and nearly everyone else—are reluctant to take personal responsibility for change. Change scares us. Yet, unless and until enough of us do take responsibility for our own change, neither performance nor change will happen.

▶ *Most of us change skills, behaviors, and working relationships best when concrete and specific performance consequences depend on our doing so.* Performance consequences give us something to focus on. They give us something to *do*, some motivation and measure of control during a period otherwise fraught with anxiety and apprehension. And the more control over the process of change that any of us feels, the more willing we are to experience change itself. If you aspire to manage through a period of change, therefore, you must learn how to transform reluctance into action and action into change by paying direct attention to the people and performance consequences that matter most.

So who are "you"? You are anyone in your organization confronted by the challenge of learning new and different ways of adding value to performance. You may be a frontline employee who must learn the philosophy and practices of total quality, continuous improvement, or customer service. You may have functional skills in finance, sales, marketing, research, engineering, or another discipline that you now must learn to contribute in team settings. You may be a middle manager who must learn to coach and counsel as well as command others in their work. You may be charged with reengineering a basic process of the organization. You may be a senior executive who needs to shift one or more core competencies of the enterprise in order to ensure continued excellence. And you may be the CEO, managing director, or executive director whose vision and hopes rest on leading a transformation of the entire enterprise.

In other words, you may be any number of people in any number of positions who are faced with the task of changing your own behaviors or managing change in others as the price of continued personal and organizational success. A significant number of you face such challenges today. If, for example, you are part of a government organization that is trying to reinvent itself, then you and your colleagues must learn new skills and behaviors. Perhaps you work for a charitable organization that must learn sophisticated marketing techniques to survive financially. Or, instead, you may work for a company in the private sector that, as a consequence of changes in technology, market structure, government policy, innovation, or competitive inroads, faces the challenge of fundamental, broad-based behavior change.

Whatever the particulars of your situation, because fundamental change will test *your* organization and *your* role, you will feel as no one else can the range of emotions from anxiety through exhilaration that any meaningful experience with change entails. It is not my purpose, then, to presume that I can predict or describe the exact number or sequence of thoughts, actions, and emotions you must employ in your own peculiar context. However, I have spent many years thinking about and managing broad-based behavior change. Over that time, I have participated in or observed scores of organizations and thousands of people going through periods of turmoil and transformation. Several major lessons have emerged that I intend to share with you throughout the book. Let me highlight some of them so that you know what to expect.

▶ *The leaders who make the biggest difference in today's organizations are those who, regardless of job or level, figure out how to manage people through the period of change itself.* Most of us already can describe the skills, behaviors, and working relationships needed to succeed in the rest of the 1990s and beyond. Yes, we need leaders with vision who can inspire us with the credibility and attractiveness of some future state. But too many of those visions will remain empty of all but aspiration unless and until we find leaders—*at all levels of the organization*—who can guide people through the period of learning and change necessary to accomplish the specific performance challenges implied by the visions themselves.

▶ *Resistance to change is used too often as an excuse for failure rather than a motive force for success.* Neither you nor I nor most people embrace behavior change on a regular basis. In fact, most of us don't like it at all—especially if it threatens our economic security and well-being. This natural reluctance, however, also constitutes a powerful potential force in favor of change—when we come to believe change is necessary. When we and others know in our hearts and minds that we *must* change, few of us steadfastly resist. In fact, the majority of us succeed. It is ignorance about the underlying nature of our reluctance and what to do about it, and not the reluctance itself, that kills change in people and organizations.

▶ *Behavior and skill change in organizations must be managed directly.* No one can change another person's behaviors or skills;

adults must learn for themselves. But many adults will fail unless you or someone is *directly managing* their efforts to change. Unfortunately, a notion sprung up several years ago and spread like a weed that people could learn only in democratic workplaces that had been liberated from all managerial direction and dictate. That is nonsense. In fact, far too many people today are stalled in their path toward change because their managers refuse or don't know how to manage change itself. Instead of creating a context that promotes both performance and change, such managers produce a vacuum that nature fills with failure, frustration, and more business as usual. People do need solution space in which to learn new ways of doing things. But they also need and benefit tremendously from managers who give them direction, opportunity, and energy.

▶ *In the absence of compelling performance challenges, people neither learn nor change how they work.* The first magic moment in any person's path toward change comes when he or she is *compelled* by the connection between that change and his or her performance at work. Until then, change remains only so much talk. Consider, for example, how rarely any of us ponder the skill of walking a straight line; yet, how quickly we focus on it when asked by a police officer to step out of our car. Threatening circumstances and challenges compel both performance and change much more effectively than mere opportunities and good intentions. But today's opportunities become tomorrow's threats in the competitive world of organizations. A compelling performance consequence can always be found, if only you choose to find, communicate, and manage toward it.

▶ *The three words most valuable to behavior and skill challenges are "both/and" and "we"; the three most pernicious are "either/or" and "they."* All of the capabilities of the high-performance organization of the 1990s and beyond reflect a "both/and" view of the world. Relative to ten years ago, we now understand that organizations cannot rely on "either/or" choices about the basis for their strategy (low cost or high value), or the focus of performance (shareholder wealth or customers or employees). Today, success demands that organizations deliver customers *both* high value *and* low cost through organizational capabilities of *both* speed *and* scale as well as *both* functional *and* cross-functional ("process") excellence. That, in turn, requires people throughout the organization to know *both* how to make the decisions previously reserved only to managers *and* to do the real work previously assigned only to the front lines. Today, we all must *both* think *and* do, and we must do so in a context increasingly dependent on *both* individual *and* mutual accountability. Unfortunately, nearly a century of organizational behavior and habit continue to favor the either/or characterization of decisions and actions—an orientation that cuts the legs out from under the collaboration and risk taking necessary to behavior and skill changes.

"We" must make these changes. Only "we" can tackle the specific performance challenges that provide us the crucible to learn and change. "They" cannot do this for us. If "we" wait for "them" to come up with yet one more way of articulating the strategy or set of desired cultural characteristics or new reporting relationships or ways of compensating us, "we" are only wasting time and opportunity. Correspondingly, leaders of change do not treat people as some abstract "they" from whom buy-in is needed. No, that kind of "they" conveys the mind-set of business as usual. Change leaders are part of the "we" who know deep in our hearts that only "we"—and no one else—can make performance and change happen.

▸ *Managing* both *performance results* and *broad-based behavior change is different from and more difficult than managing performance alone.* Managing organizations to perform under any circumstances is a tough challenge. But when the skills, behaviors, and working relationships of many *existing* employees must change to sustain or revitalize performance, the manager's job fundamentally differs from what it was before. Over most of the twentieth century, organizations worried about choosing and seizing growth opportunities through adding capacity and people. Private enterprise grew this way. So did government organizations and major charitable organizations. The objective with regard to people was finding the best way to get many new people to learn what the existing people were already very good at, namely the existing skills, behaviors, and working relationships. Today, by contrast, the challenge is to learn how to get existing and new people, at all levels, to learn new skills, behaviors, and relationships. This shift profoundly affects the job of management. No longer can managers make the best strategic and organization choices without worrying about the capabilities or readiness of people to implement those choices. And no longer can they safely equate the *decisions* they make with implementation and change itself.

▶ *Because of the risks involved in managing broad-based behavior change, any other path to sustainable performance is preferable.* Managers have many choices for improving performance. Mergers, acquisitions, strategic alliances, pricing, new product introductions, purchasing economies, cost reductions, and other choices might sustain performance and competitive advantage. In addition, managers often can build organizational skills by hiring new people instead of getting existing people to learn and change. None of those choices is easy. But experience suggests that such choices are more likely to succeed in a timely and effective manner than trying to shift performance based on many existing people learning new and different skills and behaviors. Of course, in most organizations of any size or scope today, sustainable performance depends on finding the best blend of non-behavior-driven choices as well as those that depend for their success on many existing people learning new ways of working.

▶ *A discipline built on proven managerial principles can help more people and more organizations successfully meet the challenge of both performance and broad-based behavior change.* The principles identified and explained in this book can make you a much better manager of behavior and skill change than you are today. They will not teach you anything specific about total quality, reengineering, continuous improvement, supplier partnering, mass customization, time-based competition, core competencies, or other particular techniques for improving organization performance. Nor will they instruct you about specific strategic, organizational, or operational choices peculiar to your own organization. But to the extent that any of these initiatives and choices depend on many people from top to bottom and all across your organization learning new skills, behaviors, and working relationships, success or failure will turn on how well you and others follow the discipline set forth here.

A GUIDE TO READING THE BOOK

The book explores how you can take charge throughout the period of change. It is divided into three parts. Part 1 asks you to think very differently about the principles you use to manage performance and change in yourself and others. Chapter 1 describes why traditional managerial approaches fall short when performance results depend on broad-based, behavior-driven change. It also introduces you to the ten new management principles critical to meeting the behavior-driven performance and change challenges you face.

Chapter 2 helps you avoid the mistake of equating hesitation and anxiety with determined resistance to change. Few of you enjoy the prospect of behavior change. But you can do a better job of managing yourselves and others through the period of change by understanding and responding to the sources of reluctance identified in Chapter 2. In particular, as Chapter 3 explores, you will manage change best when you use specific performance objectives and the actual experience of change to respond to reluctance and anxiety. A focus on performance results helps you connect inspirational vision and purpose to the new skills and behaviors needed to attain them. A performance orientation also helps you muster the courage to change because, as Chapter 4 asserts, your leadership must arise from living the change you wish to bring about.

Part 2 assists you in shaping and improvising strategies for leading performance and change initiatives. Chapter 5 provides you the diagnostic tools to determine whether the performance results of any particular initiative depend on broad-based, behavior-driven change. If broad-based behavior change is not required for performance, you can rely on traditional managerial principles for success. If, however, you face a performance and change effort, then Chapters 6, 7, and 8 introduce you to the strategies you can use to continually increase the number of people joining you in taking responsibility for change.

No organization transforms itself on the back of a single initiative. Part 3 discusses how you can use vision to lead entire organizations through change. Chapter 9 reviews the importance of articulating a vision of what the future holds and why. Importantly, however, Chapter 9 also demands that you form a vision of how to combine multiple initiatives, meaningful language, new organization designs, and personal actions to create and focus the energy that organizations need to get through periods of profound change. Chapter 10 insists that you use performance consequences to guide your basic organization design choices, and it describes the disciplines you must follow to ensure that those new designs focus on work instead of power struggles and decision-making authority. Finally, Chapter 11 asserts that none of you—no matter how senior—has learned all the skills and behaviors you need to meet today's performance and change realities. It challenges you, as a leader, to make change as personal an experience for yourself as it is for others.

Behavior change is best accomplished through repetitive experiences, especially in performance contexts that matter. It is a cyclical, iterative phenomenon in which you return to the same insights over and over again, each time with a deeper, more nuanced appreciation. I have structured the book to give you a similar experience, particularly with respect to the ten new management principles. Thus, please note that I discuss the principles throughout the book, not just in Part 1. Because of the way the ten principles work as a whole managerial discipline, I did not mechanically dedicate a separate chapter to each principle. They reinforce and elicit one another and, therefore, provide the common thread running throughout the book.

In light of this, you might choose to read (or reread) the book in different ways. You could, for example, start with Chapter 5 to determine whether the specific challenge you now face requires the ten new management principles. If you are primarily interested in the challenge of leadership, you might begin with Chapters 11 and/or 4. If you want to figure out a specific strategy for getting other people to commit to change, you might focus on Chapters 6 and 7. Or, if you are interested in exploring the powerful role of energy, effort, and new meaningful visions and language, you might begin with Chapter 9. Finally, if you have questions about organization design, you should look to Chapter 10.

In whatever order you read the book, however, I suggest you will gain the most through a posture of reflection instead of memorization. Self-discovery lies at the heart of changing skills and behaviors. The more you reflect on what you read here against your own challenges and experiences, the more you will cast the principles, strategies, and visions into your own set of insights and understanding. That is a good thing. Worry far less about memorizing the specific way I articulate the ten new management principles, for example, than about making their underlying meaning relevant and useful to you.

Finally, the book also exposes you to the experience of change through a number of stories of people grappling with behavior-driven challenges. All the stories are real, although some are disguised. (I indicate disguised names of companies and people with quotation marks the first time they are mentioned.) The stories span the private, nonprofit, and government sectors of the economy. Naturally, there are important differences in one sector versus another. For example, because the division of responsibilities in government organizations is often written into law and the legislators who might amend them have no accountability for performance, managing behavior-driven change in the government sector can pose unique dilemmas. However, *people* are at the heart of all performance and change challenges. And people do not respond fundamentally differently to the challenge of change by virtue of where they happen to work. The discipline for taking charge of change described in this book applies to all economic sectors.

The most important story, of course, is yours. In sharing the management principles, tools, and experiences of others, I hope to provoke you to *think hard and creatively* about your challenge and then to *act*. Much of what you read here will be new; some will not. But all of it demands that you rebalance your effort away from abstractions such as strategies, designs, and decisions in favor of keeping performance as the primary objective of change and relentlessly enlisting the people whose behavior and skill changes matter most. I am convinced that if you do practice the principles set forth in this book, you will learn the skills, behaviors, and working relationships required for performance in the rest of the 1990s and beyond. You will emerge as the kind of leader on whom all of us—and all of our organizations—most depend as we move into the third millennium. And there will be far more happy endings to the change stories now unfolding every day.

PART 1

PRINCIPLES

THE MANAGEMENT PRINCIPLES

1. *Keep performance results the primary objective of behavior and skill change.*

2. *Continually increase the number of individuals taking responsibility for their own change.*

3. *Ensure each person always knows why his or her performance and change matters to the purpose and results of the whole organization.*

4. *Put people in a position to learn by doing and provide them the information and support needed just in time to perform.*

5. *Embrace improvisation as the best path to both performance and change.*

6. *Use team performance to drive change whenever demanded.*

7. *Concentrate organization designs on the work people do, not the decision-making authority they have.*

8. *Create and focus energy and meaningful language because they are the scarcest resources during periods of change.*

9. *Stimulate and sustain behavior-driven change by harmonizing initiatives throughout the organization.*

10. *Practice leadership based on the courage to live the change you wish to bring about.*

*T*oday's most urgent performance challenges demand that you learn how to manage people through a period of change. You already know you must have a vision for what the organization will be like after change has been mastered. But such visions are not enough. People facing change need more than an understanding of the end of their journey. They need guidance about how to make the journey itself.

To provide that guidance, you must adopt a new set of management principles. Traditional managerial approaches do not work because they assume that most people already possess most of the capabilities required for performance. As a result, managers can safely focus on making wise decisions. The implementation of those decisions, however, eludes organizations when lots of existing people—from top to bottom and all across—must learn new behaviors and ways of working. In addition to making decisions, then, you must apply managerial principles that tightly link performance, behavior change, and responsibility.

Each of us must take responsibility for our own behavior change. No one else can do it for us. Yet most of us are reluctant to change when doing so risks a loss of economic security, friendship, self-esteem, and sense of purpose. Thus most of us are likeliest to take personal responsibility for change if specific performance consequences—for ourselves, our colleagues, our customers, our shareholders, and others—depend on it. Only then will we risk experiencing change itself. And the direct experience of change is far more powerful than decisions about strategy or organization in helping us overcome our reluctance to change. Indeed, without specific performance consequences, most of us quickly grow cynical. We believe managers are promoting change for the sake of change.

Maintaining an unrelenting focus on people, performance, and change, however, demands courage. When the mechanistic organization gives way to the profoundly human challenge of broad-based behavior-driven change, managers can no longer rely on traditional sources of authority or the power of decisions. In addition to learning new skills themselves and putting their own performance at risk, those who would lead people through a period of change must discover *new, solid ground for their authority over others. That takes courage. You and others can find that courage in the ten management principles that have made the difference time and again between success and failure. You can find courage by focusing relentlessly on performance and people. Most important, you can find courage within yourself by living the change you wish to bring about.*

Chapter One

Getting Through the Period of Change

In the wake of unrelenting change surging through the private, government, and not-for-profit sectors, today's most urgent leadership challenge has shifted. If you aspire to lead, you should not spend the bulk of your time convincing yourself and others why fundamental change is happening. You and they already know why. You also should avoid consuming yourself in describing the cultural characteristics of winning organizations, or the desired skills, behaviors, and working relationships of people in them. You and your colleagues already know these things, too. The balance and focus of your efforts must move. You must now take charge of change by managing yourself and others through the period of change, using management principles specifically designed to address the conditions and challenges of change itself.

The management principles you have been using don't work. And why should they? As the failure rate among organizations and people demonstrates, managing existing employees and executives who must *simultaneously learn new capabilities and deliver performance* is profoundly different from managing people who *already have the capabilities* needed for the challenge at hand. In the more familiar case, your success turns on making good decisions and then relying on technical and functional managerial expertise to guide those asked to implement them. But that won't work when neither you nor the people you lead have the skills, behaviors, and working relationships needed for performance. Sure, part of the new management answer lies in articulating why change is necessary and what the desired changes look like. But seeing the top of the mountain and climbing the mountain are different. Change, as they say, is a journey. Wouldn't it help to learn a set of principles for guiding yourself and others while on that journey? I say yes, because unless you figure out *how* to lead people through the period of change, all of the visions and strategies, all of the hopes and dreams, of your organizations will ring hollow—if they ring at all.

You Already Know Why Change Is Happening

You already know that you and your organization are on a collision course with the forces of change. Consider, for example, the following:

‣ *Technology.* Generic information, telecommunications, and transportation technologies as well as more specialized technologies (e.g., energy, biology, electronics) make it possible for almost any organization to fundamentally rethink the value of its products and services, the way it goes about delivering that value to customers and at what cost, and the markets it chooses to compete in. Substitute the word "beneficiaries" for "customers" and the same impact of technology applies to organizations in the public and not-for-profit sectors. What your organization makes, how you make it, whom you compete against, and whom you seek to serve—technology puts *everything* in play.

‣ *Demographics.* Organizations do not exist in a vacuum. Consider the implications of women joining the for-pay workforce over the past fifteen years; the multiethnic and cultural character of "workforce 2000"; the incidence of family breakups; crime, drug and alcohol abuse; the coexistence in the marketplace of the ultraskilled (e.g., those who are computer literate) and the nonskilled (e.g., those who cannot read or do simple math); and the shifting, unpredictable role and power of unions. In many organizations around the world, the people who show up for work just don't bring the same predictable habits, values, attitudes, and expectations they once did. Yes, most still believe in the basic work contract of reward for effort. Beyond that, however, labor markets are no longer a simple matter of distinguishing between white and blue collars.

▶ *Government policy.* Widespread disenchantment with social welfare and economic management policies has put in question what governments will and will not do (e.g., privatization) as well as how they will do it (e.g., deregulation and reregulation). With each shift come new opportunities and threats for affected organizations. Meanwhile, and perhaps most subtly, the language and apparatus of legally oriented democracies increasingly influence how your organization operates even in the absence of explicit government pressure (e.g., diversity, sexual harassment, drug and alcohol abuse, consumer protection, and notions of due process and fairness).

▶ *Financial markets.* Capital is not the scarce resource it once was. Yes, access to capital is neither free nor assured. But in contrast with twenty or forty or a hundred years ago, the world is awash in funds and managers of those funds looking for opportunities—across all industries, companies, geographies, cultures, and generations—to provide investors with superior returns. Consequently, competitive barriers to entry and exit fall with greater rapidity than ever before, putting organizations with internal orientations at high risk of competitive threat and failure.

Although you or others might categorize or describe this list differently, the basic story remains the same, in terms of both opportunity and threat. If *mastered*, such forces can reduce the cost base of what you do while simultaneously increasing the speed and quality with which you respond to customers or beneficiaries. If *understood*, ever mutating variations in what customers and beneficiaries need offer a never-ending source of opportunity. If *embraced*, the economic and emotional rewards of individual and collective human enterprise can be yours. However, as you now deeply appreciate, the same forces will—if *ignored* or *mismanaged*—downsize, demoralize, and defeat both you and your organizations.

You Already Know
What Your Organization Must Do

You also already know how to articulate the shifts your organization must make to master change. Whatever sector your organization participates in—private, government, nonprofit—you know success depends on abandoning the organization-as-machine archetype that dominated thought and action for most of this century. It has been several years since I have heard *anyone*—from any part of any organization—defend the pure "machine" and "command and control" approach. And it never takes more than thirty minutes or so for any group of people—again from any part of any organization—to distinguish the attributes of losers from those of winners. You know that your organization must continue to move

1. *FROM* believing *people are cogs* in a machine to be used and controlled *TO* believing *people are people* who can and must provide the basis for competitive differentiation and success

2. *FROM* relying solely on *individual* accountability and performance *TO* relying on both *individual and team* accountability and performance

3. *FROM* continuously searching for the perfect *division* of labor to make all people *specialists TO* balancing the need for both the *division and integration* of labor by people who are both *specialists and generalists*

4. *FROM* betting on *functional* excellence alone *TO* betting on both *functional and process* excellence

5. *FROM* focusing *internally* on the *boss TO* focusing *externally* on the *customer*

6. *FROM* organizing in *vertical, rigid hierarchies* around *decision* flows *TO* organizing in *horizontal, flexible networks* around *work* flows

7. *FROM* employing information and communications technology to *police* and *control* people *TO* employing information and communications technology to *inform* and *enable* people

8. *FROM* asking managers to be *overseers of uncooperative and adversarial subordinates* *TO* asking managers to be *leaders of involved and committed people*

9. *FROM* showing up at work knowing that your only organizational purpose is to *make money for shareholders* and your only personal purpose is to *get paid* *TO* showing up at work knowing that your purpose is to work with your colleagues to *delight customers, grow* as a person, and *ensure the financial success* of you and your enterprise

You Already Know
You and Your Colleagues Must Change

Finally, you also already know that the "to" side of winning organizational characteristics depends on the ability and willingness of lots and lots of people, including you and your colleagues, to learn new skills, behaviors, and working relationships. Moreover, you can describe the changes quite well:

▶ *Frontline employees* in sales, marketing, research, engineering, manufacturing, customer service, back-office operations, and elsewhere need to learn the problem-solving, decision-making, teamwork, and interpersonal skills necessary to both self-management and team performance. They must learn as many technical and functional skills as possible instead of relying only on specialized roles. They must learn to be good team leaders. They must learn the skills and perspectives required to identify and continuously improve key work processes. And they must learn how to engage their bosses and others in solving problems for customers, whether internal or external.

▶ *Middle managers* must learn how to be good coaches and team leaders as well as decision makers and delegators. They must learn how to share information effectively and how to take risks. They too must get comfortable with as many technical and functional skills as possible as well as with the skills and perspectives necessary to identify and continuously improve key work processes. They need to learn how to distinguish team performance challenges from individual challenges and acquire the problem-solving, decision-making, teamwork, and interpersonal skills needed for both. They need to learn how to engage both their bosses and their subordinates in identifying and solving problems for customers, whether internal or external.

▸ *People in staff roles* such as finance, planning, audit, human resources, and legal need to learn how to gain conformance to needed policies and directions by means in addition to policing people. They too need to learn the problem-solving, decision-making, teamwork, and interpersonal skills necessary to both team and individual performance. They need to learn how to perform as facilitators who guide others toward self-discovery as well as experts who provide the answers. And they need to learn how to add value to the performance of their enterprise, and to hold themselves accountable for doing so.

▸ *Senior managers and executives* must continue to understand what constitutes excellent functional performance and how to deliver it themselves or get others to deliver it. In addition, they must learn what constitutes excellent process performance and how to deliver it themselves or engage others to do so. They must continue to understand how to use fact-based problem solving in support of tough-minded decision making, delegation, monitoring, and evaluation. In addition, they must learn to distinguish individual performance challenges from team challenges, and learn the different disciplines required by each. They must learn how to make clear performance demands on people, and then empower and hold those people accountable. They must learn how to identify and remove obstacles to performance. They must learn how to use their own time, attention, and behavior in support of communicating direction and purpose. They must learn how to tell the truth and listen.

You know that these changes in skills, behaviors, and working relationships are today's fuel of organization change and performance.

No organization can be fast or flexible if managers do not inspire people to join the "we" who will make performance and change happen instead of treating people as untrustworthy cogs to be controlled. No organization can deliver both functional and process excellence if people, within and across all levels and functions, do not learn the skills and working relationships necessary to team performance, or if the majority of people fail to become generalists with multiple skills while retaining special competencies. And no organization can achieve any meaningful aspirations if one or more of its key constituencies— customers, employees, shareholders—remain alienated because people at all levels do not explicitly balance the needs among them.

YOU ARE NOT AS CERTAIN ABOUT *HOW*

Your most critical leadership challenge has shifted. It no longer lies in using your time and effort to make choices about what to change or in further articulating the differences between the "to" of where you are headed versus the "from" of where you are now. No, today's most significant test is in learning how to manage yourselves *through* the period of change itself—learning, in other words, how to get *from the "from" to the "to."*

Compare this novel management challenge with those dominating most of the twentieth century. Traditionally, managers worried about growth or decline. They concentrated on choosing and seizing growth opportunities through adding capacity and people as well as pointing capable people in new directions. Or, faced with recession or adversity, managers worked to reduce assets and lay people off with minimum damage to the enterprise. Corporations, especially large and successful ones, grew and shrunk this way. So did government organizations and major charitable organizations. Collectively, these opportunities and threats posed four main concerns for leaders:

▶ *Managing assets and policies apart from people.* Many performance tests turned on how well leaders dealt with assets and policies instead of people. Mergers and acquisitions, inventory and working capital, pricing, scale economies, lobbying, union negotiations, plant consolidations, centralization and decentralization of resources— those and other initiatives did much to determine the size and sustainability of any organization's performance. Change? Yes. But it was neither broad based nor deeply *behavioral* in character.

▶ *Positioning capable employees against new opportunities.* Which markets to compete in, geographic expansion, finding new and different distribution channels, product positioning, product line expansion, service and product line profitability, pricing, cost cutting, and organizing people effectively dominated the agendas of leaders seeking to exploit the *existing* capabilities and working relationships of their people. Again, decisions like these implied change. But they were changes in direction and role, not fundamental skills, behaviors, or working relationships.

▶ *Finding and getting new people to learn what existing people were already very good at.* Many growth opportunities depended on doing more of the same work versus doing the same work differently. People had to change and learn. But those people were *new* employees who had to learn skills, behaviors, and working relationships already known in the organization. Unlike today, the people who had to change had plenty of expert teachers to guide them.

▶ *Reducing the workforce with minimum damage to morale and competitiveness.* Managers have also had to deal with adversity and failure. Even before downsizing became a popular euphemism, managers went through cycles requiring them to fire small and large numbers of people. This involved change. But the test was to treat the losers humanely while maintaining morale among the survivors as opposed to today's challenge of asking people to learn new ways of working even while they and you fear the possibility of job loss.

In confronting challenges like these, managers could rely on their expertise and experience to sustain their confidence and that of their subordinates. The good news is that many of today's performance challenges still fit within those four categories. When you face them, you can and should continue to use the time-honored managerial approaches that you know well and can rely on to work.

But, as you also know, the more difficult challenges you now face are quite different. They depend on getting existing people to learn new skills, behaviors, and working relationships so that the organization can become very good at something new and different. As often as not, they also require you as a manager to learn ways of working that are not part of your experience or expertise. Thus, in considering how to manage people through such change, I suggest that the place to look for help—and for a new foundation for managerial confidence—is *not* in the practices and approaches relevant to managing assets instead of people, managing decisions that depend on existing capabilities, or managing new people who must learn established skills. Instead, you must adopt a new set of management principles specifically directed at the challenge of broad-based behavior-driven performance and change. Indeed, as the following story about "Iberian Motors" illustrates, failure to adopt a different managerial approach produces neither performance nor change.

"IBERIAN MOTORS": FACING THE CHALLENGE OF DELIVERING SUPERIOR CUSTOMER SERVICE

Iberian Motors was a two-family-controlled distributor of industrial equipment with exclusive licenses to represent several foreign manufacturers in Spain and Portugal. Iberian's business was the result of government regulation. Both Spain and Portugal prohibited foreign manufacturers from directly distributing or selling their products. Instead, such manufacturers were required to make exclusive distribution arrangements with local Spanish and Portuguese companies.

The two families—one Spanish and one Portuguese—founded Iberian Motors to take advantage of these laws. Over the years, they built a network of local dealerships and warehouses to sell equipment and provide service and repairs. By the late 1980s, both families were wealthy, with the value of Iberian Motors estimated at between $500 million and $1 billion.

When the European Economic Community moved toward creating a single, open European market in the late 1980s, a shadow fell over Iberian's business. If Spain or Portugal permitted direct distribution by foreign manufacturers, the value of the two families' franchise could diminish significantly.

Iberian Motors executives could argue persuasively why foreign manufacturers should continue existing arrangements even in the absence of government requirements. First, any foreign company would have to make a sizable investment to duplicate Iberian's infrastructure of dealerships, warehouses, and maintenance and repair services. Second, Iberian Motors had decades of experience and knowledge about the equipment sales, service, and repair needs of local business customers. Third, the customers themselves were familiar with Iberian. Why would they switch?

Not surprisingly, though, many customers easily answered this last question. Iberian Motors was a monopoly. Like all monopolies, it had focused more on producing wealth for the owners than on delivering value to customers. New equipment deliveries and even simple replacement parts and repairs often took months to complete instead of weeks, days, or hours. Although most employees believed they provided good, reliable service, they *behaved* as if they were allocators of scarce resources to lucky customers instead of maximizers of customer satisfaction. Executives at Iberian feared, in the words of one, "Most of our customers really *don't like us.*"

Iberian Motors had enough time to fix these problems. Neither the Spanish nor the Portuguese government had yet acted. Furthermore, even if the markets were opened, it would take time for foreign manufacturers to decide whether to enter. Iberian executives as well as key family members believed they could persuade enough manufacturers to choose against direct entry so long as Iberian Motors could prove that it provided *superior customer service at lower cost* than any manufacturer could do alone.

Doing so, Iberian's leaders knew, would require a period of broad-based behavior change because

- The company had to become very good at both total customer service and managing superior value delivery at low cost, neither of which Iberian Motors was any good at then.
- Many *existing* employees throughout Iberian Motors had to learn specific new skills, behaviors, and working relationships, even if the company were to hire some new blood.
- Iberian Motors had no track record of delivering superior performance while simultaneously shifting the basis for that performance to new skills and behaviors.
- Many people throughout Iberian Motors—from top to bottom and all across—lacked a clear understanding of what had to change and/or felt little to no sense of urgency that they must make it happen.

Convinced of the seriousness of this challenge, Iberian's Managing Director, with the support of both families, asked a team of twelve senior executives to take on three critical initiatives:

1. Design and implement a dealer management approach that would help dealers change from acting like resource allocators to focusing on satisfying customers at a profit.
2. Find a better way to provide service and repairs.
3. Build a culture of total customer service and quality throughout the company.

When the twelve executives gathered, they acknowledged the need for new levels of performance. Each was as anxious as the families and the Managing Director about the opening of their markets. Rumors, they said, had begun circulating that the families were negotiating the sale of the company. The Managing Director assured them the rumors were false. But that didn't dispel an atmosphere of growing uncertainty, even among the twelve executives. Several team members wanted an explicit promise from the families that they would never sell. Others argued that, unless the families lowered their profit expectations, Iberian could never change. All in all, they had a good, candid discussion. Having aired their concerns, however, the twelve agreed to do their best to produce a set of recommendations for changing the company. They decided to split into subgroups around each of the three initiatives, and went to work.

The Dealer Initiative. The leaders of the dealer initiative quickly identified the people whose skills and behaviors had to change: dealers, dealers' direct reports, and the region heads to whom dealers reported. The team had strong ideas about how the dealers and the dealers' direct reports should change. To avoid the bad habit of acting like resource allocators, both groups needed to add skills in marketing, sales, and customer service to their already strong operations and cost orientations. The dealers had to become good general managers—good local business men and women—who knew how to balance multiple and competing perspectives. Finally, the team also believed the dealers had to alter the working relationship with their direct reports from command and control to collaboration and teamwork.

The team suspected that most dealers and their direct reports would resist making these changes. In fact, they believed only one dealer—Jose Munoz—stood out as a forward thinker and doer who would champion change. Six others were so close to retirement that the group believed they would never change. The remaining eighteen were likely to resist for a variety of reasons. Some would refuse to believe the governments would open the markets, some believed they already were very good business people, and some were unlikely to take any action without a lot of explicit direction from above. All would question the seriousness of the families and top management in making these changes, and all would point out that annual budgets, plans, and compensation arrangements continued to focus on profit, not market share or customer service. Finally, in the opinion of the initiative leaders, none of the dealers except Jose Munoz was comfortable with the notion of working more collaboratively with direct reports.

To better understand how people might react, the team decided to conduct one-on-one interviews with two dozen dealers and dealers' direct reports. They were surprised to discover that most people had a much better appreciation for how Iberian might respond success-fully to the threat of open markets than the team originally expected. They also confirmed the need for significant changes in customer service, marketing, sales, and general management skills as well as more collaborative performance among dealers and direct reports. Although nearly all those interviewed openly questioned how serious senior management was about the projected changes, half of them were ready to try things differently so long as senior management asked them to do so. Last, and unexpectedly, it now appeared that three dealers in addition to Jose Munoz would champion new ways of running a dealership.

The Service and Repairs Initiative. This initiative caused a major battle within the team. For several years, Iberian Motors had run the service and repairs function on a centralized basis. Among dealers, region heads, and others, the head of service and repairs seemed dic-tatorial and unresponsive. They seized the chance to propose break-ing up his function into a decentralized arrangement of regional service and repair managers who would report directly to the region heads. The chief of service and repairs, however, argued that a decen-tralized arrangement would drive costs up and quality down.

With the battle lines clearly drawn, the people on each side went about proving their point of view. They interviewed individuals throughout the company and did a variety of economic analyses to identify the likely costs of each option. In the course of this work, the many disappointing stories of poor performance convinced the head of service and repairs that his function had to become much more ori-ented toward customers and quality. He continued to believe, however, that the best route remained a centralized function.

The debate between him and those supporting decentralization took an interesting turn. Each side agreed that, regardless of how Iberian organized itself, the only way to improve service and repairs was to spend more money on it, and the only way to do that was to increase prices. This, they also agreed, raised many questions about Iberian's strategy that only the families and the Managing Director could answer.

The Total Customer Service and Quality Initiative. The leaders of the total customer service and quality initiative believed their success depended on behavior and skill changes in frontline workers and supervisors ranging across all of Iberian's functions: accounting, parts, repairs, distribution, sales, and service. They decided to use a combination of interviews, focus groups, and surveys to find out more about the readiness and resistance levels in the front lines. They learned a lot. Although most frontline people had heard of total quality, less than 10 percent had a working knowledge of the basic philosophy and tools. However, more than half of the focus group participants and survey respondents had specific suggestions on how they might serve customers better. Good ideas emerged from people in every function. With the exception of sales, where resistance seemed particularly high, the team found a much more optimistic picture than they had expected. They estimated that up to one-quarter of the people in other functions were ready to try something different, and that many others had rather straightforward reservations, such as "I'll do this when my boss tells me to" and "I'd like to see this actually work first." The initiative leaders believed that if the senior management of Iberian made customer service and quality a clear priority, much of the reluctance to move forward could be eliminated.

After three months of hard work, as the team put together its final recommendations, their initial concerns resurfaced. All were more persuaded than ever that open markets required Iberian Motors to become much better at total customer service and superior value delivery at the lowest possible cost. But they questioned the seriousness of the families and senior management. Although most of the twelve believed the Managing Director was committed to change, they doubted his willingness to spend the kind of money they felt was needed. And they were convinced that the families wouldn't let him go ahead with such investments anyway. Moreover, they each continued to wonder about hidden agendas, especially the possibility that the families really wanted to dress up Iberian for sale.

Last, they wondered about themselves. The group members had known each other for years, and once or twice during the project they questioned whether they were too set in their ways to lead change. They even admitted they weren't sure they understood all the new skills, behaviors, and working relationships that needed to be learned. All such discussions, however, remained quite circumspect. Yes, if the families and the Managing Director made the new direction very clear and asked them to lead, they would do their best. But going into the final meeting, team members were not sure just how much of an emotional investment they themselves were ready to make.

The meeting began with the team suggesting that Iberian hire an outside consulting firm to figure out the best strategic approach to the service and repairs challenge. Once the strategy was in hand, the team argued, then the best organization structure—centralization versus decentralization—would follow. The team was far more specific regarding the other initiatives.

In response to the dealer management challenge, they recommended that Iberian Motors:

- Add customer preferences and quality assessments to profitability as key measures for dealer success
- Redesign the budgeting and planning process to include concern for customer service, market goals, and delivery costs
- Add up to $20 million of new investments in marketing, advertising, and customer service
- Establish a new training department in human resources for skill development
- Redesign compensation policies to incorporate new goals
- Start to conduct monthly dealer reviews to monitor progress against customer service, lower costs, and profits
- Reorganize the dealer regions to create a special "champion region" to include Jose Munoz and the other three dealers ready to try change
- Redefine the profile for new hires at the dealer and dealers' direct report levels to reflect the desired new skills

In response to total customer service and quality, they suggested the company:

▶ Hire a new head of customer service and quality, who would report directly to the Managing Director

▶ Establish customer service and quality positions in each major function, reporting solid line to the functional heads and dotted to the new head of customer service and quality

▶ Set up a Quality Council and ask it to work with the Managing Director and other top Iberian leaders to establish a customer service and quality vision for Iberian

▶ Hire an outside firm to train all Iberian personnel, including senior management, in total quality philosophy, tools, and techniques

The families and the senior executives were impressed. They agreed that the service and repairs issue had important strategic implications, and took the suggestion to hire a consulting firm under advisement. Next they approved all the recommendations regarding customer service and quality, although they cautioned that the budget for training would be modest. And they responded favorably to most of the dealer suggestions as well. Specifically, they agreed that Iberian needed to modify performance objectives for dealers and redo budgets and compensation schemes. But they weren't sure the team had come up with the best answer as to how, and therefore they asked the team to study the matters further. They okayed the creation of a champion region, subject to the team's working out related reporting relationships and organizational issues. They also encouraged the team to go ahead with plans to expand monthly performance reviews as well as to alter the hiring profile for new dealers and their direct reports.

After the meeting, team members felt cautiously optimistic. The discussion had been much more factual and specific than was typical. They could tell, for example, that the families and the senior leaders appreciated the detailed picture of readiness and resistance that the teams had developed. In particular, the feedback that "senior management isn't really going to do this" sobered everyone. Notwithstanding the few objections senior management and the families had made, most team members believed the decisions taken at the meeting represented concrete steps toward change.

Three months after the meeting, a new head of customer service and quality was on board, the other quality positions had been established and filled, the Quality Council was in place and working on a vision, and a training firm had already conducted three well-attended sessions on total quality. That was the good news. The bad news was that the new head of customer service and quality had difficulty getting the attention of other functional leaders who, while talking a good game, still behaved as though quality were secondary. Only the head of service and repairs seemed willing to commit to specific goals in the upcoming year's budget and plan. In fact, so many stories circulated about the lack of senior management commitment to quality that, by year's end, the new customer service head contended that he needed direct, not indirect, line authority over all customer service personnel.

Meanwhile, under the pressure of new events, most of the other initiatives had lost momentum. Six weeks after the meeting, two of Iberian's largest equipment suppliers merged. They asked to renegotiate all contracts, causing several initiative leaders, key senior people, and others to become consumed in the negotiations. Work stopped on the redesign of budgeting, planning and compensation approaches. Interestingly, the two equipment suppliers expressed pointed concern about the quality of Iberian's customer service. As a result, senior management demanded that people throughout the company develop and package a detailed picture of "how well customers were treated by Iberian".

In the middle of the contract renegotiations, the Spanish government announced a complicated tax law change with severe potential consequences to the profits the families could take out of the company. A special task force of internal and external lawyers and accountants went to work. They decided to rewrite several accounting policies at Iberian. Several months of effort went into devising and then communicating the needed changes.

Other surprises and obstacles popped up as well. All contributed to distraction from the initiatives. Eighteen months after work on the initiatives had begun, only a small amount of fundamental change had taken place at Iberian Motors. Because of the efforts of the head of customer service and quality and the Quality Council, awareness was widespread in Iberian about total quality and a vision for what it might mean to the company. Also, a few specific success stories circulated about people who had tried out total quality tools and made improvements. In the opinion of most, however, customer service and quality remained hostage to the lack of cooperation from the functional heads.

The other two initiatives told the same tale. Positively, Jose Munoz and his colleagues in the champion region had discovered a variety of ways to deliver both improved customer service and lower costs. Their accomplishments, however, were greeted with more skepticism than optimism. So much initial excitement had arisen among dealers and dealers' direct reports about coming to grips with the challenge of open markets that the isolated stories from Munoz and others seemed too insignificant to make a difference. "The dichotomy between profits and the long-term need for customer service is tearing us apart," said one disgruntled dealer. "It's worse than ever," added another. "Will the families keep this up until we all fail?"

The families, the Managing Director, and other senior executives continued to worry about the need for change—so much that they finally asked an outside consulting firm to come up with a strategy and organization for succeeding in open markets. They were delighted with the progress in the champion region but weren't sure how to replicate it. And, faced with the constant complaint that they weren't investing enough money in change, they despaired over whether their people had the will to succeed. As one senior leader summed up the situation, "We just don't have the right people in the right jobs."

WHAT HAPPENED AT IBERIAN MOTORS?

Unfortunately, the Iberian Motors story repeats itself in many organizations confronted with managing both performance and broad-based behavior change. Most of you, for example, will recognize the following explanations given by Iberian executives, dealers, and others when asked what had gone wrong:

▸ "The families and top management were never really committed to doing what was needed to drive change."
▸ "We just could never overcome the resistance to total quality."
▸ "The various initiatives too quickly became 'just one more thing to do.'"
▸ "There weren't enough Jose Munozes to get us through this."
▸ "The plans were good. But unexpected events derailed us."

Each assessment is partly correct. Some family members and top executives were not committed to the change; the resistance of certain functional heads to total quality got in the way; the initiatives did get marginalized in the perception of many people; and unexpected events did consume time of particular people.

However, the teams had identified many people—beyond Jose Munoz and his colleagues—who were either ready or only slightly reluctant to try new and different approaches. The Managing Director remained committed; many people were ready to try total quality; some people, like the head of customer service and quality, remained completely focused on their initiatives, and others like the head of service and repairs, badly wanted to improve quality. Furthermore, not everyone in Iberian was involved in responding to the various distractions. In light of this, much more progress should have been made throughout the company.

In my view, the above-quoted explanations for the poor showing, although valid, are too superficial. Iberian Motors failed not because of issues of commitment or resistance, but because of how people managed themselves and others *during this eighteen-month period.* Look beneath the surface of the comments as well as the story itself, and you will find deep-seated, familiar management beliefs that all but sealed the fate of the change initiatives from the beginning:

▶ Managers, especially senior ones, should focus most on making the best decisions.

▶ Decision making about issues of companywide importance belong to the top.

▶ Strategy, structure, compensation, and other elements of organization design—particularly when focused on decision-making power and effectiveness—are the essential engines for meeting any significant challenge.

▶ Individual accountability drives performance, and it starts with the boss.

▶ Technical and functional expertise, in addition to hierarchy, provide the basis for managerial authority.

▶ People learn by being trained.

▶ Money and investment are the scarce resources of progress.

Everyone who played an influential role in the initiatives—the families, the top management, the initiative team members, the new customer service and quality head, the leaders of the Quality Council—*managed according to these biases and beliefs.* And why not? They are time-tested and valid managerial approaches that are not wrong—so long as they fit the performance challenge at hand. As the story illustrates, however, the biases did not fit the challenge of managing performance and change at Iberian Motors.

PRINCIPLES FOR MANAGING BOTH PERFORMANCE AND CHANGE

The Iberian Motors story could have turned out differently if Iberian's leaders had applied the following set of principles for managing performance and broad-based behavior change. You will find the principles explored throughout this book. Here I simply introduce them to you and describe how Iberian managers ran afoul of them.

1. *Keep performance results the primary objective of behavior and skill change.* Few people change for the sake of change, especially in organizations. But they will change when their organization's performance and their own personal contributions to results depend on doing so. Therefore, you must ensure that everyone pays constant attention to the performance consequences of their efforts to learn new skills, behaviors, and working relationships. Otherwise, neither change nor performance will happen.

Iberian's managers spent most of their time worrying about decisions and designs, not performance. None of the team's recommendations, for example, suggested or committed to any specific performance goals regarding customer service, quality, low cost, or cycle time for repairs. Instead, the team focused on designing organization structures, compensation approaches, budgeting and planning schemes, and the like, a managerial pattern that persisted throughout the eighteen months. For example, when the new head of customer service and quality got frustrated, he turned to an organizational design solution, not to a frank discussion and commitment to specific performance goals.

2. *Continually increase the number of individuals joining you in taking responsibility for change.* No one can change behaviors for someone else. People must take responsibility for their own behavior change. But you can and should do whatever is possible to enlist more and more people to join you in taking that responsibility. Your goal must be to shape yourself and them into a cohesive group, a "we" who will make both performance and change happen. This requires constant attention to whose changes matter most; what skills, behaviors, and working relationships they need to learn; how those relate to performance; and whether progress is being made.

The Iberian team had done an excellent job of identifying which people mattered most and who among them were ready versus reluctant to change. Indeed, they found greater readiness than expected. But they ignored it. The only "we" that emerged in the Iberian story was Jose Munoz and his colleagues in the champion region. Not surprisingly, this "we" drove the greatest amount of performance, work, and behavior change.

The other managers waited for the families and the senior leaders to demonstrate their commitment through making numerous decisions and spending lots of money. While they waited, frontline people with performance improvement ideas, dealer and dealers' direct reports who wanted to try something different, and the head of service and repairs, who wanted to improve quality, as well as many others who were ready or only marginally reluctant to try change, went untapped. A year and a half after the initiatives began, few people in Iberian had taken responsibility for their own performance and change.

3. *Ensure each person always knows why his or her performance and change matters to the purpose and results of the whole organization.* Why would I go through the agony of learning new behaviors on the job unless something is in it for me? And how can I trust that I have a meaningful role unless I understand the contribution I am making to the big picture? If you aspire to lead change, therefore, you must continually help people connect their efforts to the big picture. This means understanding what's at stake for the organization and its key constituencies and what's at stake for the individuals taking responsibility for their own change. Only by keeping all the possible consequences—from opportunity through threat—fresh and compelling can you hope to guide yourself and others through the tough, trying period of change itself.

Iberian executives failed at this task. They sent out the obligatory memo both before and after the project. Beyond that, they let the rumor mill dominate. Consequently, people throughout the company—from the front lines to senior executives—never fully understood the intentions of the family regarding the potential sale of the business or what senior management and others thought could be done about open markets. Nor did they grasp what *they* could do to help. Given how little any single manager understood his or her own role, the vacuum was not surprising. Still, it had bad effects. As one Iberian manager put it, "The organization got thoroughly demoralized. They were being asked to work harder and harder, yet had no idea where all this was headed."

4. *Put people in a position to learn by doing and provide them the information and support needed just in time to perform.* Behavior and skill change is not passive. Adults learn through doing and searching, failing and succeeding. You must continually create the performance commitments and contexts that give people a chance to *experience* change. Furthermore, you should deploy help—information, training, advice, reinforcement—mostly when people need it to meet specific goals, not before they have even set any goals.

Nothing so dynamic and constructive happened at Iberian. The new head of customer service and quality, for example, fell into a classic trap by investing heavily in up-front training. Word did spread about the philosophy and tools associated with total quality, but not much happened as a result. No one demanded that people commit to specific performance challenges requiring them to use what they had supposedly learned. Most people forgot most of what had been covered in training. Seizing some specific performance challenges, and then giving people the option of receiving training when and as they needed it to succeed, would have been far better.

5. *Embrace improvisation as the best path to both performance and change.* If neither you nor anyone else has the existing skills, behaviors, or working relationships needed to perform, how can you expect to rely exclusively on what you already know? Change demands that you make stuff up, try things out, see what works and doesn't, and talk among yourselves a lot. In other words, improvise, act, improvise, act, improvise!

Improvisation is at odds with the legitimate caution in managerial concerns over decision making, strategy, organization design, and compliance. Because leaders throughout Iberian Motors focused mostly on such things, it was not surprising that many people worried more about obtaining permission than committing to performance and change. Notwithstanding clear ideas about how to respond to open markets, Iberian managers continued to search for the "right" set of decisions, directions, strategies, designs, policies, and rules.

Interestingly, those managerial habits blinded people to the large scope of permission that did exist. Remember that the Managing

Director and family members *approved* nearly all of the recommendations the team presented. There was plenty of solution space for anyone focused on performance and ready to improvise a way of delivering it. Yet Jose Munoz and his colleagues were the only ones to take advantage, even though no one—not the Managing Director, not the families, not others in senior management—disapproved anything Munoz and his colleagues did. In fact, they consistently applauded it!

6. *Use team performance to drive change whenever demanded.* No better, more powerful unit to promote both performance and skill change exists than the team. Recognize, however, that performance challenges—not the desire to be a team—are what create a real team. And not every performance challenge demands a team. Many are better handled through classic individual assignment and responsibility. Thus, if you wish to drive broad organization performance and change, you must constantly identify those performance opportunities where teams can make the biggest difference—and then exploit them for all they are worth.

At Iberian, the dealer initiative members recognized the need to build better teamwork among dealers and dealers' direct reports. But teamwork and team performance are not the same, and Iberian's managers didn't understand this. In fact, the majority continued to believe that teamwork was nice to have but only individual accountability mattered. As more than one Iberian executive said, "I'll go to my grave believing you can't run a business with 'teams.'" This bias caused trouble at times. By creating the new customer service and quality position, for example, Iberian management encouraged the notion among other executives that quality was someone else's job.

7. *Concentrate organization designs on the work people do, not the decision-making authority they have.* When organization performance depends on new behaviors and skills, only *people* can make it happen by changing how they work. New designs, particularly those that articulate a different vision for *how work gets done,* can inspire people to take responsibility for change. Many managers, however, habitually divert the focus of new designs away from visions of work to debates over decision-making authority. As a result, the people whose behavior change matters most get frozen while a select few engage in expensive and time-consuming power struggles. When the dust clears, whatever new designs emerge say much more about decisions than work.

Efficient decision-making systems give terrific power to the efforts of already capable people considering new directions. And, of course, decisions also matter to behavior-driven change. But when existing people are not already capable, then the twin of decision making—the work that transforms decisions into value—matters more. You need to focus your design visions on that.

Instead of engaging people to change the real work they did, Iberian managers spent most of their time debating designs for how best to budget, plan, and otherwise make good decisions. Thus, for example, whether the service and repairs function was centralized or decentralized mattered less than figuring out how to provide service and repairs faster, with fewer errors, and in a manner friendlier to customers. Investing managerial time and attention in decision-oriented organization design instead of real people and how they worked was a mistake.

8. *Create and focus energy and meaningful language because they are the scarcest resources during periods of change.* Money and talent matter. But changing behaviors is hard work. People who must do it on the job need lots of *focused* energy to make it happen. They also need the confidence arising from the language, pictures, initiatives, and personal actions you employ to describe purpose and approach. Indeed, the well-known power of vision comes from both the rational and emotional fuel it provides. Visions that inspire meaning about the *what, why,* and *how* of change help to create, focus, and harmonize the energy needed to accomplish behavior-driven performance and change. New language gives life to visions of what and how change can make a difference to people and performance. To do that, however, new language must make sense. You cannot, for example, abuse potentially powerful new words (e.g., "reengineering") and expect them to have meaning to people.

The all too obvious bias among managers at Iberian was this: "Change cannot happen here unless the families are willing to spend lots and lots of money." Budgets for training, marketing, advertising, customer service, quality, and consulting would need to rise dramatically. In truth, however, people's success at learning new skills, behaviors, and working relationships depends far more on the energy they invest than on the money spent educating or organizing them—something demonstrated by Munoz and colleagues, who, it turned out, neither asked for nor spent any extra money.

Finally, unexpected difficulties and events, such as the supplier merger and the tax law changes, always occur during periods of change. The option is not to ignore them but to figure out how to convert the unexpected into energy for change. For example, Iberian managers could have used the merging suppliers' pressure for customer service information as an opportunity to reinforce the monthly dealer operating reviews, the work in the champion region, and the customer service and quality initiative. They could have, but didn't, ask, "How can we use this to promote performance and change in addition to meeting the negotiating goals and schedules before us?"

9. *Stimulate and sustain behavior-driven change by harmonizing initiatives throughout the organization.* No organization has ever gained traction against both performance and broad-based behavior change without a reinforcing set of initiatives that move simultaneously from the top down, the bottom up, and across preexisting organizational boundaries. Moreover, no organization has gained traction without a set of initiatives that permit real people—individually and in teams *at all levels*—to contribute to the purpose of the whole organization and reap both inspiration and reward from doing so. Such harmony and reinforcement happen only if you consciously seek to achieve them as a key part of starting, stopping, or modifying programs and initiatives.

Almost all the Iberian initiatives were top-down. Even the approach taken by the new head of customer service and quality was dependent on direction from the top. Iberian managers missed the opportunity to use quality, dealer teams, and customer service to generate dozens of bottom-up performance and change events. They also missed the opportunity to tackle the repair initiative cross-functionally through reengineering work instead of either redefining strategy or reorganizing responsibilities. Finally, as mentioned above, Iberian's leaders never grasped the importance of using the initiatives to get real people at all levels, including the leaders themselves, to take responsibility for performance and change.

10. *Practice leadership based on the courage to live the change you wish to bring about.* Change is as change does. The best leaders from the team level straight to the top of the enterprise must clearly stake out and relentlessly insist on what they want the organization to become. But in doing so, they must make clear *the principles by which people are expected to get there*—and then prevail relentlessly upon themselves and others in practicing those principles. This demands that you search for every possible opportunity to practice the new skills, behaviors, and working relationships in the very initiatives and programs by which you hope to bring those behaviors about. Also, you must have the courage to act in the face of your own doubts and fears. Indeed, if you as a leader lack the courage to live the change, how can you expect it of others?

Iberian Motors' managers followed managerial approaches more suited to stability than to change. As a result, they focused far more on decisions instead of on people, on strategies and designs instead of on real work, and on practicing their existing skills and behaviors instead of new ones. Except for Jose Munoz and his colleagues, everyone at Iberian Motors continued to manage performance as they always had instead of finding new ways to manage both performance and broad-based behavior change.

CONCLUSION: IMPROVE YOUR ODDS OF SUCCESS

Because of their simple, rich, and mutually reinforcing character, the ten principles constitute a discipline for managing broad-based behavior change just as surely as supply and demand determine the discipline of economics, or eating less and exercising more defines the discipline for dieting. Moreover, there is a direct correlation between the degree of adherence to the principles and success. The good news is that people who practice the principles give themselves a real chance to change and perform. But the *bad news is that every change effort, like that at Iberian Motors, that has run afoul of one or more of the principles has been disappointing.* The empirical pattern alone should be reason enough to learn the principles.

Some of the principles seem more straightforward than others; all are easier to accept than apply. Few would argue, say, with the dictate that performance results ought to be the primary objective of efforts to change. Yet how often have you experienced or heard about organization change efforts that seem to have no connection to performance at all? Or consider the principle that individuals must take responsibility for their own change. Notwithstanding its obviousness, the same organizations that so clearly and effectively differentiate customers into a variety of distinct market segments persist in quite gross, undifferentiated views about who in the organization is ready or reluctant to change, why, and what to do about it. All of this raises doubts about just how well understood or practiced these pieces of common sense are as principles of management.

You know that no simple, quick-fix approaches to fundamental change exist, and they never will. That is why getting the same people to deliver much higher and different kinds of performance is the most difficult challenge you face. Armed with the ten principles, you can find the conviction needed to meet that challenge. Not that the principles ensure success—they don't—but they do materially improve the odds. And, even more important, they give you a durable, proven basis for persisting against the risks and uncertainties of behavior-driven change.

We live in a time when millions of people understand that weight loss requires discipline, but too few people have recognized that managing through a period of fundamental change requires a disciplined approach, let alone have grasped the basics of that discipline and how it differs from longer-standing leadership practices. If you want to lead change in your organization, don't confuse the challenge ahead with that of managing assets, strategic directions, or new employees. Getting large numbers of existing employees through a period of change will put you to a different test—one that promises you the rich, unparalleled rewards that come only from the principled pursuit of performance and change with other people.

Chapter Two

Enlisting People to Perform and Change: Managing Through Reluctance

There is a cold, hard, immutable truth in organizations whose performance requires broad-based behavior change: unless and until *people* take responsibility for both change and performance, neither is possible. Each of you must take responsibility for your own behavior and skill change. No one can do it for you. Nor can you, as a leader, do it for others. You can encourage, cajole, demand, reward, support, train, flatter, educate, reassure, inspire, threaten, and push. But until enough people, including you, risk some combination of choice, action, reflection, and repetition, neither individual nor organizational change occurs. Nor does performance shift to a new, more sustainable level.

This is sobering news. The majority of us only reluctantly change long-standing habits or behaviors. When an audience is asked, for example, "How many of you have quit smoking, lost weight, learned the piano or golf, or made some similar behavior or skill modification since you became an adult?" usually less than half the hands go up. When an audience is asked "How many of you have done this twice?" usually no more than 20 percent of the hands stay in the air.

This does not make us a pack of "old dogs" with hopeless attitudes toward "new tricks." We can learn different skills and behaviors—if we believe we must do so. We all know too many adults who have changed for any but the most cynical or defeated among us to believe we or others cannot change. Furthermore, most of us have the minimum capabilities needed to acquire the skills and behaviors required to perform in the late 1990s and beyond. It is just that we are reluctant to do so.

We carry our reluctance to work, where so much is at stake. You have experienced the variety of human motivations stirred up by fundamental change in organizations. When fears of losing economic security, friendships, self-respect, and self-fulfillment are widespread, it should surprise no one to observe anxiety and caution as favored responses. Sure, most of us can see and hear the upside of change. We can imagine success, especially with the help of others. But if left to ourselves, our imaginations, and our fears, most of us live in the downside—a downside in which change means risk, risk means uncertainty, uncertainty means failure, and failure means us.

From such anxieties and apprehensions arises the issue of resistance. After more than a decade of widespread change, however, I believe "resistance" has acquired more weight than it deserves. The typical discussion of resistance can leave you believing that nearly everyone is against change at any cost. The favored pronoun in such discussions is "they," as in "This never had a chance because they resisted it from the start."

Far too many leaders now use resistance as an excuse for their own failure to understand and reach out to people who, like the leaders themselves, are naturally reluctant to change. Do pure resistors to change exist? Yes. And the higher placed they are in the hierarchy, the more potentially detrimental they are to the challenge. But in any serious change effort, it usually takes no more than several months for pure resistors to show their stripes. Once they do, you must get them out of the way, either through giving them different assignments or, if necessary, firing them. But for every pure resistor, one or more people are always ready to champion change from the outset. If you enlist them effectively, these people will make extraordinary efforts to advance new visions and possibilities.

Meanwhile, the majority of people—in my experience, between 60 and 80 percent of any sizable organization—are neither resistant nor ready. They *are* anxious and reluctant about what lies ahead. And their reluctance might turn into hardened resistance if you continue to confuse the two phenomena. Your job, however, is to turn reluctance into readiness, not resistance. People's reluctance to change always has one or more specific causes that you and they can do something about—if only you take the time to listen to them, work with them, and, especially, find some performance-based opportunity for them to experience change itself.

READY, RELUCTANT, OR RESISTANT?

In mid-1993, Terry Murphy took on the job as head of Tandem Computer's "America's Solution Team," a new sales division created to help Tandem make a critical strategic change. Like other traditionally hardware-driven companies such as IBM, Hitachi, Siemens, Unisys, and others, Tandem had to figure out how to shift from emphasizing hardware alone to selling both hardware and software, and from only manufacturing and servicing machines to delivering full solutions to customers' business problems. This strategic transition required many people throughout the company to change specific skills, behaviors, and working relationships.

Terry knew he had to drive change in sales and marketing. In Chapter Seven, we will discuss the innovative approach he and his colleagues followed. Here I provide a profile of "Joan Yancey," one of the Tandem sales people Terry had to enlist in taking responsibility for performance and change.

A central challenge was to get Joan and others to learn how to move *from* selling Tandem's products *to* selling Tandem's solutions and capabilities. To begin, Terry used a full day at the annual sales conference to engage sales people in identifying the implications of solution and capability selling for how they did their work. Most people at the conference, including Joan, knew how important that was to Tandem's future. They had many reservations, but easily and productively joined Terry in working throughout the day.

They crafted an excellent "from/to" descriptic
behavior and skill changes to be made. As the chart on pa
Joan and others articulated what solution and capability sellin₅
for how they should reallocate their time, the specific skills and knov.
edge they needed, how their key internal and external contacts would
shift, the larger role that teams would have, and how the criteria for
their personal success would differ.

People at the sales conference also discussed the real concerns that
always accompany fundamental change. After more than a decade of
spiraling growth, Tandem had gone through some downsizing and
more was expected. Like nearly everyone else, Joan had seen the
recent press coverage criticizing Tandem's CEO for taking "his eye
off the ball," making key strategic mistakes, ignoring Tandem's
core strengths and customers, and underestimating a spate of new
competitors who had duplicated Tandem's traditional technological
advantage.

Solution selling had first been introduced several years earlier,
and there were examples of success sprinkled about the company.
But most informal discussions at the conference ignored the success
stories in favor of anxiety, panic, anger, and lack of confidence. One
part of Joan believed she could make the changes needed. Another
part heard herself and her colleagues saying the following:

▶ "The industry has completely shifted. Our strength is our existing
customers, where we have to do something 'awful' to lose them. But
I'm afraid we will lose them unless we do something to prevent it."

▶ "They're making way too many changes and throwing them at the
field all at once."

▶ "Too many sales people just don't honestly feel they need to use the
team approach."

▶ "The CEO only cares about getting the stock up to $1.30 a share. Is
that our 'vision'?"

▶ "We never stay the course. Solution selling will just be one more
program du jour."

"There's no sense of urgency about the changes needed. To be blunt, the basic attitude of too many is, 'I don't give a hoot about this or that 'solution'. I can still make my numbers doing what I have always done.'"

▶ "We're going through hell trying to get the marketing people to listen. They just won't. Their attitude is, 'Our job is to decide what to build. Your job is to just sell it!'"

On returning home from the conference, Joan knew she faced a major personal challenge. She remained convinced that performance depended on learning the skills, behaviors, and working relationships laid out in the from/to job description. Still, as she stared at that chart on her first day back, she asked herself, "*What* exactly should I do? *When* do I begin to change? *How* do I go about it?"

The from/to job description was not the only thing on her desk or on her mind. Other items included an appointments calendar filled with

▶ specific customer calls and follow-ups
▶ internal meetings on topics ranging from new portable technologies the company wanted her to learn and the coming year's approach to compensation and bonuses to the latest hardware proposals coming out of marketing and an explanation of what was expected in Tandem's push for total quality
▶ travel arrangements
▶ due dates for reports such as time and expenses, sales call summaries, and the first draft of the next year's sales plan
▶ personal, non-work-related matters

She also kept thinking about other complicating factors. What about her desire to make Tandem's First Cabin Club of top performers? Or her current year's sales quota that, naturally, was expressed in terms of quantity of products sold, not the sale of solutions or capabilities?

From / To Job Analysis for "Joan Yancey," Tandem Sales Person

Category	From	To
Use of time	50% alone with existing customers 10% alone with prospects 20% with Tandem product managers 20% administrative	30% team selling existing customers 20% alone with existing customers 20% team selling prospects 10% Tandem product managers 20% administrative
Job objectives	Sell new and upgraded Tandem products	Sell Tandem capabilities, solutions, and products
Critical skills/knowledge	Tandem product knowledge Customer/industry knowledge Product-based sales skills	Knowledge of Tandem products and capabilities, including who are Tandem's software and application experts Collaborative, team, and solution-based sales skills
Style	Tandem centered	Customer centered
Key external relationships	Customer's information systems executives	Customer's senior business executives, including information systems Third-party applications vendors
Key internal relationships	Marketing/product managers Technical, after-sales service reps	Tandem subject-matter experts Marketing/product managers
Criteria for success	Products sold	Products and solutions sold

Or that recent time a colleague of hers introduced a Tandem specialist to a customer only to find out the specialist didn't help as much as either her colleague or the customer had hoped? As someone at the conference had said, "Lots of sales people won't let Tandem experts near their accounts until they are persuaded they won't be embarrassed by them."

Joan had to admit that she wasn't sure she knew much about the technologies and people underlying Tandem's solutions and capabilities and, therefore, how scared she was that—truth be told—she might not be able to learn how to sell in the way the from/to job description so neatly described.

Guess what? As Joan sat at her desk and pondered these things, she was not alone. Most other sales people who had just returned from the conference were going through the same thing and asking themselves the same questions. When it came time for Joan to go to work, what do you think she chose to do? Practice the new skills and behaviors listed in the from/to chart?

No. Like most of the other sales men and women at Tandem, she concluded in her heart that neither she nor her manager, customers, associates, or family were confident that she knew how, or even whether or when, to make the changes happen. Consequently, Joan and most of her colleagues put the chart in a drawer or a briefcase, and proceeded to the next appointment.

That does not mean that the chart, and all that it implied, was forgotten or went away. For example, some of Joan's colleagues did try to apply the new skills and behaviors. Others, like Joan, continued to worry about the change because, as the conference demonstrated and future events probably would confirm, selling products instead of solutions simply wouldn't be enough to keep Tandem, and ultimately themselves, in business. Still, for all the reasons apparent in those other items on her desk and on her mind, Joan felt that proceeding with work made more sense than pursuing changes that she didn't fully grasp and lacked confidence she could pull off by herself. Joan chose, in other words, to keep pondering the changes but not to act on them until later.

RELUCTANCE AND THE INDIVIDUAL'S
WHEEL OF CHANGE

Clearly, getting Joan Yancey to learn solution and capability selling would take more than a new sales organization and a day's work at a sales conference. In opting to wait and see, however, Joan did not brand herself a resistor. She remained anxious and reluctant. And because of that, she represents the classic test for anyone who aspires to lead real change in organizations: How can you enlist the Joan Yanceys to join you in taking responsibility for performance and change?

To succeed, you must find an actionable way of identifying and responding to the root causes of reluctance in people like Joan. As we saw in the Iberian Motors story, this means paying more attention to *people* than to descriptions about such things as strategy and organization design. It also means moving beyond the familiar refrains voiced in organizations facing broad-based behavior change:

- "He says one thing but does another."
- "She just doesn't get it."
- "They'll never go along with this."
- "Sure, he seems willing to give it a try, but his boss won't let him."
- "She doesn't really believe anyone is serious about this."
- "They would do it, but they don't have the right equipment and buying it will never get approved."
- "It's all politics."
- "He is just waiting around for someone to tell him what to do."
- "They know this is just another fad. So, they're just keeping their heads low like always."
- "She hasn't changed in twenty years. Why should she start now?"
- "He's a lightweight."

Comments like those and the ones at the Tandem sales conference are inevitable. Each says something about the reluctance or readiness of "he," "she," and "them" as well as the speaker. But taken as a whole, they shed little light on why and what you might do to enlist others in joining your change effort.

So what should you do? If you pick up a self-help book, or listen carefully to expert psychologists or psychiatrists, or observe an Alcoholics Anonymous meeting or something like it, you will find a variety of explanations for what adults must do to change behavior and how to do it. You will hear about "twelve steps," support groups, taking control, and the need for both will and skill—most of which is truly fascinating and helpful, and some, to be sure, hokum.

If, however, you focus on the similarities instead of the differences in what you read and hear, you will discover a pattern that most adults go through most of the time when they learn new skills or behaviors. The diagrams on the following pages portray these similarities in their depiction of three common frameworks for explaining individual change and reluctance inside organizations.

The first, "Beliefs-Behaviors-Reality," suggests that how we behave is a function of what we believe; that what we believe is a function of how we perceive reality; and that our perceptions of reality, in turn, are a function of how we and others behave. Fundamental change, then, depends on modifying all parts of the cycle.

Although this framework can help diagnose any person's situation, it too often suggests a focus on the organization design elements (structure, compensation, career paths, information systems, and so on) that heavily determine what that person perceives as reality. Thus, for example, Joan Yancey believed that Tandem needed to make the shift to selling solutions instead of only products. But she also perceived that Tandem's "reality" had yet to seriously tackle the new challenge when she considered the company's approach to compensation, hardware-oriented R&D budgets, and reporting structures. Consequently, her behavior continued to focus on business as usual, as did that of most other Tandem people. In the chicken-and-egg question posed by this picture, too many people—like the Iberian Motors managers—chase the illusion of only fixing organization designs instead of getting people to take responsibility for change through performance-based action and experience. Indeed, a flaw of the

Beliefs–Behaviors–Reality

ORGANIZATION DESIGN

organizational structure
compensation
job descriptions
strategy

Beliefs

Behavior

**Perceived
Reality**

management information systems
career paths
technology, spending and decision authorities

ORGANIZATION DESIGN

Beliefs-Behaviors-Reality framework is its failure to even mention action, experience or performance.

The second framework, "Will/Skill," suggests that we change behavior only if we have both the will and the skill to do so. By definition, however, reluctant people facing behavior-driven change lack both will and skill. Thus, the framework provides only one suggestion: be directive. This, however, raises a problem. In many cases, you, the manager, have yet to learn the skills, behaviors, and working relationships needed for change. So, although you should be directive, you must find some basis for doing so other than your existing expertise and experience. Too often, people using the Will/Skill framework

Will/Skill

	Low		High
SKILL High	Support		Delegate
SKILL Low	Direct		Coach

Low   **WILL**   High

assume that the boss already knows the skills, behaviors, and working relationships to be learned. In addition, the Will/Skill framework, like the Beliefs-Behaviors-Reality one, overlooks the performance-based action and experience that are so critical to getting people to take charge of change.

The third framework, which I call the "Wheel of Change," overcomes the weaknesses of the other two without sacrificing any of their strengths. With it, you can identify and address the specific and actionable sources of reluctance of the people you need to enlist in change. They include the following:

▶ ***Developing both the understanding of the need for change and the desire to do it.*** These can come in either order. But without an understanding of what and why they need to change as well as the desire to do so, adults will not take the other necessary steps. People usually develop a rational, intellectual understanding of the need for change more quickly than the emotional desire to make it happen. Most of us, for example, agree with the need for such behaviors as collaborative problem solving, constructive listening, and mutual accountability in delivering team performance, total quality, customer service, process reengineering, and so forth. But behavior change is a matter for the heart, gut, and nerve as well as the mind. Until we feel emotionally compelled to change behaviors—to learn through practice something like constructive listening—we will not do so.

Our emotions, in turn, derive from complex motivations ranging across basic security, belongingness, self-respect, and meaning, which explains why threatening, "we must do this or else" circumstances cause more adults to change faster than do mere opportunities for self-improvement. Indeed, because of the power of emotions and motivations, individuals who come to desire change even before they fully understand it often move through the period of change more effectively than those who achieve understanding before desire.

Joan Yancey already understood intellectually what and why solution selling was needed. In addition, a part of her desired the chance to make the changes at hand. Thus the opportunity with Joan

The Individual's Wheel of Change

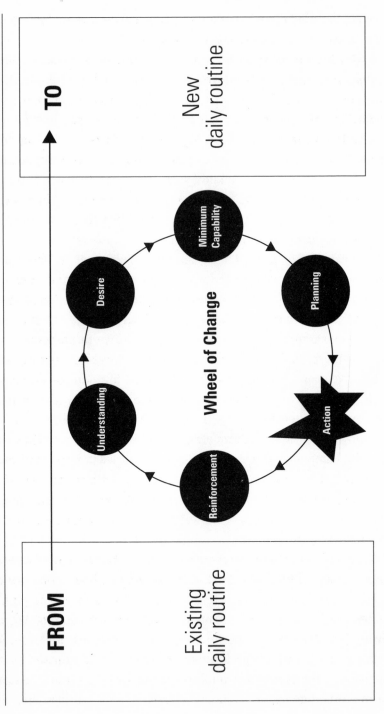

FROM — Existing daily routine

TO — New daily routine

Wheel of Change

Desire · Minimum Capability · Planning · Action · Reinforcement · Understanding

probably resided elsewhere on the Wheel, particularly in finding some way for her to *experience* solution selling.

▶ *Having the minimum capability required to learn new skills, behaviors, and relationships.* If you can't hum your national anthem on tune, then you probably won't become an opera star, regardless of how well you understand the challenge or how much you want to make it happen. But the emphasis here is on "minimum." You should avoid the all too common mistake of assuming that "he or she or I *cannot* do this" when the real problem is that "he or she or I *will not* do this." Also, do not confuse the skill or behavior to be learned with the minimum capabilities needed to learn that new skill or behavior.

Consider, for example, the challenge facing Joan Yancey. You already know that Joan does not know how to sell solutions and capabilities. The question you must ask is whether she has the minimum competencies to learn. For example, does she have the minimum questioning and listening skills needed for the consultative aspects of solution selling? Does she have the minimum problem-solving skills needed to work collaboratively with other Tandem professionals? Does she have the minimum technical and business skills needed to understand the economics of solution selling?

The good news is that, assuming basic literacy and common experience, most adults do have the minimum capability required for such desired skills and behaviors as collaborative problem solving, cross-functional perspective, mutual accountability, and self-management. Only rarely is the lack of sufficient minimum capability a real stumbling block to change.

▶ *Putting together some plan of action, however rudimentary.* Joan Yancey will never learn solution selling without a plan for converting understanding and good intentions into action. The plan can be as simple as "I think I'll invite a software expert into the next meeting with customer X." Or it can be more robust: for example, a solution-sales calling plan jointly created and committed to by a team including Joan and other Tandem professionals from marketing, service, and technology.

The best plans lead to action in a performance context. Do not, for example, equate time spent preparing plans with impact. Completeness can help. But you know as well as I that people in organizations often use planning as an excuse to deflect action instead of as a device to spur it.

▶ *Taking action.* No one ever learned golf without swinging a golf club. No one ever stopped drinking alcohol without saying "no" to the offer of a drink. And no one ever will learn customer service without serving customers; statistical process control without analyzing processes; the team performance discipline without being a part of potential teams; and so on. Behavior and skill change is a game that one must play in order to win.

Nothing does more for a person's understanding and desire than the experience of change itself. To enlist people like Joan Yancey in taking responsibility for change, you must use ingenuity and creativity to improvise ways for them to experience what otherwise remains just talk. As we will explore in Chapter Three, the most powerful experience comes in a specific performance context with goals that demand the behaviors and skills in question.

▶ *Responding to the reinforcement that follows action.* Change is all about a reinforcing cycle of cause and effect. In managing people through a period of change, you must pay careful attention to the three main sources of reinforcement:

1. *Performance results.* The most powerful reinforcer is performance. For example, when sales people like Joan Yancey actually closed deals with customers based on selling solutions and capability, they made huge strides in developing the understanding, desire, plans, and actions needed for further learning and change.

2. *Organizational arrangements.* Throughout most of a period of fundamental change, nothing is so insidious as the compensation and information systems, career paths, reporting structures, budgeting, planning and review routines, and other *impersonal* realities of organizational life. The obvious problem, with which you are familiar, is that existing arrangements never fully support the new

skills, behaviors, and working relationships needed for change. Thus, for example, Tandem asked Joan Yancey to sell capabilities instead of products while still compensating her mostly for selling products.

What may be less obvious is how time consuming, expensive, and risky it is to alter such arrangements. For example, a fundamental restructuring of the Tandem sales force compensation system would have consumed the better part of a year even to prepare and several months more to communicate and operationalize. Moreover, exactly how best to alter such organizational arrangements, in advance of learning whether the new skills and behaviors make any difference to performance, is not always clear. For example, what if Tandem had shifted dramatically to compensating solution selling, only to discover it lacked sufficient technical and marketing expertise and customer understanding to succeed?

Finally, what is not obvious about the insidiousness of organization design issues is illustrated by the Iberian Motors story of Chapter One: because changes in organization design—and particularly the decision-making aspects of design—have traditionally worked so well in getting capable people to pursue new directions and strategies, too many managers continue to put too much faith, time, and effort in them during periods of fundamental change.

You cannot ignore design issues; you must, for example, acknowledge when existing arrangements conflict with the desired changes. But neither should you focus so much on fixing them that you fall into the Iberian Motors trap of managing decisions and designs instead of people, performance results, and work.

3. *People.* Other than performance results, the most constructive reinforcement for people going through change comes from other people—specifically, you and anyone else who might be part of the "we" taking charge of change. The more time Joan Yancey spent with other people trying to learn the skills and behaviors needed for solution selling, the more likely she and they were to succeed. And the more those interactions happened in the context of experiencing solution selling, the more likely she and others would discover what worked, what didn't, and how to improvise and get better.

Yes, there are broad organization realities that constrain you. It might help if the impersonal organization were aligned to promote change. The reality of fundamental change, however, is that such alignment cannot arrive until the change is nearly complete. There are simply too many unknowns that depend on experiencing change on its own terms. Thus, if you wish to guide individuals to take responsibility for their own change, you must devote lots of your own time and attention to making certain that they receive the support and criticism needed to sustain their effort, especially from one another and from you.

▶ *Responding to each of these possible sources of reluctance over and over again until the new skill or behavior is integrated into daily life.* People rarely learn new skills and behaviors on the first try. Instead, most people continue to go through the Wheel of Change until they have fully integrated the new way of working into their daily efforts. Once that happens, you no longer have to worry about behavior change or reluctance, only performance. But until then, you cannot manage behavior and skill change in yourself or others without monitoring the progress and issues arising from each person's effort.

As you do, remember that issues can arise simultaneously from anywhere on the Wheel. The point of the Wheel, then, is not to give you a cookbook recipe by which to tick off a series of steps. Rather, it is a dynamic picture of what people go through on the path from old to new behavior. To help manage them through that effort, you need to keep the whole picture in mind at all times by continually asking the following questions and what you and the person in question can do about them:

Identifying and Responding to Reluctance

1. Does the person intellectually understand the need for change, including why the new skills, behaviors, and working relationships

matter to the larger organization's performance as well as to their own personal performance?

2. Does the person intellectually understand the specific behaviors and skills called for by the change? Can they articulate the from/to implications of the change for how they spend their time, the performance goals and objectives of their work, what they must be good at, and with whom they need to interact and toward what purpose?

3. Is the person emotionally invested in the change? Does the person feel in his or her heart that learning the new skills, behaviors, and working relationships is essential? Does the person have a compelling sense of the performance consequences, both to him- or herself and the organization, of success or failure?

4. Does the person have the minimum capabilities required to make the change?

5. Does the person have a plan of action in place? Does the plan call for action and a personal commitment to specific performance goals in a specific time frame in addition to training and awareness building?

6. Has the person taken action? Has he or she experienced change in a performance context involving specific and relevant goals (again, as opposed to attending training or awareness-building sessions alone)?

7. What kind of reinforcement did you and others provide the person when he or she took action? What kind of reinforcement might you give this person when he or she takes further action?

"WIREBOARD": MANAGING INDIVIDUALS THROUGH CHANGE

To illustrate how you can use the Wheel of Change together with a performance focus to manage specific individuals through readiness and reluctance, consider the challenge that faced "Wireboard," a manufacturer of electrical circuit panels. As a result of a major reengineering effort, Wireboard consolidated five manufacturing plants into one while simultaneously eliminating two levels of management. Under the new design, self-directed operating teams would conduct all activities from receipt of orders through shipping while middle managers were to become coaches and advisors to the teams. That required middle managers to make significant skill and behavior shifts:

♦ **FROM** *a departmental manager* who decides, plans, and delegates the work in his or her functional department, and focuses on the skill development and performance of individual operators within that department,

♦ **TO** *a team coach and advisor* who devotes time and attention to the effectiveness with which self-directed operating teams plan and deliver both performance and skill development.

Wireboard's performance now would depend on the output of the new operating teams. This meant that hundreds of frontline operators had to master multiple technical skills (e.g., people would no longer only take orders or only assemble or only ship), as well as the decision-making and interpersonal skills necessary for team performance. As is so often the case in behavior-driven change, this also meant that middle managers had to work through their own behavior change while simultaneously trying to help people on the teams work through theirs.

In preparing for the reengineering decision, Wireboard could not involve every middle manager. "Donna Davidson" and two others participated in the reengineering project from its inception. But neither "Tom Kern," "Cindy Downs," nor the other Wireboard middle managers were fully, actively engaged. The company did its best to keep the latter group informed about what might happen and why. Still, the first time most of them confronted the reality of the change followed the consolidation itself.

Put yourself in the position of the plant manager who must guide middle managers through the shift from departmental manager to team coach and advisor. You know five important things. First, the plants have been consolidated, the self-directed operating teams formally organized, and the middle managers told of their new responsibilities. Second, you are counting on Donna Davidson and her two project colleagues to champion the change. Third, the rest of the middle managers are nervous. Fourth, success requires the new consolidated plant to perform work previously assigned to five facilities. Fifth, Wireboard expects the new plant to reduce delivery times by a factor of three while simultaneously achieving zero defects.

Using the Wheel, you assess the three named middle managers as follows:

Donna Davidson: Her participation in the reengineering project has left her excited, ready, willing, and able to champion this change. She deeply understands the specific cycle time and quality goals the reengineered process seeks to deliver; what the new self-directed operating teams must do to deliver it; how training and cross-skilling efforts can position individuals on the teams to perform; and a variety of ways that she, as a director and coach of the teams, can help them develop the skills and confidence they need. In fact, she already has spoken with a number of people on several operating teams to get a sense of how she might meet their needs. Donna knows the transition will have its ups and downs, and that the reengineering project team did not figure out everything in advance. For example, the project left open whether coaches would be assigned responsibility for specific teams. But she believes Wireboard's survival depends on making this work and that there is no turning back.

Tom Kern: Tom is greatly relieved that he survived the plant consolidation, unlike several friends and acquaintances who have been let go. He has read and heard about the shift in roles expected of him. Moreover, he has spent a fair amount of time staying in touch with Donna Davidson and others on the reengineering project. He has a pretty good idea of why Wireboard has made this decision, the goals it wants to accomplish, and the key role of the operating teams in reaching them. But he still has questions. No one has told him exactly how he should spend his time or what he should seek to accomplish. Moreover, he's anxious about how he can help people on the teams learn all the new skills they need when they neither report to him nor must follow his decisions. Finally, he has always overseen between five and twenty people in a department. Under the new team structure, the number of people he may be called on to help could approach one hundred. That worries him.

Cindy Downs: Like Tom, Cindy is glad she survived the downsizing and has read and heard a fair amount about the whys and wherefores of the reengineering change. She knows that managing the increased number of people will be a tougher job, but believes she has been ready for a couple of years for a promotion and increased managerial responsibilities. She expects the operating teams to have many questions. Drawing on her skills at identifying issues and alternatives and then making tough-minded decisions, she fully expects to provide the teams all the answers and direction they need. Her major concern is how she will succeed at making sure the people on the teams get along with one another.

What do you think? Remember, you are the plant manager, the new plant is under way, customer orders are coming in, the teams have been formed, and Donna, Tom, and Cindy, along with nearly two dozen other former middle managers, need to do everything possible to help the teams deliver performance and change. In other words, this is all happening in real time. Your challenge is clear. Having identified each person's specific sources of readiness or reluctance, you must figure out how to guide them all into a position to learn by doing, then provide them the support and reinforcement needed just in time for them to perform.

As expected, Donna is a true champion for change. The classic risk with her is that you will not take full advantage of her readiness by enlisting her to join you as a peer in leading change. For example, in addition to helping the new operating teams deliver performance, Donna can help other middle managers make their own skill and behavior shift. Instead of letting the coaches decide to divide up the teams individually among themselves (a highly likely outcome for middle managers used to individual responsibility), you might suggest they form their own coaching teams. You could ask Donna to lead or facilitate one or more coaching teams and work with her and others to set specific performance objectives for the teams. This would position Donna to provide regular support and feedback to others like Tom and Cindy who are not as ready for change.

Tom and Cindy are each reluctant to change, although for different reasons. Tom wants to make the effort but lacks a clear understanding of what he is supposed to do. The reengineering project did not put together a from/to job description. It would help Tom if that were done now. Ask him to join Donna and some others to do it. Also, Tom does not appear to have a plan of action in place. Perhaps you should ask him to put together a thirty-day plan for how he will work with the new teams and what specific performance goals he hopes to help the teams set and accomplish, especially those relating to delivery times, defect rates, and cross-training. Then follow up to see if Tom acted on the thirty-day plan and with what results.

Tom, like most of the others, will need lots of reinforcement as he works his way through the change. Arrange for regular discussion and debriefing among the coaches so they can discover what's working, what's not, and how to improvise their efforts. Last, start thinking about bringing in outside expertise (in the form of books, consultants, or people at other companies who have been through this), remembering that the most effective timing will be *after*—not before—Tom and others have had a chance to work through their challenges for a while.

Cindy presents a different challenge. She seems to think little or no behavior or skill change is needed from her. In her mind, the reengineering decision granted her a well-deserved promotion and greater span of control. Her implicit plan of action is to manage people in the same fashion she always has. But, as you should know even if she does not, she will fail if she tries to personally make all the decisions, work assignments, and performance evaluations and adjustments for close to one hundred people who have been told they are supposed to manage themselves. Moreover, Cindy thinks the key to successful teams is helping people get along—another red flag that should worry you since, as you know, performance challenges are what make teams work, not the desire to be a team.

In terms of the Wheel, Cindy lacks both understanding and desire, her plan of action is defective, and, like Tom and others, she will need persistent and helpful reinforcement. None of this necessarily means that Cindy cannot or will not make the change, but you had better act quickly to adjust her understanding and help her develop the desire to make the needed changes. Both the from/to job description and a demand for a thirty-day plan would help. In addition, you probably need to speak candidly to her about the implications of the reengineering change, emphasizing your conviction that her performance as well as that of the operating teams depend on the skills and behaviors of a coach instead of a departmental manager. And since you can expect her to try to command and control the teams, you should arrange for quick, candid, and persistent feedback from the teams themselves—it may well prove the most powerful context to help Cindy learn that she must change.

Finally, do not assume, as far too many managers do to their peril, that your job is finished once you have started Donna, Tom, and Cindy down the path of change. Indeed, as the Wheel of Change illustrates, they will not have succeeded until they have incorporated the new coaching skills and behaviors into their daily work routines. Donna is probably close to that already. But it could take Tom and Cindy several months or even more than a year to learn how to coach effectively. Until each has succeeded, you must continue to monitor specific sources of reluctance. The Wheel, then, is a tool that managers must use throughout the entire period of change and not just at the beginning.

To emphasize this point, let's move forward in the Wireboard story. Assume you have taken most of the steps described above and four months have passed. Donna has adopted all the new skills and behaviors and is performing as a critical leader of the overall change. The progress of the other two, however, surprises you. Notwithstanding a clear description of the from/to challenge as well as persistent feed-back and discussion, Tom is stalled. Reports from his coaching team as well as the operating teams he works with suggest he has difficulty striking the right balance between giving directions and sitting back and letting the teams set their own directions. And those same oper-ating teams are lagging in their progress against key delivery time, defect rate, and cross-training performance goals. Finally, Tom admits that he is discouraged. He knows he must change, but he's losing confidence that he can.

The issue with Tom may now be one of capability. In terms of the Wheel, Tom understands the need for change; can articulate the from/to implications of the change; wants to make the change; and has repeatedly made plans, taken actions, and received feedback and other reinforcement. Still, he's not succeeding. You suspect that Tom's problem is in trying to deal with too many different teams at once. He's frustrated, but recognizes and appreciates that Wireboard has given him a real chance to make the shift from departmental manager to team coach. Now the question before you and Tom is whether he should continue to try, or should he shift roles? For example, he could become a member of a team, or a technical advisor available to all teams. After discussing the alternatives, Tom decides to join a team and pretty soon emerges as one of Wireboard's most effective team leaders.

Cindy, by contrast, has succeeded. The first six weeks were a night-mare. She ignored your candid warnings as well as the help from others on her coaching team and proceeded to boss around every operating team she came in contact with. Anger and confusion spread among these teams. Their performance results were poor when com-pared with those of teams being helped by Donna and others. The teams soon let Cindy know that her "help" was not really appreciated or wanted.

Her first reaction was to ignore them. Then, in anger, she told the teams, "Okay. Do it yourselves!" Having first overdirected the teams, she now swung all the way in reverse. Once again feedback from you, the teams, and her coaching team let Cindy know that that didn't work either. Only then did Cindy wake up. Using a near-term performance shortfall facing one particular team, you asked Donna to facilitate a clearing of the air among Cindy and that team. Everyone, including Cindy, worked to figure out how to meet the goal, and when they did, all credited the contributions of each other. Cindy *experienced* directly what it meant to coach and advise, and saw that it worked. Soon, armed with both the desire and the understanding to change, she worked hard to learn new techniques for coaching. Not all of them worked for her. But a few months later, Cindy was improving every day at her new role and the teams she coached were meeting their critical performance challenges. Cindy recognized the rockiness of her path to change, but readily expressed how much better she liked life in the new plant than in the old one.

CONCLUSION: HELP PEOPLE STAY THE COURSE

Managing people like Donna, Tom, and Cindy through a period of change takes a lot of time, attention, and effort. You will not succeed by assuming that decisions alone will achieve behavior change. How many people, for example, do you know who have intellectually understood the need to quit smoking or go on a diet, have made a decision to do so, and still have failed? To most of us the notion that people change personal behavior through decisions alone sounds dull witted. Why, then, does our confidence in the power of decisions inside organizations—and the disproportionate amount of time we spend debating and worrying about them—so often betray just such a notion?

The Wireboard reengineering decision was not sufficient to get Tom and Cindy through their effort. Nor was it enough for Donna, whose readiness and enthusiasm came from her participation before the decision. Individuals must work their way through understanding, desire, planning, action, and reinforcement on their path to change. They might do this before a decision, like Donna, or after one, like Tom and Cindy. But do it they shall, or else they will fail.

Consequently, you will manage change more effectively if you deemphasize decisions. And, when decisions are taken, you must build on their catalytic potential by working directly with individuals instead of naively equating decisions with action. You need to replace traditional managerial approaches by doing the following:

▶ *Take advantage of readiness and identify sources of reluctance instead of overreacting to resistance.* Resistance is more of a black and white issue when the implementation of a major strategic and organization decision depends on already capable people who either agree or disagree with the decision. Broad-based behavior change paints a grayer picture. Any particular person's failure to respond instantaneously to new decisions, directions, and designs poses a more complex challenge than implied by today's overused complaint about resistance. Still, to give up in the face of resistance is much easier than to take responsibility for engaging people to make change happen. Avoid the easy excuse. Instead, identify people who are ready for change and immediately enlist them in your effort. For those who are reluctant, understand why and do something about it. If, after providing a performance-based opportunity to change, some people emerge as pure resistors, then decide how best to get them out of the way, including firing them if needed. When you challenge people to take responsibility for change through performance-driven experiences, however, you will discover the vast majority successfully transform their reluctance into readiness.

▶ *Build on what people do know instead of underestimating them.* Too many managers freeze when they recognize that neither they nor their people have the skills, behaviors, and working relationships needed for performance. They do not go on to question and discover that most people do have the minimum capacities needed to perform and change. People can learn, and you can manage them effectively while they do. But they will not change overnight. Nor will they succeed unless you, as a change leader, believe in them and work with them. Still, simultaneously managing people through change while changing yourself is very hard work.

▶ *Improvise ways for people to experience change instead of focusing only on whether they understand why it's necessary.*

The traditional focus on strategic direction, organization design, and up-front training belies a managerial approach bent on explanations. You keep saying to yourself, "If only I can explain why and how this is going to work, they will get it and move forward." Intellectual understanding, however, is only one part of the Wheel— and the part that most people grasp most quickly. The far more powerful elements of change require experiencing it. Accordingly, you must look relentlessly for opportunities for people to experience the desired new behaviors and performance approaches. This is far more intense a challenge than contributing to debates about strategy and design.

▶ *Refuse to stop with "buy-in."* Helping people experience change and its consequences goes beyond the superficial involvement implied by the popular notion of buy-in. In the most practiced form of buy-in, people affected by decisions attend workshops or meetings so they can question, discuss, and buy in. Once they have bought in, they are expected to change. Such sessions do help increase people's awareness and understanding of change. They also help managers who listen well to identify sources of reluctance. But the kind of one-time involvement and buy-in that results from such meetings definitely falls short of the sustained understanding, desire, action, and reinforcement necessary to significant behavior or skill change.

▶ *Pay attention at all times to purpose, performance results, and work.* The primary objective of change is performance, not change. Managers who get lost debating the intricacies of strategies and organization designs, instead of managing real people and the real work that they do, always find it difficult to keep performance firmly in focus among the people they are enlisting to change. They also lose sight of the power of fundamental purpose to create understanding, desire, and action in pursuit of change. But higher purpose, whether it goes by the name of vision or mission or strategic intent, also requires concrete performance objectives to become real and tangible. Although seemingly obvious, this principle is quite slippery and difficult to follow, for reasons discussed at length in the next chapter.

Behavior and skill change is intensely personal. Managing such change is also personal. It is about enlisting the people who matter into a cohesive force, a "we" who will join you in making both change and performance happen. The combined power of reluctance and resistance to change ought to caution you against declaring victory too early. But don't confuse reluctance with resistance. Don't give up on people, or yourself, too easily. Instead, quickly sign up those who are ready, and then, together with them, work hard to identify and overcome the sources of reluctance preventing other people from joining you in meeting the challenge ahead.

Chapter Three

Performance Results: Managing the Link Between Purpose and Change

The primary objective of change must be performance results, not change. Performance makes inspirational purpose real. It makes new skills, behaviors, and working relationships relevant to people who must make change happen. Performance objectives give people the best means to assess and improvise their way through change. And performance helps people channel reluctance into motivation by giving them something real to do in their work.

Unfortunately, no management principle discussed in this book is more abused. Although common sense and common experience rail against the prospect of change for the sake of change, organization after organization conspire, almost ritualistically, to do just that. Inspiring purposes and promising initiatives stumble toward irrelevance as people go through the motions in a way that cannot sustain the tough work of achieving real change.

"This year we're doing . . ." goes the well-known refrain among people caught in this trap. Whether "innovativeness," "quality," "teams," "reengineering," "being the best," or any other flavor-of-the-month notion fills the blank, this comment hangs about the organization's hallways, elevators, e-mail, and parking lots because people neither see nor act on any compelling link between purpose and performance, and performance and change. Instead of performance grounded in new skills, behaviors, and working relationships, organizations harvest cynicism and despair.

At times, the mismanagement of the link among purpose, performance, and change is tragicomic. My favorite example comes from Ben Hamper's *Rivethead*, an autobiographical account of a decade spent on a General Motors (GM) assembly line. At the height of the crisis caused by superior Japanese imports, GM management—like other U.S. automakers—recognized quality as a key factor of success. Soon, Hamper reports, the supervisors at his truck plant were talking about "quality" with mantra-like regularity.

Interestingly, Hamper and his fellow workers already understood the connection between GM's performance and quality at least as deeply as their managers did. They could see the consequences of poor GM quality every day when they drove to work in Japanese cars along the highways of Michigan. They also felt its impact each time GM announced another round of layoffs or plant closures. And when they turned on their televisions, they heard Ford commit to "Quality as Job 1."

How did GM management take advantage of their readiness for change? The single most memorable initiative Hamper recalls was the introduction of the Quality Cat, a person dressed in a large cat costume and asked to walk the plant floor as a cheerleader! No identification, demand, and commitment to specific goals. No from/to description of the skills and behaviors that would make the new goals possible. No introduction, training, or assistance in practicing new skills and behaviors in the real-time pursuit of performance. No articulated conviction about the value of new performance and skills to the workers and GM's customers and shareholders. In other words, no persistent, tough-minded, and practical *managerial* effort to link GM market share to GM quality and both to new skills, behaviors, and personal success among the assembly workers.

Instead, in GM's version of worker involvement, Hamper and friends got the chance to submit names for the Quality Cat.

Hamper's favorite, although losing, entry was "Tuna Meowt"—
which perfectly captures what happens to adults asked to learn new
skills and behaviors in the absence of any consistently managed link
to performance.

Few management errors are as pathetic as that story. But far too
often the mismanagement of change produces the same result.
Instead of either changing or performing, people tune out. To avoid
that dispiriting outcome, *you must grasp why you have no choice
but to manage both performance and change as opposed to either
alone.* The rest of this chapter discusses the importance of performance to purpose and change, the nature of the difficulties in staying
focused on it, and how you can manage through such obstacles.

MINNESOTA DEPARTMENT OF ADMINISTRATION

Shortly after taking office as governor in 1983, Rudy Perpich challenged Commissioner of Administration Sandra Hale "to help make
Minnesota the best-managed state in the nation." Hale and others,
including Deputy Commissioner Babak Armajani, believed they could
succeed by importing to government powerful private-sector ideas
such as customer service, empowerment, productivity, measurement,
teamwork, and experimentation. Doing so, however, meant managing
their way through a period of fundamental change.

Take the notion of customer service. As noted in *Breaking Through
Bureaucracy,* Michael Barzelay and Babak Armajani's detailed
account of the Minnesota story and its policy implications, most state
employees struggled when asked to identify their customers.
"Customer" was not part of what they thought they did. And why
should it have been? They had always worked within a model of government that pursued "the rule of law" as its highest purpose, not the
"rule of the customer."

In this, Minnesota was not alone. For most of the twentieth century,
efficient and effective government has run with a clear division of
labor. Legislatures make laws and ask various committees to oversee
their implementation by line agencies. To ensure strict compliance,

line agencies must ask staff agencies for needed resources such as employees, office space, equipment, money—in short, everything. The goal is to prevent corruption, patronage, and unfairness within the line agencies asked to carry out government programs.

In this picture, staff agencies are cops who police and control the line agencies. The concept that line agencies might be customers contradicted the core beliefs and self-image of staff agency employees. Purchasing department managers, for example, quickly suggested that the customer concept would lead to line agencies' buying Cadillacs instead of Chevrolets. Personnel people believed that line agencies would routinely violate equal opportunity and other laws. Information management people predicted that line agencies would squander limited state resources. And so on. Customer, like the other concepts Hale wanted to introduce, would make Minnesota the best-managed state only if many people throughout the Department of Administration overcame their reluctance to changing specific skills, behaviors, and working relationships.

Hale, Armajani, and their colleagues wisely chose to focus first on performance and readiness. They invited state employees to voluntarily submit proposals for projects to improve performance. They placed three critical constraints on the projects. First, proposals must seek specific, assessable impacts on results. Second, proposals must rely on existing people and resources—no requests for additional appropriations would be allowed. Third, the proposals had to experiment with the new concepts that the change leaders hoped to inculcate.

The program, Striving Toward Excellence in Performance, ultimately won national recognition for innovation in government. More important, its results gave the Minnesota change leaders the confidence to push forward. Instead of condemning staff managers and employees who remained reluctant to shift worldviews and behaviors, the change leaders worked hard to expose them to the real consequences of current performance. Through interviews, face-to-face discussions, focus groups, and surveys, staff people heard themselves and their work described as "bureaucratic," "biased," "uncaring," "mechanical," "disrespectful," "rigid," "mediocre," and "frustrating." To their further dismay, the change leaders intentionally published such reports in a manner designed for broad reach and comment. "We wanted," said one, "to create a climate in which line managers' opinions had a good deal of value and impact."

Slowly and selectively, the understanding of change and the desire to participate began to spread. As they did, the leaders seized opportunities to drive performance and change. For example, when the legislature asked for a study of the personnel department, the change leaders took a novel approach. Instead of the traditional "independent" effort designed to root out problems and cast blame, the people doing the study *collaborated* with the personnel department in identifying ways to improve performance. Central to the study's emerging recommendations was the need for people in personnel to shift their purpose *from* only enforcing compliance with public policy *to* pursuing both compliance and service to line agencies.

Personnel managers realized that their new mission demanded different performance objectives. They sought, for example, to reduce the time needed to respond to line agency hiring and job classification requests. And they chose to treat line agencies as customers from day one by heavily involving the line in discussions, experiments, and eventual selection of the new performance targets.

The performance targets forced those in personnel to rethink how they did their work. They discovered that bottleneck after bottleneck arose from extreme specialization within the department. Only some people did classifying, only some exams, and only some hiring. Furthermore, all would respond only to their assigned areas of responsibility. This produced classic, bureaucratic runarounds. Line people would ask for help from the classification area and learn they had an exam problem; they would then approach the exam area and be told they had a classification problem.

The people in personnel concluded that they could best meet the new performance objectives by approaching their work as a process of related steps instead of an unrelated collection of specialties. This view of their work, in turn, led them to favor using teams so that people with different skills could combine efforts in the real-time pursuit of both policy compliance and customer service.

The focus on performance and work yielded additional insights about specific behavior and skill changes. Providing practical solutions to line agency requests required people in personnel who listened well, sought out line customer as well as team member opinions on best approaches, generated as many options as possible, communicated those to the customer, and used team-based versus hierarchical approaches to decision making. Learning these new behaviors depended on cross-training and open information and knowledge sharing. Through cross-training, the breadth of team member expertise expanded. Through continual knowledge sharing, the teams helped one another to balance compliance and service consistently.

"The idea," commented one manager, "is to deliver service-related decisions better and faster, while sacrificing a minimum of consistency. Will team leaders make different decisions, given the same set of facts, than I might? Yes. Will they make different decisions among themselves, given the same set of facts? Yes. Will there consistently be vastly different approaches and solutions among team leaders? No. That's what decision guidelines, team building, and open communications are all about."

Ultimately, the personnel department published a set of turnaround-time performance standards they aspired to meet, and continually measured themselves against them. In addition, they kept asking line agencies for qualitative assessments of service quality. As people in the department got better at the new skills, behaviors, and working relationships, both quantitative and qualitative performance increased. They improved against their turnaround-time goals. And they found a more satisfied group of customers. Contrary to the nearly uniform condemnation given at the beginning ("disrespectful," "mediocre," "bureaucratic"), most line agency people now believed personnel did a good job of offering "help" and "solutions."

This pattern of change happened in other areas of government as well. By exposing people in staff departments to the performance assessment of customers, change leaders gradually won new and different understandings of departmental purpose and mission. By challenging departments to translate purpose into specific performance objectives, the leaders facilitated a reexamination of work and the skills, behaviors, and working relationships needed to get it done. As people in other staff agencies sought to perform differently and better, they also improvised, learned, and changed. As they learned and changed, performance—in the form of speed, cost, and quality—shot up.

Not everyone changed, of course. From time to time, pure resistors blocked progress and the change leaders used whatever flexibility they had to remove them. Also, as is the case with many pioneering success stories, the effort probably took longer (seven years) than it should have. But by 1990 a profoundly different orientation permeated the Minnesota state government. That year, for example, in just one of many similar proposals received, a manager in the state's Records Center requested permission to enter competition with private storage firms because, he argued, his center could offer lower costs, superior security, and better customer knowledge. Seven years earlier in Minnesota, and in far too many government organizations today, that kind of entrepreneurial confidence and capability would seem unimaginable.

WHY PERFORMANCE?

The Minnesota story highlights the power of performance as a crucible for behavior change. Before exploring why, let me clarify what I am *not* saying. I am not saying that performance contexts are the only possible path to behavior change. For example, advanced education courses often provide the basis for important behavior and skill change. So do personal counseling and friendly advice. And there are other means. But most adults in most organizations most of the time will make faster and more effective progress toward learning new skills and behaviors if clear performance consequences depend on their effort.

Performance and Basic Organizational Purpose

Every day when they show up for work, most adults bring a solid awareness of these two concepts:

▶ "My organization can succeed only as long as it performs against the purpose—economic, governmental, educational, charitable, religious, etc.—for which it exists."
▶ "I can succeed only as long as I contribute to the organization's purpose through my own performance."

As you know, those two widespread beliefs have fueled the rise of purpose and vision as necessary components of leadership over the past decade or so. The good news is that few people today start down a path of change without discussing purpose and vision. The bad news is that they often act as though purpose alone is enough, thereby ignoring performance as the only way to make purpose and vision real.

If you take away performance, you take away the organization's reason for being—and the individual's reason for being a part of the organization. Any change in the organization's purpose or the individual's role must remain connected to performance to be credible. Ben Hamper's GM experience illustrates what happens when purpose, change, and performance come unglued. Like too many other organizations, GM simplistically introduced quality as a good thing and then ignored its role in making any difference to performance. No wonder Hamper and his fellow workers did not take the effort seriously.

Interestingly, even organizations known for effectively managing through change stumble at times over that mistake. For example, Jan Carlson has commented that, after a successful period of performance and change at Scandinavian Airlines, he and others began noticing drift. "By establishing our original goal," he explains, "we had placed a demand on our employees. But now that there was no goal, a kind of reversal had set in."

Or listen to Fran Ahl, a General Electric (GE) spray painter whose initial experience with that company's famous Work-Out program was negative. When introducing Work-Out at Ahl's plant, local GE managers had failed to discuss the relevance of Work-Out to plant and company performance. Like most other employees, Ahl considered the ensuing effort a waste of time. "If somebody can't tell me what he wants," Ahl says, "it's awfully hard to get involved."

Effective change leaders, like those in the Minnesota story, remain vigilant against losing sight of performance. They work to ensure that everyone continually understands why his or her performance and change matter to the whole organization. In Chapter Seven, we will discuss how John Champagne and Bob Guadiana used teams to lead change at Magma Metals. For now, listen to John describe why they made the effort: "We're not doing this as some experiment in sociology. We are doing this because we want to be the world's best. We want to have the highest productivity. We want to have the lowest cost. We want to have the best environmental performance and the best quality product."

Performance and Motivation

Deep emotions and anxieties emerge during periods of fundamental change. Using A. H. Maslow's hierarchy of human needs, consider the following:

▶ *Physiological and safety needs.* Hunger and fear motivate us at the most basic level. In today's highly complex market economies, "job" means "livelihood." Consequently, the prospect of job loss—with the attendant possibility of, say, losing one's home or health insurance—strikes fear in the hearts of most of us.

▶ *Affiliation and belongingness needs.* We are social animals. Most of us need to belong to a group. Yet, now that technology has superseded geography as a prime force in our lives, organizations remain one of the few real opportunities to satisfy this need. Again, job loss means the possibility of losing friends and acquaintances, of being cast out of a community where we belong.

▶ *Self-esteem and self-actualization.* We need to respect ourselves and have the respect of others. We also need meaning, a conviction that we are doing something that makes sense for how we
wish to lead our lives. The longer we have worked in a particular job
or the more we connect our future to the contribution we make to an
organization, the more likely we feel that fundamental change will
jeopardize our self-respect and sense of meaning.

When people fail to see tangible, real links between change and performance, they generally reap the whirlwind stirred up among these
anxieties. In their distress, they hear "downsizing" regardless of the
label management puts on such organization changes as "reengineering," "core competency," and "strategic alliances." In fact, many
managers—at all levels—hear themselves communicating "downsizing" when they too cannot confidently connect performance results to
behavior change. The organization turns into a giant lottery where,
instead of learning new skills, behaviors, and working relationships,
people keep their heads low, endure the stress, and hope their numbers don't come up in the next round of pink slips.

By contrast, when leaders work every day to connect purpose, performance, and change, most people convert anxieties and fears into
positive motivation. Yes, jobs may be lost. And effective change leaders do not lie about that, either intentionally or otherwise. But, by
using performance to make change real, leaders give people the
chance to take that measure of control available to them. In this, most
people recognize both an honest and constructive foundation for personal choice, responsibility, and action.

People also see there is something concrete they can do. Think
back to the day Joan Yancey of Tandem returned from the sales conference. As she sat at her desk, she felt all the anxieties, uncertainties, and doubts raised by the specter of change. Sure, she had
the from/to chart of new behaviors and skills. But it did not give her
a specific goal or performance context toward which to channel her
energy. Like most people in her situation, Joan chose to put aside
the change and go to work against her existing, non-change-related to-
do list.

People focused on *both* performance and change react differently. Consider the experience of Dorothy Jacobson, a Morgan Guaranty Trust department manager. In a private-sector challenge similar to the Minnesota government story, Morgan Guaranty's productivity required people in centralized administrative departments to learn a variety of new skills, behaviors, and working relationships. In particular, managers had to stop firefighting in favor of promoting more fundamental and enduring performance. As part of the change effort, the company challenged people like Dorothy to establish and meet short-term performance goals that would require them to practice the new skills and behaviors.

Dorothy set such a goal at a workshop designed to introduce both performance and change. When she left the workshop, she took her specific performance goal with her. Sure enough, just like Joan Yancey, when Dorothy arrived at her desk the next day, she was greeted with a different to-do list and a different set of crises to solve. Just when she was about to start firefighting, however, she remembered the workshop, the performance goal, and her commitment to meet that goal within five weeks. Unlike Joan Yancey, Dorothy Jacobson did not put the goal back in her briefcase. Instead, she said to herself, "I'd better get started."

Performance, Causality, and Adult Learning

Causality—the connection between effort and outcome—is critical to adult learning. But how can you have outcomes, particularly inside organizations, without performance results? For example, neither you nor anyone you know is likely to show up at work one day and suddenly announce, "Hey! Let's stop what we're doing and read Peter Senge's *The Fifth Discipline!*" Some people usefully do that from time to time at home, but not at work. You might, however have read Senge's excellent book and suggest at work, "Hey! You know how hard we're finding it to answer customer service inquiries within twenty-four hours? Well, I've got a few ideas about how we might tackle our problem differently."

To illustrate, consider the challenge facing Norm Gelbwaks, a systems manager at American Express Bank. Like many organizations, the bank had suffered suboptimal performance caused by the classic impasse of mutual distrust and misunderstanding between business people and systems people. In this particular dance of death, business people, on the one hand, act as though they don't appreciate how necessary clear specifications are to systems people's ability to do their work. Systems people, on the other hand, act as though they neither understand nor care what makes the business tick, causing them to fail to deliver what the business people and customers need when they need it. Like ships passing in the night, these behavior patterns generate shortfalls ranging from lost sales to late product introductions to high costs.

This situation existed for years at American Express Bank. Enter reengineering. Bank executives recognized that, by taking a horizontal process view of information technology and banking, the time, cost, and quality of product and service delivery could improve dramatically. Among other things, this meant altering the bank's basic technology architecture. But it also required systems, operations, and business people to change skills, behaviors, and working relationships.

The technology architecture could not be reshaped overnight. Bank executives asked Norm Gelbwaks to begin driving the needed behavior changes and learning immediately. To do so, he and his colleagues:

▶ insisted that marketing and sales people write their own requests for systems modifications or upgrades instead of delegating the job to systems people

▶ asked that all such requests be written in business, not systems, language

▶ gained agreement from both business and systems people to apply the same set of parameters for prioritizing all requests

▶ established joint business-and-systems reviews of projects in progress

▶ measured and monitored both quality and time to completion of all such projects

Nothing on the list is rocket science; everyone at American Express Bank had the minimum capability needed to do these things. Instead of just talking about such behavior changes, however, Norm and others insisted on the new behaviors as the price for performance.

The marketing and sales people who failed to submit requests in business language instead of systems jargon did not obtain the needed resources. Those who did, and who survived the prioritization gauntlet, did obtain the resources. More important, those who participated in the new disciplines witnessed a dramatic improvement in the on-time, on-spec delivery of systems modifications and upgrades. People on both sides of the previous impasse saw for themselves the causality between changing behaviors and performance. In addition, they built a much higher level of mutual trust, understanding, and effectiveness across the systems/business boundary, paving the way for the new technology architecture.

Performance, Change, and Administrative Effectiveness

"What gets measured," goes the adage, "gets done." If you want new skills, behaviors, and working relationships, you must find an administrative way of assessing or measuring them. Three choices exist:

1. *Examinations.* Test people for competency in the desired skills, behaviors, and working relationships.
2. *Activities.* Measure activities intended to help people learn the new skills, behaviors, and working relationships.
3. *Results.* Measure the performance outcomes that the new skills, behaviors, and working relationships are intended to produce.

All three can help; all three should be used. However, only the last—*measuring performance results*—ensures administrative effectiveness. Why? Consider examinations. Competency tests provide a sound way to assess technical or functional skills. But their effectiveness breaks down when the skills and behaviors reach beyond what individuals can do or know by themselves. It is far more complex, for example, to test for the collaborative problem-solving skills of a team of Tandem professionals than to examine each person alone for his or her product, technology, business, or customer knowledge. More important, even when examinations do help to measure learning progress, they cannot provide evidence of whether that learning actually *matters* to the organization—a defect that also bedevils measuring activities alone.

Measuring activities, of course, is administratively the easiest of all three choices. Attendance at training sessions on total quality, or the number of reengineering projects under way, or how many teams have been formed are simple to track. But administrative ease can seduce organizations into falsely equating activities with outcomes.

The understandable yet naive logic assumes that training or awareness cause people to "get it." And once they have "got it," they return to their jobs and immediately "apply it." Hence, the more people trained in "it," the more powerful the impact of "it" on overall organizational performance.

Some people do leave training sessions and quickly find opportunities to apply what they learned. Those are the "early adopters," the 5 to 15 percent of people in any sizable organization who are change seekers. The vast majority, however, mirror the behavior of Joan Yancey of Tandem. They leave the training session with greater *awareness* of the need for change and how new skills and behaviors can help; then, for a variety of reasons, they put all that aside when they get back to work.

No one has written more insightfully about the folly of only measuring activities than Robert Schaffer. He strongly urges people to "begin with results, not activities." For example, having identified something like customer service as critical to competitive success, *demand* that particular people in particular jobs and groups establish specific and measurable performance goals relevant to total customer service and deliver against them. Not only do such demands link performance to change and purpose, focus anxiety into motivation, and provide the cause-and-effect cycle that adults need to improvise and learn, but they also give change leaders the only reliable way to assess whether the whole effort is making any difference.

WHAT MAKES A PERFORMANCE ORIENTATION DIFFICULT?

Performance, performance, performance, performance. Do you get my message? Okay, but also recall my comment at the beginning of this chapter: No principle for managing behavior change is more ignored and abused. Why? If the power of a performance context to produce behavior and skill change is so clear and convincing, why are the links between purpose, performance, and change so difficult to maintain?

The short answer is that, even in normal times, risk aversion combines with habit and routine to weaken performance commitments and disciplines inside organizations. As you know, clarity, aggressiveness, measurability, and persistence always demand real effort. But periods of fundamental change make them even harder. For example, committing to clear performance objectives risks both clear success and clear failure. During a period of change, it is far easier to talk about new and lofty purposes—"We seek to be the best!"—than to test the mettle of yourself and others against clear and specific goals, especially if no one is certain how the changes at hand actually matter to performance.

Or consider aggressiveness. Left unattended, most organizations conspire to take the tension—the uneasiness—out of performance goals. Most people know the value of aiming high for "stretch" goals. Yet, at budget and planning time, too many subordinates hide the stretch. Their bosses, who play the same game with their bosses, join in the annual contest of hide and seek. What emerges is definitely not the "best that we can be." This ritual rarely prevents well-honed organizations from growth and prosperity. But during periods of broad-based behavior change, organizations are *not* well honed. Just when they most need the benefit of stretch goals, everyone's long-standing habits prevent hard-nosed, open, and constructive discussions focused on performance and change.

In addition to those well-known problems, fundamental change poses another, more profound difficulty: shifting your understanding of what performance itself means. Think back ten or fifteen years. If you asked how an organization in the private sector performed, the answer described such shareholder considerations as share price, revenues, profits, and market share. If you asked how different parts of the organization performed, the answer referred to functional measures such as sales, capacity, head count, budget variations, and costs. If you asked how specific people were doing, the answer told of performance against individual objectives. The decided preference for what to measure went to things quantifiable in terms of money. And the time dimension for setting and reviewing goals was periodic—from annual and quarterly at the whole organization level down to weekly, daily, and hourly for frontline employees.

As the chart on page 90 illustrates, all those dimensions of performance have altered. Today's goals must be both periodic and continuous. Some are best quantified in terms of money; others in terms of time or quality. Still others, such as satisfaction, skill, morale, and values, are qualitative, not quantitative. Sometimes clear and aggressive individual goals best drive performance and change. But not always—many depend more on team performance. Sometimes functional goals matter most. Often, however, process performance makes change happen. Finally, the health of the enterprise can never be summarized by shareholder value alone. Today, enterprise performance demands a balance among shareholders, customers, employees, and any other crucial constituency.

Most of today's skill, behavior, and working relationship changes link directly to these shifts in performance. Yet change leaders will not identify the performance consequences that help people focus and motivate behavior change if those leaders make no effort to distinguish team from individual, process from function, continuous from periodic, qualitative from quantitative, and time and quality from money. Nor will people understand their role in the big picture if leaders continue to emphasize shareholders or even customers to the exclusion of other critical constituencies, especially the very people asked to make change happen.

The Shifting Dimensions of Performance

	From Yesterday's Performance	To Today's Performance
Whole enterprise	Shareholder value	Shareholder value Customer value Employee value Other constituencies
Subenterprise	Business unit and function	Business unit, process, and function
Basic performance unit	Individual	Individual and team
Metrics	Quantitative Money	Quantitative and qualitative Money, quality, and time
Time	Periodic	Periodic and continuous

Instead, you must learn to make the choices of which performance results to pursue. And you must confidently operate across the four levels that translate purpose into specific goals (see the chart on the opposite page). In addition to establishing a broad purpose such as "earn our customers' loyalty every day," you must identify relevant conceptual performance achievements (e.g., customer retention, satisfaction) and quantitative or qualitative performance metrics (e.g., customer retention rate, customer satisfaction survey scores). *Then you must make specific performance demands.* You must, for example, ask some specific people to "reduce the percentage of lost customers from 10 percent to 6 percent over the next six months." Only when you have taken this last step have you helped anyone understand how he or she can contribute to, and benefit from, the big picture. (The chart on page 91 provides additional illustrations of how to move from high purpose to demanding specific performance goals.)

Part of what makes the new and richer set of performance meanings difficult to practice and learn are long-standing managerial routines,

Translating broad purpose into specific goals

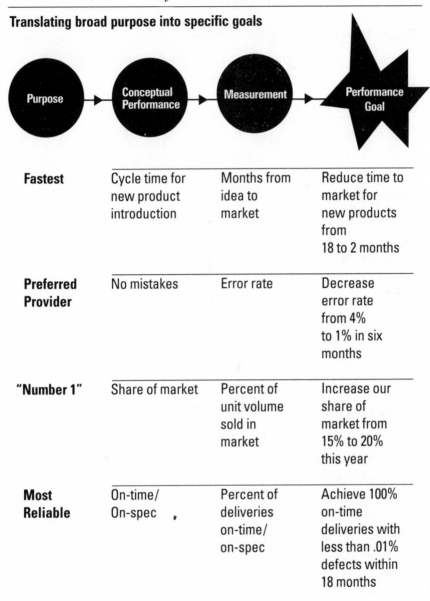

	Purpose	Conceptual Performance	Measurement	Performance Goal
Fastest		Cycle time for new product introduction	Months from idea to market	Reduce time to market for new products from 18 to 2 months
Preferred Provider		No mistakes	Error rate	Decrease error rate from 4% to 1% in six months
"Number 1"		Share of market	Percent of unit volume sold in market	Increase our share of market from 15% to 20% this year
Most Reliable		On-time/ On-spec	Percent of deliveries on-time/ on-spec	Achieve 100% on-time deliveries with less than .01% defects within 18 months

perspectives, and habits. For example, the Iberian Motors executive who said he "would go to his grave believing you can't run a business with 'teams'" will also probably go to his grave without trying to distinguish performance challenges that can best be met through a team discipline. Moreover, as you well know, such traditional managerial perspectives are reinforced by traditional organizational arrangements. Regardless of economic sector, most enterprises are still designed around function instead of process; they plan, budget, review, and reward individual performance instead of team; and they do so against periodic goals quantified mostly in monetary terms instead of continuous goals that are both qualitative and quantitative.

And so those who might use performance to drive change find themselves with a dilemma: Should they ignore existing arrangements and tackle performance on its own terms? Or should they redesign the organization to align with new and different performance realities? The best answer, of course, is both. But as we will see in the story of "Clean Keepers, Inc.," the search for organizational alignment carries with it a high risk of divorcing change efforts from performance consequences—even in a company acclaimed for its focus on performance!

"CLEAN KEEPERS, INC.": THE LURE OF ORGANIZATIONAL ALIGNMENT

"Clean Keepers, Inc." makes a variety of household cleaning products for the laundry, kitchen, and bathroom. Like most consumer product companies, Clean Keepers witnessed a transformation of its industry during the 1980s and early 1990s. Unbranded generics spawned new competitors, including several supermarket chains that also sold Clean Keeper products. Fragmenting and shifting media complicated the job of defining and delivering messages to consumers. Information technology permitted entirely new approaches to things ranging from monitoring detergent production to communicating with distributors. Distribution choices multiplied with the appearance of club and warehouse stores.

By the late 1980s, such fundamental forces had put a premium on the speed, cost, flexibility, and customer service of consumer product companies like Clean Keepers. They also increased the level of complexity in the industry. In a deft strategic move, Clean Keepers exploited this complexity by using product and promotion tactics to dramatically increase the net price it received for products without raising the price paid by the consumer. As a result, company earnings soared to industry-best levels during the four years leading up to 1992. *Business Week, Fortune,* the *Wall Street Journal,* and other publications praised the tough-minded, no-nonsense performance focus of Clean Keepers.

Then, in 1992, financial performance stalled. Fickle analysts who had earlier applauded Clean Keepers now asked whether the company's pricing strategy had come at the expense of addressing fundamental issues of speed, cost, flexibility, and customer service. The analysts' either/or suggestion, however, missed the point. The pricing strategy remained a brilliant strategic move that had not prevented Clean Keepers from dealing with other issues. In fact, as early as 1988, executives had put speed, cost, flexibility, and customer service on their agenda. And by 1992, people throughout the company had lots of ideas for making the needed improvements, including reengineering the order generation through fulfillment process, taking advantage of purchasing economies, rebalancing sales force resources, responding to the special needs of club and warehouse stores, and working directly with suppliers to improve quality.

Only a small number, however, had taken any action. Instead, nearly the entire company waited. In 1991, senior management had invited consultants to help identify the best strategic and organizational solutions to speed, cost, flexibility, and customer service. Working with people throughout the company, the consultants recommended ways to improve speed and quality as well as cost by moving to organization designs that promoted process as well as function, and team as well as individual outcomes. Everyone acknowledged that the recommendations made sense. But the magnitude of the organization changes—together with the implications for the power and positions of senior executives—cast serious doubt on whether any of them would become decisions.

Meanwhile, people still waited. And waited. And waited. Nearly a year later, few decisions had been made. Managers, particularly at the senior level, continued to believe that Clean Keepers' performance would catapult when the full set of decisions finally got taken. And they continued to vigorously challenge the organization to adopt cross-functional coordination, open communications, knowledge sharing, teamwork, customer service, and similar skills, behaviors, and working relationships. To most of the thousands of managers and employees at Clean Keepers, however, these exhortations sounded increasingly artificial and *unconnected to performance.* What evidently still mattered most, people believed, was price, market share, product line extensions, functional excellence, and individual performance. "After all," one Clean Keepers manager said, "these are what's in my budget."

Conclusion: Put People and Performance First

As so often happens, the consultants had told Clean Keepers what people throughout the company already knew: they must redefine performance in order to learn the skills and behaviors needed to deliver that performance. For example, Clean Keepers could not penetrate club and warehouse stores without modifying how it packaged, priced, positioned, and promoted its cleaning products. That would require managers from several different functions and divisions to combine efforts—a clear-cut *team* performance challenge. Instead of taking action by chartering such a team, however, Clean Keepers waited for strategy and organization solutions to that and other challenges. The whole company wasted time in the misguided hope that an alignment of strategy, structure, job descriptions, compensation systems, and budgeting and planning procedures could make the new performance challenges somehow clearer or more approachable.

It is a costly myth, however, that organization alignment must precede fundamental change. The Minnesota government change leaders avoided this mistake. They did not ignore strategy and design. For example, the approach to state funding and budgeting ultimately shifted to facilitate certain skill, behavior, and performance changes under way in the Department of Administration. But, as their story reveals, they spent most of their time—from the outset—working through change with the real people who mattered against the real performance challenges that made the most sense.

The pragmatism of putting performance and people first was a major lesson. "To have tried to 'reorganize,'" says Babak Armajani, "would have meant getting manipulated by one of the most powerful vehicles the old culture uses to perpetuate itself. It gives everyone the chance to debate roles and responsibilities. Endlessly. We wanted to get people using that energy on the bottom line."

Suppose, by contrast, that the Minnesota change leaders, like the executives at Clean Keepers, had bet on refining and aligning the descriptions of strategy and organization design to drive change. Imagine what would have happened if they had tried to get the governor and state legislature to make a series of public policy, strategy, and governmental organization decisions. If you have any doubt about the outcome, just reflect on the 1993–1994 efforts by the Clinton administration and Congress to reform health care through policy, strategy, and organization design changes alone.

Simple logic dictates that you will find it easier and more effective to manage both performance and behavior change *if you relate them to one another.* Basic organizational purpose, human motivation, how adults learn, and administrative effectiveness support this conclusion. Perhaps the power of this logic induces managers to assume that people will stay focused on performance even in the absence of explicit links between change and results. If so they are naive, given the many complex and subtle forces that divert people in organizations from performance, especially during periods of broad-based behavior change.

If you want to lead real change, you must attend to performance and the people who will make it happen—from beginning to end and all during the period of change. Only by linking performance results to purpose and change can you make all three real. And you cannot expect descriptions of abstractions like strategy and organization design to do it for you. Instead, you must do the following:

1. *Develop the performance habit of asking "So what?"* How a particular new idea might matter to specific aspects of performance is rarely obvious. Rather than find out, however, we too often join in dis-

cussions whose only apparent purpose is to conclude whether the
new idea—"teams" or "workplace redesign" or "diversity" or whatever—is "good" or "bad." If the new idea has been introduced by
senior management, we too often worry only about how we can add it
to already crowded agendas. Neither of these responses seriously
engages our attention on performance.

You can avoid this trap with two words: "So what?" Insist that you
and others discuss the specific performance consequences of possible
skill and behavior changes. Ask people, regardless of rank, *why, how,*
and *by how much* the new idea might make a difference to specific
challenges the organization faces. Yes, you must do this constructively and not belligerently. In certain hierarchical settings, you will
need to pick your spots and be diplomatic. But only when you insist on
exploring the potential impact of new ideas on the various and specific
performance contexts of your organization will you make any meaningful progress toward seriously considering whether to use those
ideas.

**2. *Demand performance results from people who must change
skills, behaviors, and working relationships.*** You must demand
performance, in the form of specific goals, from yourself and others
faced with learning and change. Don't stop, as Tandem initially did,
with the articulation of from/to skills and behaviors. Demand
the performance results that will motivate and test those skills and
behaviors.

You have two choices for doing this: you can specify the goals, or you
can demand that people specify the goals themselves. In either case,
you and others must decide on a set of specific goals to drive your
change efforts. Note, however, that this does not mean you must wait
to have the "right" set of goals, or the goals most elegantly coordinated with the rest of the organization, or the goals that everyone
involved completely agrees with. Each of those paths will snare you
into inaction. Instead, take your best shot. Pick goals that seem to link
performance, purpose, and change, and then get going.

**3. *Practice making the performance choices most relevant to
change.*** In setting performance goals, pay attention to the context.

Try to understand which of the dimensions of performance set forth in the chart on page 90 are most critical. For example, the following questions will help you distinguish between individual versus team performance challenges and function versus process performance challenges:

▶ Can we achieve this goal through the sum of individual best efforts? If so, individual assignments will deliver both performance and change.

▶ Does achieving this goal require a small number of us to integrate our multiple skills, perspectives, and efforts? If so, you face a team performance challenge.

▶ Does this challenge require us to become continuously better at separate tasks? If so, you face a classic functional challenge.

▶ Does this challenge require us to become continuously better at coordinating across separate tasks? If so, you face a process performance challenge.

You can become better at distinguishing between team versus individual and process versus function only by making choices and moving forward. If you have made a mistake—say, by miscasting a functional performance challenge as process—then you'll discover it and adjust, so long as you continue to focus on performance itself.

4. *Use both/and goals that translate across all four levels from purpose to specific performance.* The most productive change-oriented goals contain an inherent opposition. Examples include *both* profits *and* market share, *both* cost *and* quality, *both* speed *and* customer satisfaction. At first blush, people might say about such goals, "We can't have both." But when you help them move beyond that habitual either/or logic, everyone uses the creative tension in both/and goals to excel. The Minnesota personnel department, for example, became very good at *both* policy compliance *and* service.

Make certain that such both/and goals are *specific.* Help yourself and others understand the contribution to the big picture by relating overall purpose (e.g., "to be the fastest and the best") through conceptual performance (e.g., "speed and error free") and performance metrics (e.g., "cycle time and error rate") to a specifically stated goal: "Reduce product delivery time from seven days to twenty-four hours while simultaneously reducing the error rate from 3 percent to 1 percent").

5. *Communicate the consequences and benefits of performance to all who must make change happen.* A performance focus forces everyone to consider the consequences and benefits of changing or not changing. Consequences and benefits include the full range of implications from opportunity to threat. You might communicate these at a general level: "more customers with greater loyalty will spend more," "job security," "personal growth and opportunity," "greater profits leading to more investment in our products and ourselves." Or you might describe them quite specifically: "If all of us pull together in the next six weeks, we have a terrific chance of winning the XYZ account"; "By reducing our turnaround time on maintenance requests to twenty-four hours, we'll avoid head-count reductions." Either way, the more you discuss the benefits and consequences of performance, the more likely you will stay focused on them.

In addition, once performance starts to change, find occasions to ask why. You will notice a major difference in the quality and impact of such discussions. At the beginning of a period of change, people often debate why new behaviors and orientations won't work. For example, the Minnesota government workers argued that "customer" was a dangerous concept. Once change and performance were under way, however, this shifted. People began evaluating how new behaviors and skills made a difference to progress. "By treating the line agencies as customers," Minnesota staff managers explained, "we found it easier to collaborate in meeting their needs." At such moments the *theory* of behavior change disappears, and the new skills, behaviors, and working relationships get reinforced with unstoppable momentum.

In Charlie Chaplin's classic film *Modern Times*, one sequence depicts the uncaring, bureaucratic general manager who, seeing all that happens in the factory, demands a faster pace and then settles back to enjoy lunch. Chaplin's metaphors of "business as machine" and "managers as operators of the 'machine'" took direct aim at the dehumanizing tendencies of bureaucracy and big business. They also oversimplified the managerial task, even during an era of stability. In today's fast-moving, complex world, however, managers who call for new behaviors and skills without committing themselves to understanding their specific relevance to *performance results* are no better than Chaplin's bureaucrat. In making this nonsensical mistake, such managers, intentionally or otherwise, dehumanize what is the ultimate human challenge: to transform an organization's performance based on many people learning new skills, behaviors, and working relationships. By contrast, those who relentlessly demand an ever deepening understanding of the connection between new behaviors and new performance give fresh and powerful meaning to the notion of *managing* change.

Chapter Four

Leadership: The Courage to Live the Change

"We must live the change," said Mahatma Gandhi. Few of us question Gandhi's courage to make the world nonviolent by *being* nonviolent. Perhaps more of us wonder what Gandhi's precept has to do with customer service, total quality, process reengineering, innovation, time-based competition, core competencies, mass customization, empowerment, reinventing government, statistical process control, and other organization performance and change challenges. The short answer is "Everything." I believe that living the change is the most pragmatic way to take responsibility for your own change and the only solid ground on which you can lead people through a period of broad-based behavior change.

A less lofty version of Gandhi's precept suggests that "change is as change does." You cannot learn new skills, behaviors, and working relationships without *using* them. You cannot learn team performance without being part of a team that holds itself mutually accountable for achieving specific performance goals. You cannot learn a customer orientation without actually listening to customers and trying to meet their needs. You cannot empower yourself—whether you are CEO or frontline worker—without taking initiative and accountability for performance.

Useful activities such as training, reading, debating, role playing, and contemplating can prepare you for those and other changes. But until you go "live," until you employ new skills, behaviors, and working relationships in real situations demanding performance, you have yet to grapple with real change. As discussed in Chapters Two and Three, all aspects of reluctance—understanding, desire, minimum capability, planning for action, action, and reinforcement—are tested when you experience change in a performance context. It is the only way to convert anxieties into action and action into learning.

Putting your performance in play, however, means taking risks. When dozens or hundreds or thousands of people in your organization must do so simultaneously, the risks multiply well beyond the control of any single person. Moreover, many performance and change challenges, such as process reengineering and team performance, *require* you to risk your performance on the performance of others and vice versa. Both by circumstance and by design, periods of broad-based behavior change confront you with the possibility of failure notwithstanding your own best effort. They ensure failure absent your effort. With that possibility, then, comes doubt—doubt about change, doubt about others, and doubt about yourself. With doubt, in turn, comes the question of courage.

"Courage" may sound to some like an odd, perhaps old-fashioned word to apply to the world of work and organizations. But I disagree. As the third millennium approaches, the economic and psychological consequences of having a job, belonging to an organization, and contributing to that organization's performance have more importance to more women and men than ever before in history. Since we all must risk our jobs, our contributions, our friendships, and our self-esteem during periods of fundamental change, I assert that "courage" is exactly the appropriate word.

It takes courage for frontline workers to learn new skills and behaviors on the job, to collaborate with unfamiliar people from other departments or companies, and to take on expanded managerial responsibilities—all while living under the constant threat of further head-count reductions. It takes courage for senior executives to attempt ambitious and untested strategies, build confidence and direction among people at much deeper levels in the organization than ever before, take risks on unproved leaders, and master the fears of thousands of people as well as themselves. And it takes courage for the much-maligned, disappearing class of middle managers to jump from long-term, economically secure roles as information and order processors to short-lived assignments as coaches, facilitators, champions, and problem solvers, every task of which—by design—is meant to come to an end.

To *lead* people through periods of fundamental behavior change takes even greater courage. Like everyone else, leaders must work through their own doubts and reluctance as they perform and change. Unlike everyone else, leaders must go first. They must show the way. Inevitably, the leaders' personal change efforts are more visible and, fairly or not, are held to a higher standard of consistency and effort. "Change is as change does" always applies to leaders.

Although you already recognize that leaders must go first, you may not have considered what else makes leaders so vulnerable during periods of change. Think back, for example, to the challenge facing Donna, Tom, and Cindy at Wireboard. Each had to lead frontline employees through change while simultaneously changing themselves, which meant they had to reconstruct each of the cornerstones of their own authority and leadership:

▶ *Technical/functional expertise.* When performance depends on both process and functional excellence, both team and individual outcomes, and both periodic and continuous improvement, whatever functional or technical expertise you already have is important—but not enough. Accordingly, if you try to base your authority only on your existing knowledge and skills, you will fail.

▶ *Traditional managerial expertise.* Fact gathering, listening, tough-minded decision making, delegation, and monitoring of individual performance remain relevant to any managerial challenge. During periods of broad-based behavior change, however, those approaches are necessary but insufficient. When other people must empower themselves, when teams must control their own decision making and performance, and when existing employees must learn new skills, behaviors, and working relationships, they and you are likely to fail unless you find additional managerial expertise to rely on. Such new expertise may relate to team or process performance, or to managing people through a period of behavior-driven change. But it is *new*. And unlike traditional managerial expertise, most managers and leaders have neither learned nor experienced these skills yet. They have not "been there before."

▶ *Decision making.* Neither decisions regarding direction and design nor descriptions of the required changes will carry enough people through the period needed to translate reluctance into performance and change. Decisions can help people begin. But you will fail if you ground your authority only on the decisions you make.

▶ *Hierarchical position.* Of all sources for authority, hierarchy is the one least likely to disappear under the feet of those who must take charge of change. More often than not, leaders retain some hierarchical authority, even if modified. That is a good thing. Hierarchy has added immense value to the world, and pundits who call for its demise are either fools or cynics. But leaders, whether they face traditional or nontraditional performance challenges, lose respect and credibility when they base their authority on hierarchy alone. Hierarchy has never been enough.

To lead during a period of behavior-driven change, you must not only perform and change yourself but find and hold new ground on which to base your credibility and confidence as a leader. This triple feat—*perform, change,* and *find new ground for authority*—is every bit as challenging as it sounds. People expect you to have the answers. Often you don't. You expect yourself to have the answers. Often you don't. Sometimes you do have the answers, but if you provide them, you rob people of the chance to experience change and performance. Sometimes, by contrast, in *not* providing the answers, you produce the same dispiriting result.

You cannot navigate your way through such a challenge without courage. And by courage, I mean more than single, isolated acts of bravery or fortitude. Periods of behavior-driven change demand courage *every day.* You have that kind of courage inside; the question is how to develop and direct it. Interestingly, as we will see in the story of "Dan Holloway" of "Southwest Gas Electric and Power," the characteristics normally associated with good leadership are needed but not enough. To lead others through change, you must have the *courage to change yourself.*

SOUTHWEST GAS ELECTRIC AND POWER: THE COMMON WISDOM OF LEADERSHIP

In 1990, "Southwest Gas Electric and Power" faced a daunting challenge. Throughout the late 1980s, various government bodies had steadily increased competition in Southwest's market without entirely removing legal constraints, including ever more complex environmental rules, on Southwest itself. Regulators, for example, had entirely deregulated the gas side, opened up the market to any producer using new energy technologies, and allowed cities to municipalize (the right to establish their own utility). Southwest's CEO had seen this coming. He was among the first utility industry executives to promote becoming "market and customer driven" as a vision for his company.

By 1990, most people at Southwest had heard a lot about the CEO's vision but had yet to change much. The utility, for example, performed only marginally better at differentiating among customer needs while optimizing its own economics. In asking "Dan Holloway" to run the Marketing and Distribution Division, the CEO hoped to dramatically increase the pace of change at the customer interface.

Dan Holloway was both an engineer and a lawyer in a utility run by engineers and lawyers. He had combined his technical, leadership, and people skills to deliver a string of important contributions during the turbulent 1980s, including persuading one major city not to municipalize and gaining approval for a new nuclear facility. He challenged regulators, Southwest's powerful staff and policy makers, and even, on occasion, the CEO to move faster with change. Many people expected he would one day run Southwest.

Dan's appointment generated excitement in the Marketing and Distribution Division. Everyone knew he would do something; no one was disappointed. He started by spending half his time with employees and customers. He leapfrogged the division's managerial ranks and appealed to frontline workers to make the CEO's vision "real." Dan regularly appointed teams to come up with recommendations for his approval and always delivered a swift response when they did. He visited customers with the intention to listen instead of talk or promise. He engaged a consulting firm to work with his group of senior division executives to craft a market strategy for how best to distribute energy to Southwest's many different customer segments. When that study was complete, Dan threw out the current budget and asked managers to submit new plans based on the new strategy. Finally, he worked with the CEO and others to keep pressure on Southwest's Power Supply Division (which supplied energy to Holloway's Marketing and Distribution Division) to lower its costs because, as Dan argued, being customer driven would also require being lowest cost.

By the end of Dan's first year, enthusiasm for change was high. He was convinced he had the right strategy. He was also more comfortable delegating legal and engineering matters to managers in his division. He continued, however, to reserve all critical marketing issues for himself.

Although generally optimistic, Dan knew that more challenges lay ahead. Customer awareness of Southwest's new vision, for example, had risen faster than the utility's capabilities. Consequently, customer satisfaction had actually declined. Moreover, as far as Dan was concerned, the Power Supply Division remained stalled and the powerful central staff units continued to prevent him from making decisions critical to the Marketing and Distribution Division's success.

Dan was also troubled by the absence of personal initiative and accountability among managers in his division. Too many people, from supervisors up to some of his own direct reports, insisted on the safety of higher approval—often many levels of approval—before taking action. He had discussed this throughout his first year, but had found no solution. Accordingly, he asked a team of his direct reports and consultants to figure out an organization approach to overcome the problem. Given the complexities of Southwest's business and operations—regulatory constraints, environmental and safety concerns, technical requirements, differing customer segment needs—Dan cautioned the study team to take whatever time it needed to really "get the organization right."

Meanwhile, Dan redirected much of his personal time to challenging the CEO, the head of the Power Supply Division, and the chiefs of Southwest's centralized legal, engineering, and other staff units to become more aggressive about change. He asked the CEO to transfer decision-making authority from the staff units to the Marketing and Distribution Division. He also continued to speak out within the division about change, about the need to be customer driven, and about working more like a team. And he continued his signature practice of appointing teams to come up with recommendations that he could act on quickly.

The reorganization team completed their work toward the end of Dan's second year. They told him that division progress required a complete rewiring of the decision-making process in order to push authority down the line. In addition, the team asked Dan to adopt a bottom-up annual planning and budgeting cycle as well as to roll out a major financial training program to frontline supervisors and middle managers.

Dan approved the team's recommendations and, recognizing their complexity, asked them to invest a few months communicating the new decision-making arrangements. Another round of excitement and energy swept through the division. Managers and supervisors applauded the new approach and eagerly attended the financial training sessions. In at least one major way, the whole effort paid off. The annual plan submitted at the end of Dan's third year was the best ever created by any Southwest Division.

That plan, however, seemed to be Dan's major accomplishment in year three. Centralized staff continued to fight him at every turn. The Power Supply Division hadn't lowered its cost structure enough. And the CEO, in Dan's opinion, continued to move too slowly on the decision-making authority that Dan wanted. Now, however, when he voiced his criticisms, Dan heard others asking, "What has Holloway actually done?" And he feared, their motivations aside, they had a point.

His division wasn't stuck. In fact, it was better positioned than ever for the world of deregulation and competition. Beyond the impact of the pricing strategy, the quality of the new planning effort, and a series of modest cost-cutting improvements, however, overall performance seemed modest. Dan believed he had failed to translate enthusiasm into results.

He also felt that too many people were letting him down. Too few managers and supervisors had learned to act decisively notwithstanding their new decision-making authority. Dan agreed that their latest explanation—the lack of a good management information system—made sense. Yet, after three years, it also sounded like an excuse. He was depressed. He admitted to close friends that he was not sure what to do and would welcome a different assignment.

GOOD LEADERSHIP IS NOT ENOUGH

Dan Holloway was a good leader. Unlike many potential leaders who permit self-doubt and weakness to overwhelm them, he demonstrated the courage—the spirit, bravery, endurance, and guts—to step up to one of his organization's most critical challenges. Yet, although he used such attributes to lead, Dan did not call on them to *drive change in himself or in his basis for authority.* As a result, although he did an excellent job of preparing the Marketing and Distribution Division for change, he failed to achieve enough real performance or real change.

Dan's good leadership was necessary but not enough to guide people through a period when their collective performance depended on changing skills, behaviors, and working relationships. His story illustrates why so many commonly held perceptions about leadership only partially identify what leaders need to do during periods of fundamental change:

▶ **Top management commitment.** Obviously, change will not happen if top managers are not committed to it. Dan Holloway, however, was fully committed to the effort he led. So are most leaders who take on performance and change challenges. Something more than commitment is needed.

▶ **Empowerment.** Dan regularly empowered frontline teams to recommend changes. He delegated legal and engineering matters to others. And he approved the rewiring of decision-making and spending authorities. Finally, he held people accountable for the matters he delegated, avoiding a common pitfall of those who use empowerment. Still, empowering others was not enough.

▶ *Symbolic behavior.* Dan used his time, attention, and symbolic behavior to model what he wanted the division to do. He spent time with customers, confronted the Power Supply Division and central staffs, and acted swiftly on all decisions. His own actions demonstrated the importance of such behaviors. Most division people got the message. Yet too few made the necessary changes.

▶ *Vision.* Dan ceaselessly communicated the CEO's vision of becoming market and customer driven. He also discussed why and how people had to change, such as managers becoming more action and risk oriented. Powerful and compelling as they were, however, Dan's words and vision fell short of leading enough people to change.

▶ *Inspiration and enthusiasm.* Dan created a tremendous amount of enthusiasm and energy. People throughout the division liked and supported him and where he wanted to take the organization. Nevertheless, by his own admission, he failed to translate that energy into performance and change.

▶ *Teamwork.* Dan emphasized teamwork from the frontlines straight to the top. In fact, teams making quick recommendations became part of his unique signature of leadership. Moreover, his senior colleagues shared his vision for change in his division and in Southwest as a whole. Still, too many of them, like too many people throughout the division, remained painfully slow in taking action.

Change is as change does. Although a very good leader, Dan Holloway changed neither his own behaviors nor the ground for his leadership authority. Look more closely at his story, and you will see that his leadership depended on traditional managerial practices. For example, he

▶ emphasized decisions about strategy and organization design instead of focusing on performance, people, and how they could work to make a difference

- reserved a disproportionate number of decisions for himself, including all those affecting the division's core marketing challenges

- delegated only when he believed that people had enough capability, and then only in matters within his own comfort zone of expertise (legal, engineering, low-level spending)

- required analytical completeness before action, thereby betraying greater concern for his own conviction than the conviction of others

- sought to grab turf for himself away from the central staffs instead of building common ground for collaboration with them

Such managerial practices can make sense when performance results depend on coordinating decisions and actions of already capable people across an organization headed in new directions. Southwest, however, faced a different challenge. Its performance depended on many existing people experiencing and learning new ways of working. Dan's managerial approaches did not promote the *experience* of change. Instead of building a "we" who would make both performance and change happen, Dan left unclear just how much he would entrust his performance to other people. All of which explains why, his traditionally strong leadership skills aside, he did so poorly at leading the division through change.

BLACK & WHITE FILM FLOW: EXPERIENCING THE VISION

When Steve Frangos became chief of Kodak's Black & White Film Manufacturing Division in late 1989, the company was having a terrible year. Instead of the record profits promised to investors, Kodak reported double-digit declines. To get back on track, the CEO announced a major workforce reduction, a companywide pay freeze, and the intention to divest nonperforming businesses. This mollified investors but deeply upset employees. In an enterprise that gave extra meaning to "lifetime employment" (the parents and grandparents of many workers had also worked for Kodak), people now openly debated unionizing. Meanwhile, customers were also unhappy. Kodak was too slow, too late, and too error ridden. Company executives decided to reorganize manufacturing into what they called "flows," hoping that a horizontal, cross-functional process approach would turn performance around.

The selection of Steve Frangos to run the Black & White flow made sense. He was a thirty-year Kodak veteran who always delivered results. Morale would be a major issue, and Steve was known for his strong interest in people. Moreover, he was loyal—senior managers considered him the ultimate "good soldier" whom they could count on to take a conservative, determined approach to any challenge. As one executive recalled, "Steve was not considered a star. He wasn't showy or flashy either. He wasn't going to do anything too risky or radical."

On taking charge in September, Steve immediately reached out for help. "I made it a personal goal to talk with the fifteen hundred people who would make or break the effort," he says. "Every single one of them." Throughout that autumn, he met repeatedly with the thirty-three most senior managers of Black & White, the sixty frontline supervisors, and, in small groups, the fourteen hundred frontline workers. His topics never varied: performance; why performance mattered to people in Black & White and beyond (families, customers, others at Kodak, shareholders); and the challenge Black & White faced in turning performance around.

His first gathering of the division's thirty-three top leaders set the tone. Kodak had a long history of treating information confidentially, which made sense for chemical formulas and patent-related matters. As happens in so many organizations, however, Kodak's legitimate concern for trade secrets had mutated into a disease. Information simply wasn't shared at all, making it difficult for anyone to know anything about the big picture. Although Steve knew the senior managers each could identify performance problems in their own areas, he suspected that neither they nor anyone else in the division comprehended the full dimensions of Black & White's troubles. When he asked the group, for example, how often Black & White missed on-time deliveries, people could only guess. No one knew the division was late one-third of the time. By the end of that first afternoon, the top group also learned that Black & White tied up tens of millions of dollars in excess inventory; threw out one-third of its product each year as waste; took forty-two days to process material that, if done in a perfect world, would take ten hours; and contributed to Kodak's being late to market with new film products by as much as a year.

The senior leaders were sobered, but grateful for Steve's candor. Others in Black & White were less receptive when Steve spoke with them. Just before the September flow reorganization, Black & White had eliminated the fourth shift, an important source of income to workers. Many of them, angered over this and Kodak's earlier announced layoffs and pay freeze, questioned Steve's intentions and capabilities. "Turnaround?" went one typical comment. "This guy probably can't even parallel park."

Moreover, Steve's wide-open discussion of performance gaps and change scared many people. Throughout the fall of 1989, a steadily increasing number of employees requested transfers out of Black & White. Most did so because they felt the division would fail; others, such as supervisors who did not like the prospect of becoming coaches, because they did not want to change.

Steve and his senior colleagues persisted. They were determined to get as many people as possible to join them in collaboratively solving Black & White's challenges. And they continued to use open communications, information sharing, and improvisation as the primary fuel for change. They knew, for example, that the division would need a vision. In attempting to shape one, however, the group could only agree on a number of common themes. These included meeting performance challenges relevant to speed, on-time and error-free deliveries, and lower costs as well as establishing a higher sense of purpose in Black & White—among other things, for example, the division's products played essential roles in activities ranging from life-saving medical procedures to cutting-edge scientific exploration.

Rather than force such complex thoughts into a single vision statement, the leaders decided to post different possibilities they had crafted throughout the Black & White complex and invite smaller groups of supervisors and workers to participate. By early 1990, Black & White did not have one single Vision. Instead, dozens of groups had adopted small-v visions filled with relevant and important performance goals such as "One Day" for vastly reducing cycle time. In addition, discussions about the division's impact on society, Kodak, Kodak's customers, and the Rochester, New York, community offered a more positive sense of self and purpose to those ready to seize it.

The leadership group's improvised approach to vision turned out well. But four months into the new flow, Black & White's performance continued to deteriorate, prompting the first of two unexpected crises. Kodak's worldwide manufacturing executives decided to recommend transferring most of Black & White's film production to other, color-film plants with newer, more efficient equipment. Having worked hard to build openness, ownership, and commitment, the Frangos team knew this decision would kill any turnaround.

They also thought the senior manufacturing executives were mistaken about the promised efficiencies of transferring the work elsewhere. In making more than seven thousand different film products, Black & White was a classic job shop requiring experience and flexibility for shorter production runs, lower volumes, and greater product variability. By contrast, color plants needed long runs and high volumes to remain efficient. At Steve's urging, his colleague Rich Malloy made this case to Steve's boss, Ron Heidke. Ron, in turn, convinced the worldwide manufacturing leaders to switch course.

The transfer scare gained the Frangos team credibility for their commitment to Black & White—as well as a rich opportunity to drive change and performance. They wrote and presented a skit to division audiences that portrayed how "Mr. Corporate" and "Mr. High Volume" sought but didn't gain the production work handled by the skit's hero, "Mr. Job Shop." Everyone enjoyed the show. Most people attending also took away a few critical messages. First, unless "Mr. Job Shop's" performance improved, "Mr. Corporate" and "Mr. High Volume" would be back. Second, the capital-V vision of the division was now clear: to be a "superior job shop producing high value, specialty products" that were important to themselves, their customers, the company, and the world.

Frangos and friends also improvised their way through the second unexpected crisis during the winter of 1989–1990. Shortly after the fourth shift was eliminated, production planners informed division leaders that volume would rise to the point of requiring overtime. The irony didn't escape anyone. "We had just told people we needed to cut back," says Bob Brookhouse. "Now we were going to have to ask them to work overtime!"

Kodak had two ways to handle overtime. In the first, called "declared," the company committed itself to a defined period of paying overtime—regardless of actual need or use—in exchange for the right to require people to work longer hours. The second, "casual" overtime committed neither the company nor the workers to anything. The risks of declared overtime are committing workers to time they don't want to work and the company to money it doesn't want to spend. The risk of casual overtime is that production stalls because not enough people volunteer when needed.

Bob Brookhouse recalls that everyone on the Frangos team "wanted to do right by the workers." They assumed that meant two things. First, they decided to hold preference meetings to gain frontline collaboration on the choice between casual and declared overtime. Second, because they assumed workers would choose declared to assure themselves of income in troubled times, division management agreed to incur the risk of extra expense at a time when financial results were unacceptably low.

The managers were startled by what happened. Employees who remained angry about life at Kodak in general accused management of manipulation. Other, more constructive workers split evenly between those favoring casual and those preferring declared. And in their debates, people argued as clearly about their personal issues of money and time as they did about the division's needs to meet production schedules. In the end, casual won by a narrow margin, presenting management with a dilemma—whether they could depend on enough volunteers to meet production demand.

Steve and others didn't hesitate. They went with the casual approach. Black & White's frontline workers came through. With the overtime and Mr. Job Shop crises behind them, as well as the growing understanding and desire to meet the challenge of performance and change, the division finally stopped its decline. Six months into the new flow, Black & White produced enough improvements that Steve and others saw the first real glimmer of hope.

Black & White had turned a corner, but not *the* corner. Steve remained convinced that the only way to win was to get everyone focused on high performance and learning different ways of working to achieve it. He also believed performance and change had to start with himself and his fellow leaders. In putting together their 1990 objectives, for example, the management team realized they lacked the right information to understand and manage division performance. But the team decided to do the best they could with what they had. As Steve recalls, two team members "pulled numbers together from thin air" that provided a baseline picture of current division performance. The team agreed to hold themselves mutually accountable for a 130 percent improvement over the next twelve months—a commitment that, for many in the group, required a clear act of faith.

"When the time came to commit to the numbers," says one executive, "I really had to do a lot of believing in the team. Because I really did not know if the performance improvement opportunities in other parts of the division would pan out."

Next, the team decided they needed a set of values and principles to guide them. Everyone knew how tricky this would be. "It never takes much effort or a lot of time," said one team member, "to generate cynicism about new values and principles. Our job was not only to craft them, but to make them *real*."

Consequently, after spending an enormous amount of time articulating and defining the values and principles (shown on the opposite page), they committed themselves to act on them. "Our focus," says Steve's colleague Marty Britt, "was really on ourselves. We kept searching and trying to behave the way we needed to in order to get done what we had to do."

No one was more determined than Steve. "I vowed to myself," he remembers, "that when I saw behaviors that were inconsistent with the values and principles, I would call people on it. I wasn't going to fire anyone, or be vindictive, or rate anyone down. I would make sure my approach was not recriminating. But I would seize such opportunities to talk among ourselves about the behaviors we did need for performance results to improve versus those we didn't, and do so publicly and out in the open."

Steve and others discovered just how hard it was to follow through on such promises—mostly because it meant changing their own behaviors. "It is very, very hard," Steve says, "to let go." He and others had to let go of personalizing criticism in order to sustain a learning context. They also had to let go of the relative safety of conducting such discussions privately.

To connect behavior to performance, the leaders had to learn how to tell the whole truth. This too was hard. Sometimes they did not know the whole truth themselves, which meant admitting ignorance (not easily done by Kodak managers) and promising to get back to people

---

KODAK BLACK & WHITE FILM FLOW
VALUES AND PRINCIPLES

Customers
  ‣ We will focus our efforts to provide customer delight.

Partners
  ‣ We will develop an enjoyable, safe, participative environment where
  • We will trust each other and communicate openly.
  • We will use teamwork to get things done.
  • We will continuously build everyone's capability for excellence.

Flow
  ‣ We will add value to the company by being a superior job shop.
  ‣ We will commit to flow thinking.

Continuous Improvement
  ‣ We will be data driven and constantly strive to improve our performance.

(soaking up time they didn't think they had). Other times, telling the whole truth required honesty about painful realities. Most of them, for example, believed that part of a manager's job was to "take care of his or her people." Now they had to tell people to take care of their own careers. Lifetime employment was dead at Kodak and not coming back.

Finally, they also recognized that people would not take responsibility for performance and change so long as managers made all decisions. This too meant changing themselves. "I like to be in control," Steve says. "And after thirty years at Kodak, I knew that everyone—my boss, my people, and myself—expected me to have the answers. But I had to learn how to let go. The second hardest part of this was learning to ask people, 'How would you do this?' or 'What do you think?' The first hardest was to actually do it. To go along with what they suggested. Because that was the only way to build their commitment to change and performance."

"I also had to learn," he continues, "that this did not mean I would just be a facilitator. I still had to make some decisions, just not all of them. I couldn't abrogate my responsibilities as boss. But I got much more skillful at interjecting my thinking through nonhierarchical methods such as 'Have you thought about this?' or 'Have you talked with such and such a person?'"

With Steve leading the way, the Black & White managers changed themselves and their approach to leadership. It paid off. Their practice of nonjudgementally discussing negative behaviors took hold. "Before you knew it," Steve says, "others were doing the same thing. I was amazed at how fast turfism and other unneeded behaviors disappeared and got replaced with more productive approaches."

In addition to using behavior discussions as learning experiences, the Frangos team became world-class at positively reinforcing other people who were trying to learn new skills, behaviors, and working relationships. They spent a lot of time learning how to positively reinforce one another, they put "positive reinforcement" explicitly on their meeting agendas, and they continued using skits, songs, and home videos to spread their news about performance and change around the division.

Steve himself never missed an opportunity to celebrate and publicize a performance success. He always handled such events with the same purpose. First, he congratulated people for making a difference and, when good cheer was established, he asked, "Now, tell me what you did to bring this about?" Inevitably, the conversation turned to how the performance achievement could not have happened without specific changes in skills, behaviors, and working relationships.

As the spring, summer, and fall of 1990 rolled by, Steve found himself quite busy celebrating. Along with their collective effort to educate themselves and everyone else about performance, purpose, economics, and finance, the leaders had also introduced new thinking and techniques such as total quality, inventory management, and process control and improvement. In all cases, they emphasized delivering training just in time for people to perform. For example, they sent groups to the famed Pecos River leadership program only if those groups had specific performance challenges—error reduction, on-time delivery, and so on—that would be explicitly addressed.

The reinforcing cycle of people, purpose, performance, and change became unstoppable. Midway through year one, it took on its own unique imagery and style. Perhaps unsurprisingly among fifteen hundred people making black-and-white film, there was talk about zebras. As in everything else, the leadership group improvised on the chance to drive performance and change. One among them did a little research and discovered that zebras were an endangered species who could survive only in herds. Remember how "Mr. Corporate" endangered "Mr. Job Shop's" survival? Remember how determined the Frangos team was to build a single, cohesive "herd" of "we" throughout the division to make performance and change happen? In Steve's new math of leadership, one plus one equaled fifteen hundred. He and others began wearing zebra costumes, displaying pictures of zebras, visiting local zoos, making videos called *Dances with Zebras*, writing and performing zebra songs and poems, and granting zebra awards.

To some at Kodak, the zebra imagery seemed overdone and hokey. Even within Black & White it only superficially captured the phenomenon of real performance built on real behavior and skill change. By the end of 1990, for example, the ambitious performance goal of 130 percent improvement had itself been surpassed by more than one-third. And year two delivered comparable results. The herd of zebras slashed late deliveries by nearly 90 percent, reduced key cycle times by a factor of four, brought waste to record lows, cut inventory by tens of millions of dollars, and reduced overall production costs by more than $40 million.

Hundreds of people in Black & White were far more capable, both individually and collectively, than they had been before. They understood statistical process control, total quality, customer service, reengineering, and the economics and finance of film manufacturing. People from Steve Frangos to the frontlines knew about teamwork, team performance, and when to use both. Many were cross-skilled in multiple specialties. And they deeply understood how to integrate work and fun to promote mutual trust, learning, and performance. As Phil Leyendecker, one of the non–Black & White Kodak executives who truly understood what had happened, commented, "You couldn't just do this with zebra hype. You could only do this with deep conviction and belief."

CONCLUSION: LINK PRINCIPLES, PURPOSE, PERFORMANCE, AND PEOPLE

Both Dan Holloway and Steve Frangos demonstrated common elements of good leadership: commitment, empowerment, vision, inspiration, symbolic behavior, and teamwork. As their stories show, however, these elements are not enough *to lead yourself and others* through a period of behavior-driven change.

To grasp why, reread the italicized phrase of the last sentence: *to lead yourself and others*. Change is as change does. You cannot lead behavior-driven change in others without changing your own behaviors. Everyone knows, for example, that good leaders must practice the golden rule ("Do unto others as you would have others do unto you."). The Frangos team went further. They discovered and applied the golden rule of leading change: *Do unto yourself what you would have others do unto themselves.* As a result, the team traveled well beyond the boundaries of good leadership:

▶ In addition to top management *commitment,* they developed the *conviction* that everyone in Black & White must collaborate together to transform the division.

▶ They tried their hardest to help people take responsibility for their own change and to provide those who did the resources needed just in time to succeed. But they also realized that the only people they could truly empower to change were themselves.

▶ In addition to generating a common vision of *what* and *why* Black & White should aspire to accomplish, they built a common vision of *how* the division could get through the period of change.

▶ They created huge amounts of energy and enthusiasm, and then focused that scarce resource on the specific performance, behavior, and skill changes that would make a difference.

▶ In addition to using good teamwork, they demanded team performance against specific goals ranging from cycle time reduction to skit preparation.

▶ They did not use behavior symbolically. They lived the change they wished to bring about.

The process was not easy or natural. Like most managers at Kodak and other organizations, everyone on the Frangos team needed courage to simultaneously deliver division performance, change their own behaviors, and change the basis for their authority as leaders. Their story echoes the central themes in Part 1 of this book:

▶ ***Principles.*** You already know that effective leaders and managers are principle driven. All the best traditional managerial approaches are principle based. Fundamental change, then, poses a different quandary. Well-understood management principles for meeting traditional performance challenges—managing assets, getting new people to learn existing skills, directing already capable people toward new opportunities, and maintaining morale and competitiveness in the face of adversity—simply won't work during periods of behavior-driven performance and change. You need different ground to stand on.

But you do need some solid, principled ground for your authority. Too many potential change leaders naively think authority and control are antithetical to change. That is a mistake. Nothing is worse for anyone, including leaders, than being tossed about by an effort out of control.

When Steve Frangos and his colleagues describe the importance of letting go, they are not saying to let go of authority or leadership. Rather, they are emphasizing the need to let go of *managerial means* that get in the way of the performance and change. Dan Holloway, for example, did not let go of traditional principles for decision making. His additional and more profound mistake, however, was in failing to find a *new set of principles* to guide his role as leader.

Unlike Dan Holloway, the Frangos team succeeded because they both let go of what would not work and grabbed onto what would. As Marty Britt describes, "We had to let go of managing in ways we had always thought we needed and replace them with managing in ways we knew we needed *now.*" They could not do this without enduring a lot of self-doubt. But in crafting and using the management principles they needed to do their job, the Frangos team gave themselves something positive to focus on and do. That, in turn, provided a critical source of courage to change their own skills and behaviors as well as their foundation for authority and control.

This raises a subtle but essential point. None of the management principles discussed in this book is beyond your capability to adopt. Take, for example, the principle of keeping performance results as the primary objective of behavior and skill change. You have the minimum capability to know whether any change initiative is focusing on performance results versus change for the sake of change. Or how about ensuring that everyone understands how performance and change matter to the whole organization's purpose? You have the capability to work with people to ensure they understand how their personal contributions make a difference to the big picture. Or consider providing people the support they need just in time to perform. Again, you have the capability of knowing whether you are deploying training, information, reinforcement, and other resources just in time for specific people to meet specific performance challenges.

The same applies to the other principles. You have the capability to use them. Therefore, you can avoid relying on inappropriate management principles or no principles at all so long as you choose to change your own behaviors and the basis for your authority to lead.

‣ *Purpose, performance, and change.* In relentlessly focusing on performance and its specific links to purpose and behavior change, the Frangos team found a way to make all three real. Dan Holloway failed at this. He discussed, described, and emphasized vision, change, and performance to audiences throughout his division. But he invested more in decisions and descriptions about strategy and organization design instead of finding ways for himself and others to *experience* the challenge at hand. As a result, he succeeded in connecting purpose, performance, and change only in theory, only to himself, and only on paper.

The Frangos team confronted serious organization design constraints. Black & White had too many managerial levels, the Kodak pay freeze demoralized everyone, and they lacked the best information needed to monitor results. Instead of trying to influence people *indirectly* through fixing the organization chart, compensation approaches, or management information and decision-making systems, Black & White's change leaders preferred more personal, direct methods aimed squarely at performance and the people who could improve it.

They created energy for change through candor about the whole picture at Black & White, including the negative consequences of continued poor performance and the positive benefits of turning the situation around. They focused that energy by demanding specific performance outcomes from themselves and others, and then gave people the training, information, and other assistance just in time to change and perform. When they did discuss organization design, it was to portray a picture—the flow—of *how* people could work together differently instead of ways to divide up decision-making authorities. Finally, they regenerated and refocused energy through constantly reinforcing people—both for their successful performance contributions and for the new skills, behaviors, and working relationships that would sustain Black & White as it moved ahead.

▸ *People*. When an organization's performance depends on many existing people learning new skills, behaviors, and working relationships, leaders cannot succeed without people. You cannot succeed by firing enough of them, or compensating for their deficiencies with deft strategies, or deploying assets or technology to replace them. Instead, *you* can succeed only if *they* succeed at both change and performance.

The good news is that most adults have the minimum capabilities to learn today's most important skills, behaviors, and working relationships. As a leader, therefore, you can entrust your performance to the people of your organization—if you have the will to do so. Dan Holloway never did this. He demanded a lot of change from people in his division, but demonstrated neither a willingness to change himself nor the confidence or trust to put his performance in the hands of others.

The bad news is that you cannot change behaviors for other people. Adults must take responsibility for their own behavior and skill change. The vast majority do so reluctantly. Your job as leader is to identify and respond to their sources of reluctance. And the single most effective vehicle is to find ways for them to *experience* the change at hand.

Dan fell short there, too. Although he involved many people in many activities, the efforts were directed at finding and making recommendations as opposed to delivering performance results. To be sure, people in the Southwest Marketing and Distribution Division grew much better at making recommendations. But they—and Dan—would have benefited far more from the experience of both making and implementing their own decisions about how best to differentiate service and economic arrangements among various customer segments.

By contrast, the Frangos team never stopped improvising ways for people to experience change in contexts relevant to performance. Whether through encouraging people to adopt their own small-v visions for performance improvements, or okaying experimentation aimed at meeting specific performance goals, or converting unexpected events into education and performance opportunities ("Mr. High Volume"), the Black & White leaders were always searching out ways, in Steve Frangos's words, for "people to empower themselves."

Principles, purpose, performance, change, people—all fueled the courage to change within and beyond the Frangos team. The whole of their focus was on performance and the "we" who would make it happen. Unlike Dan Holloway, who fought "we/they" battles with the Power Supply Division and the central staffs, Steve reached out to anyone—whether in or beyond Black & White—who might collaborate with him in making a difference. Marty Britt, for example, was just one of Steve's team members who reported not to Steve but to centralized Kodak staff units.

To Steve, such organization boundaries were meaningless, nonexistent. All that mattered were performance, change, and people. It is not that he saw and chose to ignore formal distinctions based on function or hierarchical position. He didn't *see* them. If you were on the scene, you were a full-fledged zebra. This habit of enlisting people to make a difference was very powerful. Midway through the Black & White transformation, for example, people in one Kodak centralized staff unit took a straw poll on which of the company's half-dozen flows they most preferred to assist. Black & White won 100 percent of the votes. "Black & White just wasn't threatening," explained one who voted. "It wasn't 'we' and 'they.' It was only 'us.'"

PART 2

STRATEGIES

THE MANAGEMENT PRINCIPLES

1. *Keep performance results the primary objective of behavior and skill change.*

2. *Continually increase the number of individuals taking responsibility for their own change.*

3. *Ensure each person always knows why his or her performance and change matters to the purpose and results of the whole organization.*

4. *Put people in a position to learn by doing and provide them the information and support needed just in time to perform.*

5. *Embrace improvisation as the best path to both performance and change.*

6. *Use team performance to drive change whenever demanded.*

7. *Concentrate organization designs on the work people do, not the decision-making authority they have.*

8. *Create and focus energy and meaningful language because they are the scarcest resources during periods of change.*

9. *Stimulate and sustain behavior-driven change by harmonizing initiatives throughout the organization.*

10. *Practice leadership based on the courage to live the change you wish to bring about.*

Organizations navigate through periods of change by using many different initiatives—total quality, continuous improvement, reengineering, new strategies, pricing shifts, acquisitions and divestitures, geographic or channel expansion, joint ventures and alliances, and so on. Some require many existing people to change behaviors and ways of working. Some do not. You must distinguish the two cases to know which management discipline and principles to apply.

To lead an initiative whose performance results do require broad-based behavior change, you must shape a strategy for making both performance and change happen. This strategy should aim to get an ever increasing number of people to take responsibility for their own performance and change. Most important, you must guide people to make the personal performance commitments they need to experience change itself. In addition, you must grow and deploy resources to provide support and reinforcement just in time for people to perform. Finally, you must assess whether the initiative's performance depends on coordination and control. All or nothing, bet-your-company initiatives requiring tight linkages across whole organizations do demand tight control. By contrast, most behavior-driven change initiatives (e.g., continuous improvement) benefit from a looser approach to coordination.

In shaping your strategy, do not assume that top management commitment and buy-in are enough. People take responsibility for change when specific performance consequences cause them to experience change itself. Top management commitment provides important direction and support, but rarely produces a far-reaching enough series of specific performance demands to trigger real change. Meanwhile, buy-in generates awareness and understanding, but does not lead reluctant people to personally experience change in ways that resolve anxieties and fears.

With respect to any particular person or group, ask yourself, "How can I shape their personal performance commitments?" Three possibilities exist. If you are the person's boss, you can use hierarchical *authority to demand specific performance results. Whether or not you are the boss, you can ask any small number of people to* mutually

commit to a specific team performance goal. Finally, you might pro-
vide people resources and opportunities in exchange *for personal*
performance commitments. Most initiative strategies benefit from a
blend of hierarchy ("tell"), mutuality ("team"), and exchange
("trade"). Few initiatives succeed without improvising strategies as
you go along. Indeed, with performance as your primary objective,
remember that you and all who join you must try whatever it takes
to make change happen.

Chapter Five

Existing Employees, New Behaviors: Do You Face This Challenge?

Any good manager reflects on the scope, complexity, and type of challenge at hand. Assume, therefore, that you have agreed to lead a *single initiative* that matters to the performance of your organization. This chapter will help you determine whether your initiative depends on getting many existing people to learn new skills, behaviors, and working relationships, or whether you face a more traditional, performance-only management task. If broad-based behavior change is required, this chapter will also help you identify the *people whose behavior changes matter most* to performance and *the sources of readiness and reluctance* among them.

Given the topic of this book, you might expect a bias in favor of finding behavior-driven performance challenges. And, frankly, I would be surprised if the majority of readers were completely exempt from such situations. It is hard to think of any organization of significant size or scope, whether in the private, public, or nonprofit sector, that can sustain performance without getting various people to change the way they work. But not all organizations face such challenges all the time. Many critical initiatives can succeed without lots of existing people having to change skills, behaviors, or working relationships. And because managing both performance and change is so new and difficult, if you can find an alternative path to success for your initiative, you ought to take it.

FOUR QUESTIONS TO USE FOR ASSESSMENT

Whether you face the combination of performance and change depends on the magnitude of the behavioral changes required from existing people and the mix of readiness and reluctance among them. Each factor varies according to the history, context, and performance requirements of the specific initiative in question. Experience and observation, for example, suggest that what constitutes a behavior-driven challenge for many government institutions—such as the many excellent market and competitive skills introduced in Osborne and Gaebler's *Reinventing Government*—would not as seriously test most private-sector enterprises. Similarly, learning the project management capabilities critical to innovation poses a tougher challenge in large, functionally oriented industries like, say, consumer products than in commercial aerospace or defense businesses that have historically customized most of their major products. Meanwhile, the dream of mass customization implies many more hurdles for companies that have served the Defense Department over the past fifty years than for those who have produced high-quality products and services for commercial markets.

Four questions—two about magnitude and two about readiness—can help you assess your own situation. Consider the specific initiative you have agreed to lead (e.g., implementing an aspect of the organization's new strategy, or reengineering a core process, or institutionalizing total quality or self-directed work teams). Ask yourself:

1. Does the organization have to become very good at one or more basic *capabilities* that it is not very good at now?

2. Do large numbers of *existing* people throughout the organization have to change *specific behaviors* (i.e., do things differently)?

3. Does the organization have a *track record* of success in changes of this type?

4. Do the people who matter most to performance—from top to bottom and all across the organization—*understand* the implications of the change for their own behaviors and *urgently believe the time to act is now?*

If your answers (in order) are more like "yes," "yes," "no," and "no" than the opposite, then your initiative's performance depends on broad-based changes in skills, values, and behaviors. *Success requires you to adopt the ten new management principles.* If, by contrast, your answers are closer to "no," "no," "yes," and "yes," then you can confidently rely on managerial techniques with which you are already quite familiar. That would be good news because, although a far better job of managing behavior-driven change is possible than the weak track record to date, more traditional paths to performance are always preferable. Most people do not like to change. If you can attain performance without behavior change, why not do so? Indeed, so long as you are confident in the sustainability of the gains you would make, the following logic ought to govern your approach:

▶ Can we succeed through managing assets and policies quite apart from people?

▶ If not, can we succeed through redirecting the efforts of already capable people who work for this organization?

▶ If not, can we succeed through selectively adding new people instead of getting many existing employees to learn specific new skills and behaviors?

▶ If not, can we minimize

1. the number of the existing employees who must change;

2. the number of new skills, behaviors, and working relationships they need to master; and

3. the extent to which they need to master such skills by collaborating in real time across functions and other organization boundaries?

Taking a Deeper Look

This chapter discusses the diagnostic issues you need to take a deeper look at the implications of the four questions. In exploring them, the discussion revolves around the six specific initiatives described and highlighted in the following situations:

"TeleCable." As a manager at "TeleCable," you have contributed to the dramatic growth of cable television. Indeed, by 1993, cable's success combined with the advent of the information highway to attract more attention than ever before. The Federal Communications Commission began to regulate rates for the first time. The phone companies have invested in technologies and strategic alliances designed to enter the business. Satellite technology continued to get cheaper and better, encouraging nonwire-based enterprises to make a major marketing push for "direct TV." Competition at TeleCable has always meant winning and keeping the exclusive cable franchises granted by local governments. That too is changing. Sometime in the next two or three years, the company will wage a daily battle for customers against both wired and satellite competitors. Senior management has highlighted two critical implications. First, the company must improve its **customer service.** Second, it must shift from debt to **equity financing** to relieve itself of heavy cash-flow burdens during what promises to be a very uncertain environment. Management turns to you for suggestions on how to make the **customer service** and **equity financing** initiatives a success.

"State Courts." You are a judge in the State Court system. The twin epidemics of drug-related crimes and civil litigiousness have overwhelmed the courts, making a near mockery of the goals of swift and fair justice. The chief judge of the State Courts has repeatedly asked the legislature to increase the number of judges and administrative personnel. Just as often, the legislature has said no. This past year, however, the governor persuaded legislators to fund a new law permitting broad use of binding **arbitration** as an alternative to court trials in civil matters. As the quid pro quo for this effort, the governor pressured the chief judge to do a much better job of getting judges to adopt new **case flow management** tools and techniques to improve

the scheduling and disposition of both criminal and civil disputes. The chief judge has now asked you for suggestions about implementing the **arbitration** and **case flow management** initiatives.

"Helping Hand." You work at "Helping Hand," one of the country's oldest and most respected charities. Helping Hand was founded in the late nineteenth century to assist immigrants in finding the shelter, education, and other services needed to settle in North America. By the mid-1980s, however, Helping Hand chapters found themselves responding to the crisis of homelessness. Such efforts put heavy strains on the financial and human resources of the organization. Nevertheless, at its 1992 convention, Helping Hand chose to adopt "responding to the needs of the homeless" as its new vision. The strategy its national headquarters has crafted for achieving that vision includes, among other planks, two important parts. First, Helping Hand needs advanced **direct marketing** skills to increase dramatically the number of financial donors and service volunteers. Second, both paid staff and volunteers must learn logistical, counseling, health, linguistic, and other skills needed to deliver **frontline response** to the unique needs of homeless people. The president of Helping Hand has now asked you for advice on how to make the **direct marketing** and **frontline response** initiatives succeed.

When people at TeleCable, at State Courts, and at Helping Hand asked themselves the four questions about their organizations as a whole, all recognized that they faced a period of broad-based behavior-driven performance and change. Many of you might reach the same conclusion about your whole organization. But whole organizations rarely change themselves as whole organizations. Instead, they employ *specific initiatives* to drive performance and change. *Importantly, not all initiatives require behavior change for success, even if the organization as a whole does.* Therefore, although asking the four questions at the whole-organization level can indicate broad directions and realities, it is far more pragmatic to analyze them with respect to specific initiatives.

As the table on page 135 shows, when leaders of the six initiatives probed further, they discovered that three of the efforts—TeleCable's customer service, the State Courts' case flow management, and Helping Hand's frontline response—demanded that many existing people learn new skills, behaviors, and working relationships. The other three—Telecable's equity financing, the State Courts' arbitration, and Helping Hand's direct marketing—did not. This and the other distinctions shown in the chart made a critical difference. To effectively build customer service capability at TeleCable, for example, demanded the application of the ten new management principles. Obtaining equity financing, by contrast, could be accomplished through more traditional managerial approaches. As you read the following discussion, therefore, pay close attention to the issues raised because how you answer them will determine how you should manage your own initiative.

1. *For the initiative to succeed, must the organization become very good at one or more basic capabilities that it is not very good at now?*

▶ *How clear is the link between performance results and the capabilities the organization must become very good at?* Question 1 asks whether your organization *must* become very good at new things for your initiative to succeed. The clearer and stronger the link between any new initiative and performance, the more compellingly you will answer "yes." Consider, for example, the notion of the learning organization. That learning is a powerful response to an environment of instability and change makes intuitive sense. But if you were asked to lead a learning organization initiative, you would be lost without some firm connection to existing performance challenges that matter.

By identifying clear links between your initiative and specific aspects of performance, you enrich your understanding of the challenge even when, as with most of the six initiatives described in TeleCable, the State Courts, and Helping Hand, a fairly strong connection to performance already seems to exist. Thus, for example, the link between case flow management and the performance of the State Courts seems strong on the surface.

Not All Initiatives Demand Broad-Based Behavior Change

	Requires new organization capabilities?	Many existing people must learn specific behaviors?	Track record with this type of change?	Broad-based understanding and sense of urgency?
TeleCable Customer Service	Yes	Yes	No	No
State Courts Case Flow Management	Yes	Yes	No	No
Helping Hand Frontline Response	Yes	Yes	No	No
TeleCable Equity Financing	No	No	No	Yes
State Courts Arbitration	Yes	No	No	Yes
Helping Hand Direct Marketing	Yes	No	No	Yes

Anyone taking on this initiative, however, would do a better job if he or she probed for the specific aspects of performance that the chief judge and governor most wished to improve. These might include the speed, cycle time, volume, and accuracy of scheduling and resolving disputes; the productivity of the State Courts' resources; the perceptions of fairness and service by litigants and lawyers; and the level of satisfaction, opportunities, and morale of bailiffs, clerks, judges, and other State Courts employees.

▶ *Just how new and how different is this challenge?* Three broad patterns emerge when you further test this aspect of question 1.

First, some challenges, although important and pressing, turn out on closer examination to be neither new nor different. The shift from debt- to equity-based financing at TeleCable, for example, demands a different direction but not new or different skills from existing finance and senior executives. Similarly, many organizations routinely face productivity-gain or cost-reduction initiatives that demand that people work only harder and smarter, not differently.

Second, some challenges are so new and so different that it makes no sense to ask existing employees to change. In the mid-1970s, for example, Xerox engineers invented nearly every major aspect of personal computing. But just about every skill in making and selling computers substantially differed from making and leasing copiers. Xerox could have exploited this innovation, but not by trying to transform copier people into computer people. Similarly, although Helping Hand's direct marketing initiative requires new skills, it makes little sense to try to convert many existing Helping Hand staff and volunteers into direct marketers.

Third, some challenges require many existing people to learn to work very differently. Consider total quality management. It does not demand that employees learn new or different businesses. Instead, such TQM skills and behaviors as analysis, problem solving, decision making, and teaming are meant to transform *how* people conduct their *existing* business. Or think about TeleCable's customer service initiative. For the company to succeed, everyone at TeleCable who comes into meaningful contact with customers needs to learn the skills and behaviors required to delight customers with the timeliness, completeness, specificity, user friendliness, and convenience of TeleCable's programming, installations, repairs, upgrades, billing, and other activities.

▶ *How many new capabilities must the organization master?* The shorter the list, the more manageable the challenge. At Helping Hand, for example, the statistical, creative, testing, development, and deployment skills needed for effective direct mail and telemarketing programs make up a clearer and shorter list than the logistical, managerial, counseling, medical, psychological, agency relationship, substance abuse, linguistic, and other capabilities any organization seriously trying to respond to homelessness might need. In fact, the latter list is too long and too murky. The leaders of the frontline response initiative will need to clarify, shorten, and pace their efforts if they hope to have an impact.

▶ *How much time does the organization have to learn the new capabilities?* If an organization is on the brink of dissolution, then performance cannot wait for existing people to learn new skills and behaviors. Managers need to apply turnaround techniques instead of principles aimed at performance and broad-based behavior change. However, if there is no discernible time frame within which the organization must become good at new things, then the organization's performance really does not depend on making any fundamental behavior changes. Instead, whatever capabilities are being discussed fall in the category of "nice to have."

Somewhere in the middle lies the case for change. Once again consider the case of Xerox. When they invented personal computing in the mid-1970s, company scientists certainly gave Xerox an opportunity. Opportunities, however, are far less likely than threats to induce people to take responsibility for their own behavior change. For example, think back to Chapter Two's Wheel of Change. Understanding, desire, planning, action, and reinforcement all emerge more easily and urgently in the face of threat than of mere opportunity. And that reality for a single individual expands geometrically when hundreds or thousands of people must change to survive.

In the mid-1970s, no one knew that personal computers would become a megabillion-dollar industry. The opportunity was ill defined in terms of how long the window of advantage would remain open and how best to exploit it. Without a sense of time urgency, the computer opportunity never became real at Xerox. By comparison, with each passing year in the late 1970s and early 1980s, Japanese copier competitors took away more and more market share, with no end in sight. Eventually, a critical mass of people throughout Xerox felt a sense of urgency about having only a limited time within which to become very good at producing more innovative, lower-cost, and higher-quality copiers supported by much more responsive and higher-quality customer service.

Compare both Helping Hand initiatives with the case flow management initiative at the State Courts. Helping Hand's solvency is not at stake. But people throughout national headquarters and the chapters know that their new vision will not wait forever. The needs of the homeless—and the organization's needs for the skills and funds to respond to them—are too urgent. By contrast, it is inconceivable to anyone in the State Courts that the legislature would shut down the courts or impeach life-appointed judges because of their failure to learn case flow management techniques. The sense of time urgency and threat is far more abstract here. Consequently, leaders of the case flow initiative will have a tougher time getting people to take responsibility for change.

2. *For the initiative to succeed, must large numbers of existing people throughout the organization change specific behaviors (i.e., do things differently)?*

▶ *Can you change assets or policies instead of people?*
Perhaps the initiative can succeed without requiring many people
to learn specific new skills and behaviors. Performance opportunities like mergers and acquisitions, overhead cost reductions,
pricing and positioning of products or services, expanding or
shrinking of distribution channels, or establishment of strategic
alliances do not necessarily call for fundamental behavior modifications. They do demand tough-minded decision making, careful delegation of responsibility, and active control and monitoring
of performance. But such is the stuff of long-standing, well-
understood managerial practice. The shift from debt to equity
financing at TeleCable, for example, is a policy change that calls
for changing shareholder expectations more than employee skills
or behaviors. Similarly, effectively deploying arbitration to ease
the burden on the State Courts involves a number of classic asset
and policy issues for existing employees rather than behavior
changes.

▶ *Can you redirect the efforts of already capable employees?*
Just because people might need to do something different with
their time, skill, and effort does not mean they face behavior
change. Some State Courts administrators, for example, will
need to pay attention to managing the flow of disputes that shift
into arbitration. But they already possess the scheduling,
communications, decision-making, oversight, and reporting
skills needed. And, as noted earlier, the finance and senior executives at TeleCable already have the skills needed to seek equity-
based support.

▶ *Can you hire new people instead of changing behaviors
and skills of existing people?* This option is far less difficult to
manage than the prospect of getting existing people to overthrow
"how we do things around here." Technology-based changes, for
example, often present this alternative, either in whole or in part.
Take the direct marketing of financial products as an illustration. It is a major opportunity for banks, insurance companies,
and others with established brand names and good products.

But why would you ask a phalanx of loan officers practiced in face-to-face selling to sit at terminals and sell or service customers over the phone? Instead, it makes far more sense to hire new people who have the required combination of telephone, computer, sales, and servicing skills. The same applies to the direct marketing initiative at Helping Hand—the charity's success depends mostly on hiring new people who have the required skills.

▶ *How many existing people must learn new skills and behaviors for the initiative to achieve its desired performance aspirations?* The fewer the number, the less likely your initiative depends on *broad-based* behavior change. In this regard, the number of people affected by the arbitration initiative at the State Courts is far less than the number who must change skills, behaviors, and working relationships to incorporate case flow management approaches in the daily administration of justice. Similarly, fewer people are needed to make TeleCable's equity initiative succeed than its customer service initiative.

▶ *Which specific jobs are affected?* Tip O'Neill's wisdom about politics also applies to change: "All behavior change is local." Initiatives that depend on behavior change do not succeed until individuals in specific jobs learn new skills, behaviors, and working relationships. You must identify which jobs have to change and what specific new skills and behaviors the people in those jobs must learn. Eventually, every jobholder needs to understand a from/to job description analogous to the one described in the chart on page 51. Few single initiatives, however, demand behavior and skill change from every jobholder in the entire organization. For example, the behaviors and skills of installers who connect up customer homes for TeleCable are far more pivotal to the customer service initiative than those of people who negotiate and purchase programming from studios.

▶ *How much will people have to collaborate, especially across organization boundaries?* Skills and behaviors that depend on collaboration with other people are more difficult to master than those that don't. The Tandem sales people described in Chapter Two, for example, will more easily learn to use laptop computers in their individual work than to incorporate the consultative, team-based skills demanded by solution and capability selling. Similarly, establishing and communicating a set of policies favoring arbitration in the State Courts demands less ongoing collaboration than does getting judges, bailiffs, clerks, and others to learn how they can work together in real time to improve case flow management.

Collaborations across organization boundaries, whether functional or hierarchical, are more difficult to achieve than collaborations within such boundaries. People rely solely on themselves and their familiar functional or hierarchical colleagues far more easily than on others with whom they have rarely worked and little understand. Consider again the challenge of selling solutions instead of products at Tandem. Among other things, it requires people from sales, marketing, and service to collaborate with one another as well as Tandem and third-party technology experts. Few of them have ever really worked together.

In this respect, TeleCable's customer service challenge is perhaps the toughest of the six initiatives discussed in this chapter. Much of the effectiveness of the people who directly serve customers (sales people, telephone operators and installers) depends on the upstream activities of those who don't. Collaboration across organization boundaries is at the heart of this performance challenge. Accordingly, anyone leading the effort will do a better job by viewing customer service as a core process instead of as a series of separate responsibilities allocated among various functions.

3. *Does the organization have a track record of success in initiatives of this type?*

▶ *Has the organization ever tackled something like this before?* Behavior-driven performance and change challenges have become prevalent over the past decade. People in your organization have probably struggled with managing such things even if you have not. And although the particulars of their initiatives might differ, the underlying causes of success or failure will provide lessons learned. You should identify who has faced such challenges and seek out their counsel. For example, given the life tenure of judges at the State Courts, leaders of the case flow management initiative can learn about the readiness or reluctance of specific judges from anyone who has ever tried to win voluntary judicial participation.

▶ *Was it successful?* The test for whether a behavior-driven initiative succeeds lies in affirmative responses to the following three questions:

- Throughout the period of the change, did the initiative consistently improve performance results for each key constituency (e.g., customers/beneficiaries, shareholders/ funders, and employees)?

- Did the foundation for performance shift from the "from" set of skills, behaviors, and working relationships to the "to" set?

- Did enough existing people in key jobs learn enough new skills, behaviors, and working relationships to make performance sustainable?

By discussing such issues with colleagues who have participated in behavior-based initiatives, you can learn from their experiences whether or not they succeeded. Think back to the story of Iberian Motors in Chapter One. People who would subsequently take on the inevitable customer service or total quality initiatives that Iberian Motors still required would benefit from carefully reviewing these three questions with the executives, dealers, and others who participated in the earlier efforts.

4. *Do the people who matter most to this initiative—from top to bottom and all across the organization—understand the implications of change for their own behaviors and urgently believe the time to act is now?*

◗ *Which people in which jobs understand the need for and nature of the changes at hand?* In the issues raised on page 140, you identified the specific people and jobs that matter most to the performance of your initiative. Probing their degree of understanding, like the other subissues raised here under question 4, will help you assess their specific sources of readiness and reluctance. A person understands the need for and nature of change if he or she can

- describe the link between overall organization performance results and your initiative (the big picture)

- describe the forces at work (e.g., technology, customer need, competitor capability) that make your initiative critical

- articulate the specific from/to skills, behaviors, and working relationships he or she must learn

- articulate their own peronal performance goals and contributions that depend on mastering the from/to changes

◗ *Which people in which jobs want to make the needed changes?* Which people who matter most to performance believe that they *must* change? More than any other subissue, this can help you identify the people most ready to change. Such early adopters can make critical contributions to your initiative as experimenters, promoters, champions, and active coleaders. They are also essential to focusing your initiative on performance and change from day one. Because of the life tenure of judges, for example, the case flow initiative will inevitably depend on demonstration, persuasion, and peer pressure. No one, not even the chief judge, can order life tenure judges to manage cases differently. Finding early adopters among sitting judges, therefore, is key to its success.

◗ *Which people in which jobs have the minimum capability required to learn the new skills, behaviors, and working relationships?* As discussed in Chapter Two, the emphasis here is on *minimum.* It probes for the likely effectiveness of people's efforts to learn the new capabilities that you already know they lack. Most of Helping Hand's volunteers, for example, probably have the literacy, questioning, listening, and decision-making skills required to learn how to assist homeless people access various government and nongovernment service providers. But many current volunteers may lack the minimum capabilities needed to acquire specialized expertise in such fields as mental health and substance abuse.

▶ *Which people in which jobs have made plans or taken action to experience the change?* Once people experience change, especially in a performance context that matters, their reluctance or readiness becomes far more concrete and tractable. Simply distinguishing between people who have only talked about change and those who have experienced it can help. Do not assume, however, that all people who have experienced change will be supporters. The executives who participated in the Iberian Motors task forces, for example, may or may not have soured on change. Similarly, the judges, bailiffs, clerks, and others at the State Courts who may have used case flow management approaches might or might not advocate their statewide adoption.

▶ *What kind of reinforcement can people expect from existing organizational arrangements?* Organizational arrangements such as reporting relationships, compensation and information systems, budgeting and planning approaches, and so forth almost always conflict with initiatives that depend on broad-based behavior change. They inevitably invite complaints, anxieties, and misunderstanding. Consequently, you can expect many people to question the seriousness of the organization and top management. You must understand those obstacles in order to communicate and lead effectively, including knowing when and to whom you will have to give personal reinforcement.

THE CHANGE BOARD

The Change Board (page 146) portrays a visual summary of the diagnostic issues underlying the four questions. The rows identify individuals and groups who need to change. The columns consider each part of the Wheel of Change discussed in Chapter Two. Once completed, the Change Board tells you whether your initiative depends on broad-based behavior change. It also shows the big picture of who has to change, why, and what are their respective sources of readiness and reluctance. In effect, it helps you differentiate and segment your people challenge, forcing you and others beyond we/they generalizations about resistance and top management commitment.

The more nuanced and specific your understanding, the more pragmatic your response. The chart on page 147, for example, comes from the Change Board analysis people at TeleCable used to gain a richer understanding of the implications of their customer service initiative for several key groups of jobholders. As you can see, many key frontline workers (e.g., installers and telephone operators) know they must make the necessary changes, although few understand what they will specifically need to do. Few have actually experienced the changes at hand. From/to job descriptions could help them a lot. So would a series of short-term customer service improvement projects aimed at providing positive experiences with change.

A variety of middle managers (from frontline supervisors to cable system general managers) remain unclear about what really matters to good customer service. And many do not appear to believe that *they* must change. They point to contradictory pressures ranging from the way TeleCable organizes, plans, and rewards people to the continuing cash flow required to service the company's debt. Short-term projects to improve customer service might buck up the conviction of those managers. A good place to begin would be with the ones who have identified themselves as ready for change. Eventually, however, the initiative's success depends on getting a critical mass of middle managers to take responsibility for redesigning the cross-organizational work flow processes that are critical to TeleCable's customer service aspirations.

The more specific the analysis behind any Change Board, the more effective the picture. Theoretically, you could insert a row for every individual by name. At the other extreme, you might distinguish only among top management, middle management, and the front lines.

Change Board of the organization regarding the specific initiative being analyzed

		Understanding		Desire	Minimum Capability	Planning	Action	Reinforcement	
		Link of change to performance	From / To Job analysis					Organization Design	Personal
Top Managers	Person A								
	Person B								
	Person C								
	Group 1								
Middle Managers	Person A								
	Group 1								
	Group 2								
	Group 3								
Staff	Person A								
	Person B								
	Group 1								
	Group 2								
Front-line Employees	Group 1								
	Group 2								
	Group 3								
	Group 4								

TeleCable's Customer Service Initiative

	Understanding	Desire	Minimum Capability	Planning	Action	Reinforcement
System GM champions	Can describe needed changes specifically	Want to make changes happen	All have it	Customer service goals in their plans	Have experimented and learned what works	Chief executive is determined to make customer service a top priority
Other system GMs	Unclear about what good customer service is	Believe frontline employees must change, not them	All have it	No plans in place	No actions taken to date	Reporting structures, compensation and career paths, and budgeting and planning emphasize cash flow generation in ways that conflict with investing in customer service
Supervisor champions	Focus groups identified supervisors with clear ideas about customer service	Focus group identified several champions ready to lead change	All have it	No plans in place	No actions taken to date	
Other supervisors	Confused about what customer service means	Many are reluctant to be team leaders and coaches	All have it	No plans in place	No actions taken to date	
Installers	Survey shows 4 out of 5 understand need for superior customer service, but few can describe the needed changes	Many have specific suggestions for changes they would like to try Many express concern over needed management support and training	Some might not make shift to optical fiber technology	No plans in place	No actions taken to date	Emphasis on individual accountability conflicts with need for teams Few have access to information about what makes a difference to customer service results
Telephone operators	Same as installers	Concern over possible job losses	All have it	No plans in place	No actions taken to date	

You must find the right balance of specificity and practicality between the two extremes. That balance will depend on the scope and complexity of your initiative. Going through several iterations can help. For example, the champions among TeleCable's general managers and supervisors emerged only after a series of discussions, focus groups, and other analyses.

Try to describe specifically the causes for understanding, desire, minimum capability, planning/action, and reinforcement instead of using "high," "low," and "medium" evaluations alone. Using high, medium, and low is a good way to begin, but eventually you need to know *why* an individual or group is ready or reluctant to change if you are to find a way to enlist them. Finally, use the Change Board throughout the period of change required by your initiative. It provides an effective scorecard for evaluating whether you are building the "we" who must make change happen.

CONCLUSION

The following 2-page survey asks you to agree or disagree with a series of statements regarding the initiative you might lead or join. If you predominantly agree, use the ten new management principles to guide your efforts. Such was the case with TeleCable's customer service effort, the State Courts' case flow management initiative, and Helping Hand's frontline service skills expansion.

By contrast, your analysis might reveal a different, less difficult path to performance. You might succeed through managing policies, prices, assets, alliances, or other factors instead of the simultaneous performance and change of many existing people. TeleCable could replace debt with equity financing in this way. Or, as with Helping Hand's direct marketing challenge, your performance aspirations may depend more on hiring new people instead of modifying the behaviors of existing people. Or perhaps you can redirect already capable people. This option made sense for the State Courts' arbitration initiative.

SURVEY

In considering your single initiative, do you agree or disagree with the following statements?

	Agree	Disagree

1. We understand the link between specific performance outcomes and the changes being discussed.

2. Performance depends on becoming good at something new, not just better at what we already do today.

3. This new challenge does not require entering a fundamentally different business.

4. There are many behavior and skill implications of this initiative or change, not just a few.

5. We have enough time to become good at these new things, but not forever.

6. We cannot achieve performance by changing assets or policies instead of people.

7. We cannot achieve performance mostly through hiring new people.

8. We have many existing people who must learn new skills and behaviors.

Agree   **Disagree**

9. Our skill and behavior challenges require collaboration across organization boundaries.

10. Those of us involved have not succeeded at this kind of challenge before.

11. Many affected people do not yet understand the need to change.

12. Many affected people cannot specify their particular performance contributions to the big picture.

13. Many affected people do not yet understand what new behaviors and skills they need to learn.

14. Many affected people have not yet emotionally figured out they *must* change.

15. Many affected people have yet to develop any plans of action or take action itself.

16. We have existing organization arrangements and attitudes that will not support and reinforce the changes we wish to bring about.

Even when your analysis indicates that you face behavior-driven change, brainstorm possible alternative approaches. Technology might allow you to deploy assets differently instead of changing people's behaviors (or at least reduce the number of existing people who must change behaviors). Consider TeleCable's customer service initiative. The company might try getting hundreds of customer service telephone operators—currently spread across dozens of locations throughout the country—to learn new skills and behaviors. Or it could centralize the telephone response unit in one location and use an 800 number. If it selects the latter route, it could hire mostly new people, thereby reducing the number of existing telephone operators who need to learn new skills and behaviors. The overall customer service initiative would remain behavior driven because so many managers, installers, sales people, and others would still have to change old habits and ways of working. But the scope of the challenge would be reduced.

Answering the four questions and related list of subissues can take ninety seconds or ninety days. The same is true for completing the Change Board or the survey. You might do such analyses alone or with colleagues, in regularly scheduled meetings or at offsite workshops. You might rely on your own impressions and judgment, or you could employ surveys, interviews, focus groups, or other research techniques. Regardless of the time and effort you invest, however, you cannot expect to *manage* performance and change without knowing a lot about the nature of the challenge at hand and the extent of the behavior change necessary to make performance happen.

You will do a far superior job of enlisting people in the "we" who make change happen if you know who those people are, how they must change, and what is standing in their way. That sounds obvious— a matter of common sense. But many executives, supervisors, frontline workers, and others ignore such common sense. Countless initiatives in organizations throughout the world (and, perhaps, in yours) have yet to benefit from the diagnoses set forth in this chapter. As a result, if both performance and change must happen, such initiatives are likely to fall short. By contrast, the leaders who succeed will be those who work hard to understand whether and how performance depends on behavior changes, who must make those changes, their degree of readiness or reluctance, and how to apply the management principles described in this book to the initiative at hand.

Chapter Six

Getting Beyond Decisions and Awareness
to Performance and Change

Assume that your initiative's performance results depend on many people learning new skills, behaviors, and working relationships. Perhaps you must guide fifty people from different functions to collaborate in ways that will dramatically increase the speed of new product introductions. Or perhaps five hundred people must change to implement a different business strategy. Or perhaps you must help five thousand employees embrace and adopt total customer service. Whether it is fifty, five hundred, five thousand, or any other large number of people, when your initiative's success depends on broad-based, behavior-driven change, you must shape a managerial strategy for making change and performance happen.

Both this and the next chapter will introduce you to perspectives and approaches for crafting such strategies out of the ten new management principles. To work, your strategy must continually increase the number of people joining you in taking responsibility for change. Too many initiative leaders fail to recognize and respect that challenge. Guided by deep seated, traditional managerial approaches, they assume people will implement decisions and directions so long as they are sufficiently communicated and bought into.

I call this overworked and unimaginative approach the "decision/awareness/design" strategy. It starts with a significant decision, typically made by senior people. Those leaders then communicate the decision as broadly as possible, hoping to build awareness and buy-in. Simultaneously, the leaders debate and often shift reporting relationships and other formal organization elements in order to align direction and design. This approach worked for most of the 20th century because the decisions in question did not require many existing people to change fundamental behaviors.

But your initiative is different. Performance results depend on broad-based, behavior-driven change. You probably will fail if you adopt the decision/awareness/design approach. People must take responsibility for their own behavior change. No one else—and no one else's decisions—can do it for them. Decisions can trigger the beginning of a period of change. But decisions alone rarely get many people to take charge of their own change, and decisions never get organizations through the entire period of change itself.

Awareness-building and buy-in campaigns can increase understanding of and desire for change. As we discussed in Chapter 2, however, such efforts fall short of guiding people with differing blends of readiness and reluctance to embrace change. For that, people must experience change in performance contexts that matter. Typical communications, training programs, and other buy-in efforts focus mostly on getting a new message across efficiently to large, undifferentiated groups of people rather than the hard, more protracted person-by-person and group-by-group challenge of continually increasing the number of individuals taking charge of change.

Behavior change is a personal matter. It demands personal commitments to both performance and change. Concern for gaining such personal commitments, however, too often disappears when discussions shift to new organization designs and the need for alignment. Again, the ingrained assumption, inherited from nearly a century of mechanistic organization theory and practice, is that getting the organization to perform will follow easily from the more difficult challenge of making sure all of its various formal design elements (structure, strategy, planning and budgeting, compensation, and so on) are aligned. The focus of the decision/awareness/design strategy, then, is more on the formal, mechanistic, and impersonal aspects of organizations rather than the informal, very personal challenge of behavior change and performance.

There are alternatives to the decision/awareness/design strategy. You can begin to generate them by adopting a fresh perspective. Imagine for a moment that you are a marketing executive in a business that provides specific opportunities and resources to people in need of behavior change. This point of view forces you to consider people, position, and performance with a more inventive eye. People form the "market" you want to win, your position and resources determine how you can win their "business," and performance is what you want people in your market to do. As the following Dun & Bradstreet performance quality story illustrates, strategies crafted from this perspective can powerfully assist you in gaining the *personal* commitments needed to build the "we" who make change happen.

TOTAL QUALITY AT DUN & BRADSTREET INFORMATION SERVICES

Dun & Bradstreet's Information Services Division (DBIS) gives customers a plethora of information and analysis about millions of businesses. The company's credit report is so well known that many people even refer to competitive products as "D&B's." Fueled by it and scores of lesser known offerings, DBIS has dominated its market for more than a century; Abraham Lincoln, for example, was a D&B credit reporter. Along with profits, however, this strong position has produced a tendency toward inertia and internal focus. Like most market leaders, DBIS must work hard to avoid the pitfalls of arrogance.

When Ron Glover became president of DBIS in 1990, the warning signs of trouble were flashing. Financial performance had dipped after decades of predictable growth. Internally, the heads of various functions were so powerful that they literally considered their individual parts of DBIS as separate companies and rarely communicated with one another. A culture of isolation and relentless profit pressure had taken its toll. The year before Ron Glover arrived, the *Wall Street Journal* ran a scathing article about unfair pricing practices, poor products and atrocious service at DBIS. Most DBISers discounted the *Journal* story. But Ron knew there had to be enough truth in it to merit closer examination.

That spring, Ron asked Mike Berkin to introduce total quality management to DBIS. Mike began with steps common to most TQM programs. He formed a Quality Assurance Committee and, with them, spent several months reading about total quality and visiting companies that had led the way. With what quality experts call the "period of enlightenment" behind them, the Berkin committee then turned to educating others. From December through February, more than two hundred senior and middle DBIS managers attended intensive training sessions taught by Japanese and American TQM experts.

The managers completed a mock Baldrige examination that yielded predictably low scores. When combined with inspiring tales from Xerox, Federal Express, Motorola, and other companies, these harsh self-appraisals jarred long-standing assumptions about the quality and effectiveness of DBIS's customer orientation, products, and services. At least intellectually, the Berkin committee had made its case for TQM at DBIS.

Everyone wanted to get going but no one was confident about how. The training sessions had conveyed many cautionary lessons. Ron, Mike, Quality Assurance Committee members, and other managers worried about involving everyone, ensuring support from the powerful DBIS function heads, focusing on customers, and training the division's eight thousand employees in TQM. Throughout January and February, the following elements began to define the strategy the committee would pursue:

▶ ***More training.*** The December through February sessions had gone so well that committee members believed they should conduct similar training throughout the division.

▶ *More infrastructure to coordinate and control total quality.*
Managing the training and involvement of DBIS's thousands of
employees posed a major coordination and control challenge.
Infrastructure for planning, budgeting, and oversight was needed.
The committee's representative from sales, for example, worried
about assembling sales quality committees at the national, regional,
and local levels.

▶ *More decisions.* Committee member proposals ranged from incor-
porating total quality resources in each functional budget to requiring "performance contracts" between each individual in DBIS and
his or her boss.

▶ *More teams.* Managers were encouraged to form as many "quality
teams" as possible.

Ron, Mike, and the others felt good about the enthusiasm and
support for their total quality initiative. Yet, with all the activity
getting under way, they also shared a sense of foreboding. Perhaps,
they told themselves, this was what the experts had meant when
they warned DBIS to expect a "period of struggling" to follow
the "period of enlightenment." Still, as one executive despaired
that February, "This doesn't feel like what we saw at the Federal
Express airport hub in Memphis when all the planes came in at
midnight."

WHY A MARKETING STRATEGY FOR CHANGE?

The DBIS total quality initiative was about to tumble over a familiar
precipice. In emphasizing decisions, awareness-building, designs, and
up-front training, the committee's plans betrayed mechanistic practices antithetical to broad-based behavior change. Behavior change
happens when people, not blueprints, take charge. Had they proceeded, Berkin and his colleagues would have spent their time focusing on *activities* instead of *performance* and managing *descriptions
and decisions* instead of *people*. Their effort would have crashed.
Having received the message that "total quality is important," thou-

sands of employees would have been left hopelessly wondering, "Okay, but so what? What exactly should we do now?"

To avoid leading your change initiative down this ill-fated path, you need to shape a strategy grounded in the ten new management principles. Begin with the following: *People must take responsibility for their own behavior change; no one can do it for them.* You cannot, as DBIS was about to do, equate one-time training with behavior change, or appoint "quality teams" and assume the people on those teams will then "do quality." Nor can you command people to change. Yes, the basic contract of work for pay provides you leverage on people, but behavior change itself remains a matter of free will. People must exercise their own choice and take their own action.

Your strategy, therefore, must be humanistic, not mechanistic. It must focus on people. In this, you are like a marketing executive in a behavior change business such as Weight Watchers or Smokenders. You can no more learn new behaviors like total quality for other people than you can lose weight or quit smoking for them. To get people signed up, Weight Watchers and Smokenders must go beyond such bald marketing contentions as "Losing weight is good" or "Smoking is bad." People already know that. Why then, as the DBIS leaders were doing, position your initiative solely on the ground that "change [in their case, total quality] is good"? Nor can Weight Watchers or Smokenders succeed only by training people in the importance of dieting, exercise, and saying no. They must get people to *apply* those diets and disciplines. Similarly, you must get an ever increasing number of people to take responsibility by *experiencing* the change you want them to bring about.

As a marketeer for change, then, you must guide people through the three critical stages of becoming part of the "we" who will make your specific initiative happen:

▶ *Awareness.* People achieve awareness when they understand the need for change and the new skills, behaviors, and working relationships that they must learn in order to continue contributing to organization performance. Critically, they must also understand how your specific initiative will help them both to perform and to learn.

▶ **Trial.** "Trial" is gained when your initiative has helped people experience change by identifying and seizing specific performance opportunities in which to try out new skills, behaviors, and working relationships. You also must give them resources and reinforcement just in time to ensure their success.

▶ **Repurchase.** "Repurchase" happens when your initiative has helped people experience the link between performance results and change. Motivated by what they have learned during trial and the personal reinforcement you and others have provided, they continue using the new skills, behaviors, and working relationships until such changes become routine.

Of the three, trial and repurchase—the experience and repetition of behavior change in real performance contexts—far surpass awareness in importance. Too many change initiative leaders, however, mistakenly manage awareness to the near total exclusion of trial and repurchase, especially in the early stages. As a result, even when the message of change penetrates the organization, people are left unsure about what to do. Like the DBIS managers, they ask, "How can we make this real?" Change leaders who have overinvested in awareness cannot answer such questions. When they don't, the initiative dies of its own weight, a victim of change for the sake of change.

The top graph on page 160 shows the precipitous decline in the number of people involved in awareness-driven initiatives. As the middle graph on page 160 illustrates, organizations that fail to learn from such experiences repeat them—over and over and over again. Flavor-of-the-month or program-du-jour comments crop up like weeds. So does frustration over the absence of any real change or any real performance gains. You can avoid this fate by paying more attention to managing trial and repurchase than awareness. Awareness, of course, is always important. But your goal, as the bottom graph on page 160 depicts, is to create an entirely different pattern of people's participation over time.

The curve in the bottom graph has several implications. First, your objective from day one is to build trial and repurchase through getting people to experience change directly in performance contexts.

Use experience more than awareness to continually increase the number of people taking charge of change

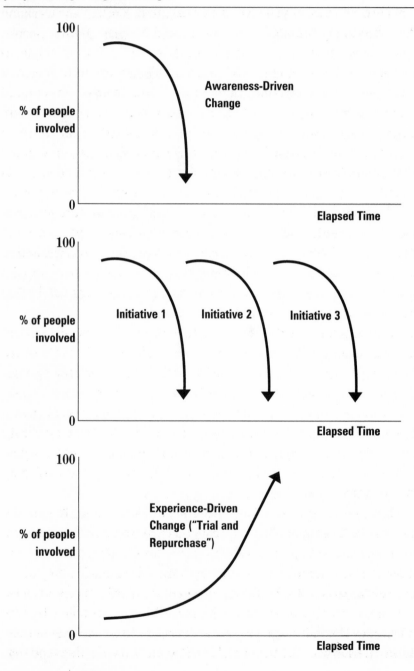

Ultimately, you want to enlist all the people who matter in the "we" who will make your initiative succeed. In a marketing sense, you seek 100 percent share of your target market. Your strategy for attaining that goal starts with yourself, then a small number of other people, then a small number more, and so on. At some point, the fundamentals of your "behavior business"—the specific performance objectives and metrics, the specific people who matter, the specific behavior and other changes they must make, the specific ways your initiative can deploy resources and help—will be so compellingly clear that you can expand your "share" dramatically. That is when the curve in the bottom graph rises sharply. Rarely, however, are such fundamentals sound enough to support rapid expansion at the start of the initiative.

This approach has many advantages. First, you can start with people who are ready to embrace change. Between 5 and 20 percent of the people in most organizations are like those customers that marketing people describe as "early adopters." It never takes much to get trial out of such people. If you have done the diagnostic work in Chapter Five, you have a pretty good idea who they are.

Second, you normally don't have to look hard for specific performance challenges that ready people can tackle. Sometimes these are low-hanging fruit—challenges so easy that you can expect early wins. Sometimes the most pressing performance gaps are more obvious than easy. Either way, by joining ready people to specific performance challenges, you give your initiative a sound basis for gaining clarity about what you are trying to accomplish; the specific new skills, behaviors, and working relationships that work; and the people who will help you lead the effort.

Third, you give yourself and other leaders the chance to gain the courage to "live the change." Conviction requires more than commitment and intellectual understanding; it requires leaders to incorporate intentions and knowledge into their own skills, behavior, and working relationships. To illustrate, consider the performance orientation at the heart of total quality. Mike Berkin and his fellow Quality Assurance Committee members had learned this lesson during their initial "period of enlightenment." Intellectually, they understood that performance results were the reason for pursuing total quality. And certainly, they were committed to helping DBIS take advantage of what they knew. But they had not absorbed the performance–total quality link holistically. For example, in proposing that DBIS employees establish "performance contracts" with their bosses, committee members often referred to the "total quality performance opportunity for secretaries to make contracts about the number of times they would get coffee for the boss."

Perhaps, you might assert, you would never make such a silly mistake. My experience is otherwise. Change initiative leaders who have yet to begin living the change have also yet to begin differentiating—even for themselves—what truly matters to the challenge at hand. In focusing immediately on trial and repurchase through real performance and real change, you allow yourselves as leaders to go first—not by talking about how important change is, but by actually experiencing the change you hope to lead in performance contexts that can make a difference.

TOM SAWYER'S QUALITY SHOP AT DBIS

Like others at DBIS, Mike Berkin was anxious to see total quality in action. But he remained uneasy about his committee's plans for more training, infrastructure, budget, and other total quality decisions. So when two colleagues offered to help him craft a strategy focused on trial and repurchase instead of awareness, Mike jumped at the chance. Starting small, starting with readiness, and starting with performance all appealed to his imagination and common sense. Working together, the three strategists formulated a plan for Mike's initiative around three central ideas they called "the Quality Shop," "performance quality," and "Tom Sawyer."

"What if," one of Mike's friends asked, "you were the head of a DBIS business called the Quality Shop that had to survive on the strength of its products and services? Would you be asking your 'investors' (Ron Glover and other DBIS executives) to commit sizable amounts of money to training, infrastructure, head-count increases, and so on *before* you had a product or service that demonstrated your 'business' could attract and keep 'customers'? Would you sell 'investors' on a hope and a prayer? Are you sure you would ask Ron Glover and the others to build demand for your 'business' by insisting on total quality from everyone when you haven't even got the products or services to meet that demand?"

These questions sparked an intense discussion that led to Mike's vision for the Quality Shop. First, the Quality Shop would consider itself a business for developing and offering products and services to DBIS 'customers.' Second, the Quality Shop would keep overhead low by avoiding full-time staff dedicated to quality. Third, the Quality Shop would apply total quality management to itself. It would be customer driven, set goals, measure itself, and seek to continuously improve. Fourth, DBIS's performance would be the primary concern of the Quality Shop. Mike wanted to introduce total quality tools and techniques into the culture of DBIS, but not for their own sake. The Quality Shop would succeed only if it made a performance difference to DBIS's customers, employees, and shareholders.

Job one was to identify a 'product' that worked. Berkin turned to Robert Schaffer's "breakthrough strategy." The breakthrough strategy challenges small groups of people to set and meet specific, near-term performance goals. Criteria for breakthroughs include

▶ a discrete, measurable, and stretch goal
▶ that is urgent and compelling,
▶ that is achievable in roughly six to eight weeks, and
▶ that requires only the existing resources and scope of authority of the people involved.

Mike recognized that the breakthrough strategy was not designed specifically for total quality management. But he also grasped that people could not achieve breakthrough goals without applying one or more tools (e.g., root cause analysis) and perspectives (e.g., customer orientation) common to total quality programs. By marrying breakthrough performance to total quality, he and his two colleagues believed they had the Quality Shop's ideal first offering, something they dubbed "performance quality breakthroughs."

The three planners then turned to how Mike should market test the new product. Instead of emphasizing awareness building (e.g., by asking top management to promote "performance quality" throughout the division), Mike chose to manage trial and repurchase. He wanted to let "customer demand" for breakthroughs grow organically. "Why not," Mike's friends suggested, "follow a Tom Sawyer approach?" Recalling Mark Twain's story of how Tom Sawyer made painting a fence so much fun that others volunteered to help, Mike decided to initiate only eight to ten performance quality breakthroughs over the next few months and build a sense of performance, learning, and excitement around them.

After describing the criteria for performance quality breakthroughs to his Quality Assurance Committee, Mike asked them each to identify a few potential opportunities. Within a month, the committee had picked eight teams to tackle the first round of breakthroughs. They hired a consultant familiar with breakthroughs to conduct one-day workshops in which each team could learn about breakthroughs, set a razor-sharp performance goal, and get started. In addition, the consultant agreed to help teams learn whatever analytical techniques they needed—and only those techniques—in a just-in-time fashion to meet their near-term goals. In this way, Mike assured himself that the consultant too was on the line for performance results as opposed to teaching things for their own sake.

By the end of May 1991, all eight performance quality breakthrough teams had made a number of small but important contributions to performance. Mike asked Ron Glover to schedule a special Executive Committee meeting for frontline team members to describe what they had accomplished and learned. DBIS's senior executives heard the following:

▶ One of DBIS's main production centers had reduced turnaround time on customer requests for new credit reports from seven days to less than three.

- A joint sales/production team doubled the conversion ratio of prospects-to-closed-sales among potential customers identified through bankruptcy proceedings.

- A finance team reduced the capital acquisition cycle for new computers and fax machines from several months to under three weeks.

- A sales/marketing team recovered a single, major lost customer account.

Mike Berkin's Tom Sawyer gambit had worked. Positive word of mouth about performance quality breakthroughs spread out from frontline workers and middle managers as well as down from senior executives. The total quality stories now being told in DBIS came from DBIS instead of Federal Express, Motorola and other companies, helping to make concepts such as "empowerment" and "customer focus" more real and tangible for people. Two senior Information Resources executives, Doug Nay and Tal Phillips, saw that performance quality breakthroughs could help them achieve a number of critical goals. They offered to work with Mike in any way possible to expand the use of breakthroughs in their function (which collects, inputs, assembles, and otherwise manages all the information behind DBIS's reports and other products).

Encouraged by this growing demand, the Quality Shop strategists put together the rest of their grand plan. They would limit the number of performance quality breakthroughs in round two to between twenty and twenty-five. In this way, they could ensure the quality of their own "product" by avoiding what they called "bastard breakthroughs" (goals that did not meet the breakthrough criteria and/or teams more interested in activities than results). Moreover, Mike himself could join the outside consultant in facilitating the teams, setting the stage for a key plank of the strategy.

Leading teams through a one-day goal-setting workshop does not involve rocket science. It does require people with a performance orientation, facilitation skills, and command of breakthrough and related total quality techniques. Mike knew that plenty of DBISers, including himself, could learn those skills. Accordingly, at the conclusion of round two, he and his coplanners decided to invite volunteers from the thirty or so completed breakthrough teams to become qualified as performance quality facilitators.

Working with Ron Glover, Doug Nay, Tal Phillips, and others, Mike established the following arrangement. Facilitators qualified by the Quality Shop would be permitted time off from their regular jobs to help get breakthrough teams started. This deal attracted people interested in learning new skills and working with different parts of the division. It also kept the Quality Shop's overhead low by building and tapping into spare capacity. Instead of the salaries, benefits, office space, and other costs that would have been incurred by adding full-time staff, DBIS would face increases in travel expenses alone. Moreover, once the in-house facilitators were doing the work, DBIS could eliminate the cost of the outside consultant.

Round two provided another exciting series of performance accomplishments. In addition to word of mouth, Mike now began fueling demand more actively. For example, Doug and Tal promoted friendly competition across the nearly one hundred Information Resources offices in the United States. More people than ever applied for round three—not because they had to, but because they wanted to. Two dozen people asked to be qualified as facilitators.

Again, Mike decided to limit the number of performance quality breakthroughs. This time he wanted to ensure success among the new DBIS facilitators. He asked the outside consultant to train the volunteers and focus mostly on helping them as opposed to the round three breakthrough teams directly. Finally, as round three proceeded, Mike began identifying additional "products" and "services" for his Quality Shop.

By the end of 1991, seventy-five performance quality breakthrough teams had contributed to the following:

▶ *Customers.* Teams had reduced cycle times and error rates to established customers, introduced new products, increased the number of new customer sales, and won back previously lost customers.

▶ *Shareholders.* Nearly $5 million of annualized impact on DBIS's bottom line came from both the revenue side (roughly 60 percent) and the cost side (40 percent).

▶ *Employees.* Nearly seven hundred DBISers had learned specific total quality tools by participating in the teams, and thirty were qualified as facilitators.

Under Mike's leadership, the Quality Shop continued to expand its "business," "customer base," and "product and service" line. With each new product or service, Mike carefully managed trial and repurchase by finding small numbers of people ready to try something new on real performance challenges. Then he leveraged the performance successes and new capabilities of the early adopters to market the Quality Shop's latest product elsewhere. Not all of his efforts worked. One process improvement technique, for example, failed to sustain interest; Mike dropped it. Most of his additions, however, repeated the success of breakthroughs.

By the end of 1994, when leaders in many organizations only dreamed of institutionalizing total quality, Mike Berkin had done it. The graph below shows the number of performance quality breakthroughs from 1991 through 1994. Customers of his Quality Shop had implemented thousands of performance improvement ideas

Growth of DBIS "Quality Shop"

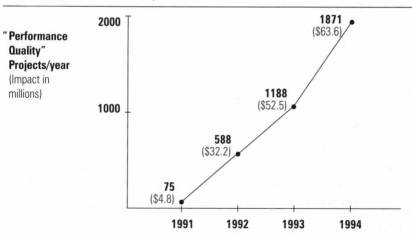

worth tens of millions of dollars annually to DBIS's shareholders. DBIS customers benefited from information products that became continuously faster, more accurate, more useful, and more innovative. And thousands of DBIS people were using a variety of new skills, behaviors, and working relationships. Indeed, so many people in the division had learned the basic quality and breakthrough tools that, in mid-1993, they asked Mike and his facilitators to redesign the one-day kickoff workshop to include more flexibility and advanced techniques. Moreover, 110 facilitators—all holding other full-time jobs—continued to serve as the main workforce of the Quality Shop. The Quality Shop itself had only five full-time employees.

Reflecting back on his committee's original intentions, Mike now chuckles. "I was delighted," he says mischievously, "that we learned how to lose the awareness-building and training race."

HIERARCHY, EXCHANGE, AND MUTUALITY

People take responsibility for their own behavior change when performance consequences depend on it. Most leaders, however, mistakenly assume that hierarchical authority is the only way to gain performance commitments from people. This explains why so many change initiative leaders rush to gain new organizational designs and top management commitment when, as is often the case, initiative leaders themselves lack the hierarchical authority to command performance and change from all of the people who matter.

This deep-seated habit stymies far more change initiatives than it helps. The DBIS committee was headed in this direction. Like too many potential change leaders, their strategy would have amounted to the following: "Let's get top management commitment. We need all the bosses to really commit to total quality, incorporate it in their budgets and plans, and order their people to do it! Let's get them to 'walk the talk.'"

Hierarchical authority, of course, *is* a powerful vehicle for demanding personal performance commitments when it is available to you and employed according to the ten principles. As we saw in Chapter Four, for example, the Kodak Black & White leaders effectively deployed hierarchical authority to lead change. The DBIS committee's original plan, however, reflected more traditional, nonchange-oriented management principles. As a result, even if they had gained hierarchical leverage over people, they were likely to fall into traps similar to that of Dan Holloway of Southwest Gas Electric and Power.

In fact, however, they lacked the necessary hierarchical authority and were unlikely to gain it. By pursuing top management commitment and new organization designs, the committee members would have condemned themselves to three dilemmas:

▶ ***Illusion.*** Imagine for a moment that the DBIS bosses had committed to total quality through budgetary and other decisions. *So what?* The bosses knew less than Berkin and his committee about total quality management. And they certainly knew no more about leading behavior-driven performance and change. Worse still, if they had done the committee's bidding, bosses throughout DBIS would have ordered people to "do total quality" (read: "Change for the sake of change"). Instead of approaching the bosses themselves as one additional group of ready or reluctant people in the internal marketplace of change, the committee was about to naively equate top management commitment with behavior change. An orientation toward performance would soon have disappeared behind the illusion of change. And, paradoxically, whether they signed up or not, the bosses would soon have garnered the blame for a lack of top management commitment.

▶ ***Complexity.*** Neither Mike Berkin nor the committee members had the authority to command specific performance from the thousands of DBISers they needed to join in the performance quality movement. In seeking to influence people *indirectly* through the formal DBIS hierarchy, however, they courted a nightmarish web of decisions and designs. To have gained any person's participation, for example, would have required a decision from that person's boss. If it had not been forthcoming, the committee would have had to go to the boss's boss, and so on. When total quality opportunities crossed

organization boundaries, the committee would have found itself perpetuating the kind of "up, over, up, across, and down" bureaucratic
communications that characterize organizations in *need* of total quality. The entire effort would have bogged down in battles over budgets,
decisions, and directions. It made much more sense for them to work
directly with people who mattered, even if that meant finding informal, nonhierarchical sources of leverage.

▶ *Diversion.* Illusion and complexity lead to diversion. The committee would have focused on activities instead of performance and on
abstractions instead of people. Like those of similarly ill-fated initiatives, 1991's report of progress would have stressed the number of
people trained, the number of "performance contracts" signed, the
number of quality committees and "quality teams" formed, and the
size of budgets devoted to total quality. A small number of DBIS
experts would have specialized in conducting mock Baldrige examinations and distinguishing among Juran, Deming, and other methods.
And in the midst of all the hue and cry, no one other than the newly
minted quality experts themselves would have given much of a damn
one way or the other.

As a change leader, you need to consider informal and nonhierarchical as well as formal, hierarchical ways to influence people's performance agendas. For example, assume I am a person whose
performance and change matter to your initiative. Remember your
challenge is to get me to make a *personal* commitment to one or more
specific performance goals that will cause me to experience the
changes at hand. You have three alternatives for directly influencing
me to do so:

1. *Hierarchy ("Tell").* **By virtue of our respective positions in
the organization, *you can tell me to meet certain performance
objectives.*** Mike Berkin could not command quality from anyone
in DBIS. He was, however, the head of the Quality Assurance
Committee. That gave him the hierarchical authority to command
other committee members to find the first round of opportunities

that met the criteria for breakthroughs in their respective parts of the organization.

2. *Exchange ("Trade").* **By virtue of the resources and opportunities that you have and I need, *you can trade things in exchange for my setting certain performance objectives.*** Mike Berkin controlled the resources and opportunities associated with performance quality. By starting small, he could identify people ready for change and trade them limited opportunities and just-in-time consulting help in exchange for their setting the specific, near-term goals required by Robert Schaffer's breakthrough strategy. By contrast, if he had been more ambitious up front, he would not have had sufficient resources to deliver effective change *experiences* to the large number of reluctant and resistant people he would have had to deal with.

With growing demand, Mike could exercise exchange leverage over an expanding number of people ready to change. As those people made increasingly positive impacts on DBIS's performance, the resources and opportunities controlled by Mike's Quality Shop also grew—giving him more exchange leverage. This positively reinforcing cycle permitted him to set conditions on the performance goals of people hoping to become part-time facilitators, to avoid "bastard breakthroughs," to introduce new products and services, and, ultimately, to control the deployment of "performance quality" as a powerful internal "brand".

3. *Mutuality ("Team").* **By virtue of our combined sweat equity, *you and I can mutually commit to meeting certain performance objectives.*** Mike and his two costrategists committed to finding and implementing a strategy that would profoundly impact DBIS's customers, shareholders, and employees. They held themselves mutually accountable for the strategy's success. They were not "trying to be a team." Rather, they wanted to deliver team performance.

Mike used mutuality to gain specific performance commitments in other ways early on. First, the breakthrough strategy itself requires team performance. In reaching out to small groups of people who were ready for change, Mike benefited from the team discipline that arises among people driven to perform together because *they* want to, not just because a boss wants them to.

Also, Tal Phillips and Doug Nay joined Mike in mutually committing to using performance quality to transform the capabilities and contributions of the Information Resources function. Phillips and Nay got personally involved in specific breakthrough projects, stimulated friendly breakthrough competition throughout the function, found high-potential facilitators, and provided a testing ground when Mike wanted to try out new products and services.

Like Mike Berkin, you need to figure out which of the three approaches—hierarchy, exchange, or mutuality—is consistent with your position vis-à-vis the people you need to enlist. My next point is equally critical. Anyone who has become part of the "we" helping you make change happen has the *same three alternatives* for influencing the performance goals of other people. You may not have hierarchical leverage over a person you hope to influence. But one of your change coleaders might. Or perhaps someone who has joined your initiative can use exchange or mutuality in ways unavailable to you. The point is that by employing hierarchy, exchange, and mutuality to enlist others, everyone involved can multiply the options for leading change.

In teaming up with Doug and Tal, for example, Mike substantially extended the hierarchical leverage available to the performance quality initiative. That was so not because he negotiated for budgeted funds, committee participation, or other declarations from busy executives trying to "show the flag" in DBIS's latest program, which was the unpromising path initially preferred by the committee. Rather, Doug and Tal joined up because they believed Mike's initiative could help meet the performance goals of the Information Resources function. As a result, they took the time to understand Mike's strategy and to manage their participation accordingly.

When Doug and Tal used their hierarchical positions to command specific performance quality goals from people in Information Resources, they kept performance as the primary objective, preferred trial and repurchase to awareness, arranged for just-in-time support, used teams wherever possible, and improvised, improvised, improvised. They did not bother themselves or Mike with abstractions such as complex new organization structures, committee assignments, and decision flows, or with awareness-building activities like massive training efforts. Instead, Doug and Tal got the point. They lived the change they wanted to bring about.

CONCLUSION: BE PRAGMATIC

Change leaders who adopt the perspective of people marketing behavior change to other people take a giant step "outside of the box." They know that people must take responsibility for their own change and that personal commitments to specific performance goals provide the best crucible for doing so. Accordingly, they worry more about the experience-based trial and repurchase at the heart of real performance and real change instead of the awareness-only campaigns that inevitably stir up the troops and then fall short.

As illustrated by the curve in the bottom graph on page 160, their goal is always to increase the number of people joining them in the "we" who will make change happen. They focus on shaping strategies for directly gaining personal performance commitments from people instead of finding alignment between organization design and the decisions made by top management. If they have the hierarchical authority to influence the performance agendas of the people who matter, change leaders should use it. But effective change leaders avoid the illusion, complexity, and diversion associated with unavailable hierarchy. Performance is their objective. In seeking to directly engage other people, change leaders improvise among all the means available to them and their colleagues, including nonhierarchical as well as hierarchical leverage. Change leaders are pragmatists. They pay relentless attention to what they can *do* to make change happen, avoiding the "if only" trap that often ensnares those who rely solely on top management commitment to overcome resistance in organizations facing broad-based change.

Chapter Seven

Exchange, Mutuality, and Coordination

A serious imbalance confronts most of you whose initiatives depend on broad-based behavior-driven change. Success requires enlisting many people who must learn new skills, behaviors, and working relationships. But the majority are reluctant to take responsibility for change and will do so only if specific performance consequences depend on it. Meanwhile, few of you have the reach or the resources at the beginning of your effort to directly influence the goals and sources of reluctance of a large number of people.

In other words, you are David, not Goliath. Some of you are constrained by *position*. Terry Murphy of Tandem, whose story we complete in this chapter, did not have authority to set goals for the sales managers and account representatives on whom solution selling depended. Others of you lack *time*. Mike Berkin of Dun & Bradstreet could not directly set performance quality goals for eight thousand employees even if he had had the authority to do so. Still others of you lack *resources*. Steve Frangos and his fellow change leaders at Kodak's Black & White could not expect millions of new dollars for training, consulting, compensation, hiring, or other support in the midst of the company's pay freeze and severe cutbacks.

Constraints dictate pragmatism. You must use whatever means are available to you and avoid wasting time on those that are not. Too many change leaders worry more about what other people might not do instead of about what they themselves can do to lead change. They waste time negotiating for the realignment of hierarchical authority and the top management commitment of those who have it. And they waste resources trying to overcome resistance through broad-brush awareness-building activities.

Shape a strategy for your initiative that avoids such mistakes. To stay out of the commitment and resistance traps, for example, you might start by seizing only the performance and change opportunities that you can actually influence—however limited in number— and expand from there. That would force you to candidly assess when, how, and with whom you can use hierarchy, exchange, and mutuality to set specific performance goals and just how much or how little coordination and control you need to ensure that your initiative succeeds.

Whatever approach you adopt, remember that your effectiveness during the period of change depends on how well you apply the ten new management principles. The Wireboard, Minnesota, and Kodak stories, for example, illustrated the power of hierarchy when focused on people, performance, purpose, and real work. The same applies to exchange and mutuality. Neither will make a difference if you ignore the fundamentals of managing both performance and behavior change. Both exchange and mutuality, however, demand additional discipline for success. This chapter explores the issues most critical to pursuing each as well as to deciding on the appropriate level of coordination and control.

THE SOLUTIONS EXCHANGE AT TANDEM COMPUTERS

Recall from Chapter Two that Terry Murphy took on Tandem Computer's solution sales initiative in mid-1993. Solution selling was not a new idea at the time. Several years earlier, the open systems movement in information technology had begun weaning a number of customers off the proprietary approach that had dominated the computer industry from its infancy. In the proprietary world, hardware manufacturers like Tandem sold computing architectures that could not operate with competitors' machines because they didn't "talk to one another." From the mid-1950s through the mid-1980s, customers preferred that approach, believing they needed customized systems to meet the unique circumstances of their own enterprise. The combination of proprietary hardware and customized software produced what the computer industry called "lock-in." Once customers invested in a hardware choice, it made little sense and cost a lot of money to switch. Vendors like Tandem who won the hardware game were set for life.

Open systems changed the rules. More and more customers viewed proprietary hardware plus customized software as an undesirable life sentence for their organizations. They preferred nonproprietary architectures open to third-party, even off-the-shelf, applications. In-house information technology people began to shift from building customized applications to helping their companies choose wisely among open systems vendors. In this new world, Tandem's performance, especially its new business, increasingly required a complete solution of Tandem hardware, Tandem software, and third-party software to meet customer needs. In fact, as often as not, customers were more interested in the software than the hardware. Tandem, like other hardware-based firms, now needed software expertise to sell its hardware.

Most of Tandem's direct sales force lacked that expertise. As early as 1987, Tandem had started hiring subject matter experts (SMEs) who had the software and networking skills to help the direct sales force package solutions for customers. But most Tandem sales people, like Joan Yancey of Chapter Two, were reluctant to take the risks associated with solution selling. Everything from hardware-oriented managers to compensation and bonus systems to R&D/marketing promises of new, home-run architectures discouraged them. So did the mixed performance of Tandem's SMEs—some of whom underdelivered, but most of whom suffered from the lack of real opportunity to make a difference.

Tandem was caught in a negative reinforcing cycle. Account representatives would not embrace assistance from SMEs in seizing solution opportunities because they lacked confidence of success and reward; success and reward eluded account representatives and SMEs because they failed to collaborate in seizing the opportunities at hand. Meanwhile, Tandem's performance plateaued. It became financially strapped, began to downsize, and turned up the pressure on account representatives to sell—especially to sell hardware, since that produced substantially more revenue than software.

Going into mid-1993, the company had yet to break this cycle. The hiring of the SMEs had not borne real fruit. Nor had an attempt in the late 1980s to have the SMEs train account representatives in solution selling. A 1989 reorganization, which placed SMEs directly into Tandem's sales districts, did not work. Instead, it allocated scarce expertise to managers without enough opportunities in their geographic areas to exploit it. For example, the Tandem district sales manager for the Detroit area could not fully use the help of the Tandem expert on decision support systems assigned to Detroit. Then a 1991 reorganization attempted to rectify that deployment problem by matrixing SMEs across the company's four major geographical sales regions. But it failed also. The accountability previously felt by district sales managers disintegrated; the reluctance of account representatives to work with SMEs remained rampant.

Thus, when Terry Murphy and his colleagues took charge of all SMEs in Tandem's new solution selling division, they realized that further organization design changes were unlikely to drive either performance or change. Nor would focusing on top management commitment. Tandem's senior sales and marketing executives supported solution selling, but none had made it a top priority. They had not, for example, fundamentally shifted Tandem's approaches to new product development, budgeting, planning, or compensation in favor of solution selling. Viewed from the position of Joan Yancey or just about any other Tandem employee, solution selling was a "nice to have." But trying to get senior management to demonstrate more commitment in an environment of financial pressure and downsizing would take too much time with too little prospect of impact. Terry Murphy wanted to drive tangible performance and change in 1994.

As mentioned in Chapter Two, Terry began with an appeal to intellectual understanding. At the 1993 sales conference, he asked people to identify the key jobholders who needed to change and the specific from/to nature of those changes (see the chart on page 51). This gave the new solution sales leaders a preliminary road map. But as Joan Yancey's story in Chapter Two illustrated, a single day's insight could not dislodge years of habit, routine, and reluctance. Account representatives would learn how to sell solutions only by *selling* solutions.

That required finding ways for sales people to experience the change in a performance context that mattered. And that, in turn, meant facing a harsh truth: neither Terry nor anyone in his division could command specific performance results from any of Tandem's account representatives. Direct use of hierarchy was not an option for leading their change initiative.

Terry turned to exchange. Together with Debbie Gassman, Rich Novak, and others in the solution selling division, he chose to treat his division as a "business" and package and market SME availability and expertise. This forced Terry, Debbie, Rich, and others to self-consciously adopt the marketing perspective that Mike Berkin had used effectively at Dun & Bradstreet. As they planned and executed their business for 1994, Tandem's solution division leaders discovered the following critical factors required to make an exchange strategy succeed.

1. *Carefully identify the "customer."* In the exchange strategy, you trade resources and opportunities in return for specific performance commitments. You cannot do that without identifying *who* matters to your initiative and *what* specific performance goals you want them to set. Terry and his colleagues debated a wide range of possible "customers," including Tandem's real, external customer, the account representative, the district sales manager, more senior sales managers, and key people in Tandem's marketing and R&D functions. Two groups emerged as most important: the account representative and the district sales manager. After much discus-

sion, they decided to offer products and services to district sales managers in exchange for their commanding specific performance commitments from account representatives in their districts. In the terminology of change initiative strategies, Terry would use exchange to influence the performance agendas of district sales managers and a combination of exchange and hierarchy to influence the agendas of account representatives.

2. *Understand customer needs.* In the real world of business, marketing and sales people do not treat customers as resistors. Instead, they identify customer needs and motivations. When the customer's own behavior change is at issue, this requires a dispassionate understanding of the sources of reluctance. You need to identify specific customer objections to change and then work to overcome them.

Terry, Debbie, Rich, and their colleagues were Tandem veterans who knew from experience why district sales managers and account representatives were reluctant to try solution selling. Instead of complaining about resistance, they specifically hypothesized a set of objections and then confirmed them through interviews with their customers. Four major areas of concern, or what they called "pain," emerged. Each major area had between six and eight underlying causes. For example, many district sales managers lamented the lack of enough qualified leads for account representatives to make their goals. To deal with that major objection, people from the solution sales division would need to overcome poor-quality leads, inconsistent prospecting efforts, inadequate knowledge of solutions by account representatives, and too few people available to do prospecting.

3. *Create products and services that answer the customer's question, "What's in it for me?"* The exchange strategy demands that you package available resources or opportunities—in Tandem's case, SME expertise—in one or more products and services that deliver clear benefits. This forces change leaders to go beyond moralistic and generic approaches like "Change is good" or "We're here to help!" Real-world customers rarely respond to such vaporous propositions. Why should internal customers?

Once the solution sales leaders understood the specific causes of pain, they designed products and services that directly appealed to the self-interest of district sales managers and account representatives. Five initial service offerings emerged, ranging from new business development planning to closing strategies. Each service explicitly laid out a set of deliverables and benefits. For example, the prospecting service promised to deliver profiles of prospect accounts, specific contact lists of key decision makers, and a customized solution sales pitch for initial meetings with those key decision makers. The overall benefit to district sales managers was made very clear: "to supplement your resources in order to assure a pipeline of qualified prospects."

4. Set a "price" that requires specific and personal performance commitments from the customer. Perhaps no aspect of the exchange strategy is more difficult or important than this one. First, it requires asking people to make performance commitments that no one, including their boss, says they *must* make. Second, it requires specificity; generic appeals for "more change" will not work. Third, the "price" must be a *personal* commitment to performance. The exchange strategy is not about transfer pricing, compensation schemes, or other *impersonal* elements of organization design. Those inevitably require hierarchical authority to implement and tend to be mechanistic. Exchange, by contrast, does not require hierarchy. Instead, it gives you the means to reach out and trade much-needed resources or opportunities to people who matter in exchange for their personal promises to you to deliver performance.

Fourth, and finally, exchange requires the resolve to walk away if the person refuses to make the needed commitments. This last aspect is particularly counterintuitive for change leaders given the charter to "provide help." But if people in positions like that of Terry Murphy of Tandem or Mike Berkin of Dun & Bradstreet do not value their own resources enough to reject "nonpaying customers," why should those customers make performance commitments? Few people value anything that is free. And that aspect of human nature does not evaporate just because people are part of the same organization.

The solution sales leaders made the "prices" for their five services clear and specific. They would provide their new business development service, for example, only to district sales managers who submitted current district sales plans along with a summary of recent new business attempts; who spent two and a half days participating in the preparation, review, and presentation of the "new business" plan; and, most important, who agreed to hold sales representatives accountable for meeting the specific goals and action steps identified in the "new business" plan.

5. *Identify early adopters who can help get the "product" and "pricing" right.* The abstract posture that "change is necessary for everyone" lures many change leaders into non-customer-friendly, monopolistic behavior. Too often the underlying logic goes like this: Since everyone must change and since the leaders control the change effort, anything the leaders offer—no matter how sloppy, generic, or poorly conceived—should be bought into. As discussed in Chapter Six, such leaders emphasize broad-brush awareness instead of trial and repurchase. But that will not work with exchange. Real-world customers do not purchase products unless their tangible benefits outweigh their prices. Real-world businesses, therefore, do not roll out new products without testing them first. Exchange strategists must be equally deliberate.

The people who will help most are the early adopters whose readiness and enthusiasm for change allow for experimentation and mistakes. Terry, Debbie, Rich, and their colleagues identified three champions among Tandem's twenty-five district sales managers to help with the design, testing, and modifications of the five services and performance commitments ("prices"). In addition, as Terry's "sales campaign" unfolded, these three district managers provided valuable reference and word-of-mouth support.

6. *Invest in the "advertising," "promotion," and "sales" effort.* Change leaders in most private-sector organizations either have, or have access to, professional marketing and sales skills, but they rarely use such skills in the service of broad-based behavior change. Exchange strategists who self-consciously adopt the "business," "products and services," and "customer" perspectives force themselves to do otherwise. They inevitably become quite creative in how they "advertise," "promote," and "sell."

Tandem's change leaders, for example, paid particular attention to "sales." They designed a 1994 "sales campaign" for calling on district sales managers and assembled a step-by-step Call Guide for identifying prospects among district sales managers and closing sales with them. The Call Guide included service and pricing descriptions, illustrative prospect and follow-up letters, successful reference stories, and specific instructions for identifying objections and describing how solution sales services provided answers.

7. Hold the "business" accountable for specific performance and change goals. Performance is the primary objective of change. Exchange strategists are not trying to win arguments; they want people to take responsibility for change in a way that produces results. This orientation must start with their own "business." As we saw in Chapter Six, for example, Mike Berkin established aggressive performance goals for his Quality Shop. So did Terry Murphy. New revenues, new application sales, new accounts, and productivity per person measured the solution sales division's bottom line contribution to Tandem. "Share" goals measured how many district sales managers and account representatives became "customers" who actually experienced the new changes.

Change is as change does. In effect, the exchange strategy forced people within Terry Murphy's division to *sell* solution selling as the *solution* to the needs of district sales managers and account representatives. In terms of the golden rule of change, it caused them to do unto themselves what they wanted others to do. And it paid off.

The specificity, professionalism, and responsiveness of the division's internal sales effort impressed district sales managers, many of whom entered 1994 believing that SMEs were a liability in front of customers. By the end of the year, most district sales managers and account representatives had a different attitude. "They were thrilled," commented one executive. "It was the first time they really understood how to utilize solution selling resources in a way that could move their district results. And they were far less worried that SMEs would somehow embarrass Tandem in front of customers."

The 1994 campaign convinced nearly two-thirds of the district sales managers to pay the "price" for the services of Terry's division. They personally committed to specific performance goals for themselves and their account representatives because they believed they would receive value in return, not because Tandem's budgeting process made them do it. Better still, they obtained the value promised. In many districts, for example, new revenues shot up more than 20 percent—an extraordinary jump from the flat to declining results of prior years. New applications and new accounts rose just as dramatically. As a result, the productivity per person of Tandem's solution sales effort was nearly *four times* what it had been the year before. No wonder that Terry entitled his annual results letter to division people with a single word: "OUTSTANDING!"

MUTUALITY AT MAGMA METALS

"War." That was how everyone—labor, management, journalists, local officials—described the situation at Magma Copper Company in the spring of 1989. No one spoke of "being the world's best," "redesigning work," "self-directed work teams," or "empowerment." June 30 would mark the end of the triennial contract cycle that had punctuated labor-management relations in the copper industry since midcentury. Magma's ten unions had rejected an offer made by the company's new management group in January. Now all sides were preparing for a bitter battle. People were often injured, even killed, in copper strikes; no one believed this one would be different.

The new management group was scared. They had gained control of Magma Copper through a financial technique similar to a leveraged buyout. "We were hundreds of millions of dollars in debt, paying more than 15 percent interest, and we had little to no cash," recalls one executive. "That's why we made an attractive offer to the unions in January. But instead, here we were coming down to the wire with no contract and very, very far apart in our positions. It was make or break for us. We spared no expense in preparing ourselves for a long strike and the decertification of the unions. And for violence."

The unions were scared. "Management's stated intention," comments one union official, "was to scab the property. They were installing trailers to house replacement workers, and getting helicopters and squads of guards to police the area. They were sending employees home with videotaped warnings. It was an intimidation process. Preparation for a real, all-out, gut-busting war."

Workers were scared and had already begun fighting. A handful of violent incidents flared before June 30. A different kind of violence—sabotaging operations—strangled the company. "There was guerrilla warfare inside the plant," says Don Shelton, a thirty-year Magma worker. "Our concern about actually producing anything was gone. We felt that Magma wasn't going to survive very long, and we certainly weren't going to do anything to help."

As it happened, management's fierce resolve ruled the day. Shortly after the June 30 deadline, the unions capitulated. They accepted a worse settlement than the original January offer. Magma had avoided a potentially business-ending strike. But no one had won. When management and union representatives gathered to sign the new contract, not a word was spoken. And the silence continued for months. "There was no dialogue at all," says Don, "except over a grievance table. At no time in the history of this place had it gotten so bad."

"It was lose/lose," agrees John Champagne, a Magma executive.

Productivity kept eroding, costs rising. By autumn, Magma's performance languished near the bottom of the industry. Management continued to worry about solvency. In late October, the company's chief human resources executive, Marge Campbell, asked to speak privately with Bob Guadiana, the United Steelworkers director who oversaw that union's contracts in the western region that included Magma. Each recognized the need for dialogue. They agreed to ask their respective colleagues to come to an air-clearing session in Scottsdale.

Months of pent-up anger, frustration, and ill will were vented at Scottsdale. But, while the session produced candor, it failed to gain collaboration. Everyone believed everyone else was responsible. Still, they promised to continue speaking. Over the next year and a half, management met regularly with union officials, and both met regularly with workers. The discussions had all the dynamics, both good and bad, of marriage counseling. Dialogue was better than no dialogue, and each side received a solid education in the other's point of view. The workers repeatedly heard that management needed higher productivity, lower costs, and a better safety record. Management learned time and again that the unions wanted a restoration of the 20 percent rollback in wages and benefits given in 1986 when copper prices were abysmally low. But neither side seemed prepared to act.

Like others, John Champagne was frustrated. He believed Magma could overcome its difficulties—indeed, become the world's best copper company—if everyone would figure out a very different way of working together. Throughout the long months of dialogue, he repeatedly sought chances to explore a new arrangement. But every time good ideas surfaced, they just as quickly got lost in the basic impasse over management's pleas for productivity and the unions' demands for the restoration of wages. "We were talking," he says, "but we were talking past one another."

Finally, in early 1991, John's management colleagues took the first step. They unilaterally established a gainsharing scheme unrelated to the collective bargaining contract. Both union and nonunion employees would receive bonuses for achieving productivity, cost, and safety goals. Management hoped this show of good faith would unfreeze the glacial dialogue and set a constructive tone for 1992's contract discussions.

It was a good move. Both the unions and the workers appreciated the promise of shared reward for shared effort. Still, management's new pledge only accentuated a set of deeper issues. For months, people at Magma had been arguing over productivity, costs, safety, and wages. Gainsharing signaled a new way of reaping the rewards of performance. But no gainsharing at all would take place until thousands of people, from top to bottom and all across Magma, learned new skills, behaviors, and working relationships. And so far, no one had taken personal responsibility for making change happen.

John Champagne and Bob Guadiana grabbed their chance to lead the way as 1991 drew to a close. Magma Copper Company decided, starting in January 1992, to put its smelting and related commercial operations into a separate subsidiary called Magma Metals under John Champagne as president. John immediately reached out to Bob Guadiana, telling him that he wanted Magma Metals to become the best in the industry by making a total break from the past. He believed that management, union officials, and salaried as well as hourly employees must seize the formation of the new subsidiary as a historic chance to build a completely different approach to working together. To begin, he formed a council that would act like a board of directors for Magma Metals. He asked two things of Bob. First, would he agree to be on the council? Second, and most critical, would Bob personally join John in leading fundamental change at Magma?

"John told me he was talking about real change," says Bob. "He wanted to use the subsidiary as a totally clean slate and he wanted true collaboration from the beginning. It was the only way he believed that both company performance and job security could be assured. He came to me and said, 'We're going to have to be partners. This will work only if we do it together.'"

In the terms of this book, John was using mutuality to lead change at Magma Metals. He and Bob could influence each other's performance agendas only by teaming up to reach certain common objectives. Against the background of the previous several years, John had no other choice. "Yeah, I was president," he says. "But there was no way I could order people to change. I simply didn't have that kind of authority." That was odd, but true for the unionized workforce at Magma. And it was certainly the case with Bob, who, as a Steelworkers Union official, did not work at Magma.

In asking for Bob's help, John chose someone he respected for taking the risk to bring the unions to the Scottsdale session in late 1989. Bob also had a good opinion of John. Mutual respect, however, was enough only to get the two men started.

Agreeing to team up is certainly more difficult than perpetuating the status quo. The much harder part, as any of you who have tried it know, is following through on promises to collaborate. That requires applying each of the six basic aspects of the discipline for real team performance that Jon Katzenbach and I explored in *The Wisdom of Teams:*

1. *Small number.* The most effective teams number between two and twelve members. Although *theoretically* any number of people can pursue common goals, groups that climb much above fifteen to twenty find it difficult to navigate through the logistical, social, administrative, and economic challenges of the team discipline. Ten people are more likely than one hundred to take advantage of individual, functional, and hierarchical differences; to find the time and space needed to reach common understanding and agreement; and to identify specific performance challenges that actually require them to work together. By contrast, twenty or thirty or fifty people tend to get stuck in vague generalities about purpose ("We've got to change!") and approach ("We've got to be a team."). Such abstractions never sustain people through the hard work required for real team performance.

"Small number" imposes a pragmatic constraint on change leaders who seek to use mutuality as a strategy for change. It forces you to respect both your own capacity for team performance commitments and the capacity of those people you hope to enlist in joining you. To be a member of more than two or three real teams at the same time is difficult. Mike Berkin of Dun & Bradstreet, for example, initially ignored the impossibility of asking hundreds of managers throughout his Division to be a team that supported total quality. In later working with his costrategists as well as Doug Nay and Tal Phillips of DBIS's Information Resources, he much more effectively deployed his capacity for using mutuality to influence the performance agendas of people who mattered. In reaching out to one another, John and Bob also took advantage of "small number" to get serious about making a difference to themselves and Magma.

2. *Complementary skills.* No team ever succeeds without the right mix of skills and perspectives needed for the performance chal-

at hand. Three skill areas matter most: (1) technical/functional, (2) problem solving and decision making, and (3) interpersonal. Teams do not need all the required skills up front. In fact, experience suggests that most teams identify and develop skills *after* they get started, which explains why teams should be used to drive change wherever possible.

John Champagne and Bob Guadiana complemented each other extremely well. John was an executive who had worked in and around copper for most of his career and was an acknowledged industry leader in trading and technology. Bob had more than thirty years' experience both as a union worker and union official. He thoroughly understood the operations of copper smelting. More critically, he knew from experience what made the difference—technically, administratively, legally, and organizationally—between management-union relationships that worked and those that did not.

However, guiding hundreds of Magma Metals' people to take responsibility for redefining how they worked and then implementing the changes would require both John and Bob to learn a variety of new skills, including teaching, questioning, facilitating, and active listening. Each man had the potential to learn those skills; by teaming up, they positioned themselves to help one another do so.

3. Common purpose. Real teams always have a common purpose that they own as a team. Management beyond the team can provide direction and set boundaries. The Kodak Black & White leadership group, for example, established a variety of themes (e.g., "Kodak's premier job shop") and goals (e.g., cycle-time reduction) that conditioned the purposes of the teams they hoped would contribute to the division's turnaround. But every real team finds some way to put a personal stamp on its purpose.

In making purposes their own, teams produce three powerful sources for success. First, they develop the sense of pride, responsibility, and enthusiasm in pursuing "their baby," something truly their own creation. Second, the intense and purposeful communications in real teams generate rich and varied specific meanings and directions that team members can draw upon to meet both expected and unexpected circumstances. Third, team purposes give teams an identity that extends beyond the sum of the individuals involved.

Common purpose, just like common performance goals and common working approach, does not mean absolute and complete agreement. It does mean that two conditions pertain to any disagreements. First, each party can articulate to the other party's satisfaction the other party's point of view; second, the team has some mechanism for making a choice and moving forward. Neither is easy.

The next time you are in a debate, for example, try articulating your opponent's point of view to your opponent's satisfaction. You will discover that it requires you to listen and speak much more carefully than you usually do. Without making that effort, however, neither you nor those you hope to influence will develop a common purpose. Instead, you will find hidden agendas and other problems continuing to undermine your collective performance and change.

John and Bob worked hard to ensure that they had a clear and commonly understood purpose. "We spent a lot of time together talking and understanding one another. We wanted a joint vision about making Magma the world's best copper company," says Bob. "We knew Magma's people themselves would have to come up with an approach so radical and so different that not even those opposed to change would be able to avoid it. But we also knew we would have to lead them to do it. And we were determined to prove that an executive and a union official could partner together in making that happen."

4. *Common performance goals.* No team realizes its purpose—however lofty or inspiring—without a series of concrete performance goals and accomplishments along the way. Performance goals transform broad purpose into action. They make the aspirational real. To work, team performance goals must be specific (unambiguously clear), assessable (whether quantitatively or qualitatively), attainable (something the team can do), and compelling (stretch goals that fulfill the team's purpose).

Moreover, team goals must define something unique for people on the team to do. Leadership teams often overlook this aspect. They tend to confuse the purpose and performance of the *organization* with that of their *team*. As a result, they often fail to discover anything concrete for themselves to do as a team beyond the generic challenge of leading. By contrast, teams that make or do things and teams that recommend things find it easier to distinguish organization from team. For example, the frontline Tandem teams of account representatives and subject matter experts found it straightforward to set goals like "sell Customer X a new solution for doing electronic commerce by year's end." Similarly, the Dun & Bradstreet performance quality breakthrough teams had little difficulty identifying specific six-to-eight-week objectives.

John Champagne and Bob Guadiana avoided this trap. As *organization* leaders, they wished to transform Magma Metals' performance. As a *team*, they hoped to find and seize specific opportunities for Magma people to set their own destiny, steer those people toward performance and work instead of debate about power and legalities, and, most critically, figure out how to get the people to implement the changes they proposed.

Over time, John and Bob could look to the company's performance record to see if they were succeeding. However, they also had a nearer-term way of assessing their progress as a team. Although more qualitative than quantitative, they paid attention to the number of opportunities they found for people to take charge and how many of those opportunities produced the desired outcomes. In effect, they kept watch over their team's own private win/loss record in getting people to take responsibility for performance and change. This helped them track their own progress and gave them a concrete way to judge and improve their effectiveness as a team.

5. *Common working approach.* Teams must agree on how they will work together to accomplish their purpose and goals. Real team members always do equivalent amounts of real work beyond and between meetings where things are discussed and decided. Over time, a team's working approach incorporates a number of spoken or unspoken rules that govern contribution and membership. Examples include thinking out of the box, candor in discussion, relying on facts instead of opinions, end-product orientation, constructive communications and conflict, confidentiality, having fun, and, as men..... above, doing real work.

John and Bob developed a series of practices that were critical to their success. They agreed to share all information, even financial. Although unusual for an executive and a union official, that was essential to their desire for open communications. In looking for opportunities for people to redefine Magma Metals, John and Bob wanted to focus on *work* and *performance* instead of legalities, rights, or power. Moreover, they agreed to give people opportunities, not answers, and hold people accountable for implementation. Other than the information-sharing compact, perhaps the most difficult part of their working arrangement called for saying yes to the recommendations people developed and then spending the time necessary to help those people make change happen.

6. *Mutual accountability.* No group delivers real team performance until the members hold themselves mutually accountable as a team. Mutual accountability comes on top of, not instead of, the individual accountability necessary to all human enterprise. But individual accountability is never enough for real teams, which inevitably discover that only the team can succeed, only the team can fail.

Mutual accountability thrives on the commitment and trust essential to team performance. Commitment and trust cannot be manufactured, however. Instead, people earn both through a reinforcing cycle of making and fulfilling promises. This cycle works as follows: by committing ourselves to the team's goals, we earn the right to be heard; in finding our positions heard and respected, we promise to hold ourselves accountable; by working toward team performance, we maintain the mutual commitment and trust needed to continue contributing to both team direction and team results.

Mutual accountability is the ultimate test of common purpose, common goals, and common working approach. All of the fine sentiments and plans in the world meant nothing to John Champagne and Bob Guadiana unless they held themselves mutually accountable for leading change at Magma Metals. Each knew the other would have to take significant risks to make their team succeed. "Neither of us," says

John, "could be sure of any of the outcomes. What we were doing was unprecedented. And a whole lot of people—both my management colleagues and Bob's union friends—thought we were dangerously nuts."

John and Bob never let each other down. Shortly after teaming up, they took advantage of a breakdown in productivity to empower a joint hourly-salary team to "redefine how we need to work together to become the best copper company in the world." This team too applied the six basic aspects of team discipline in eventually crafting a set of recommendations that the team members thought were too radical to get adopted. They suggested replacing Magma's multilayered decision-making hierarchy with three concentric circles of teams who would work together by staying in constant communication with one another. The council that John had established would be in the inner circle, surrounded by business teams of managers and workers overseeing Magma's most critical functions and processes, which themselves were composed of natural work teams.

The redesign team believed management would reject the restructuring of authority and that the unions would refuse proposed operating principles requiring flexibility and cross-skilling that violated traditional interunion jurisdictions (e.g., Steelworkers versus Electricians). Neither John nor Bob blinked. Even before the redesign team had finished, the two men had led Magma and its unions to sign a new fifteen-year collective bargaining agreement that reflected their vision of the future. With the redesign team's recommendations in hand and approved, they went to work helping Magma implement them.

John and Bob employed all the management principles of leading behavior-based change. They continually increased the number of people taking responsibility for change and gave them the information, training, and support just in time for success. They spoke endlessly to anyone who would listen about their vision for making Magma the best and the specific performance goals of productivity, unit costs, and safety that mattered most. They also made sure that everyone understood their role in Magma's new big picture, including how overall performance would translate into gainsharing benefits. In the process, their commitment to one another and to their vision for Magma grew more profound. Bob eventually took a different union assignment that would allow him to spend the time needed to lead change with John.

Not everyone, of course, took responsibility for change. Nor did all who tried succeed. A number of Magma's new teams, for example, fell short of delivering real team performance. But from 1992 until today, a critical mass of the people and teams at Magma Metals have delivered unprecedented performance and change. Copper output rose to record-setting high levels. The number of accidents or safety incidents dropped by 80 percent. Unit costs were down and cash flow up, providing a steady increase in the gainsharing payout to employees. In fact, over the three years they followed John and Bob's guidance and example, Magma Metals workers reaped annual bonuses that exceeded 10 percent of their wages—three to four times the average pay increases they had won through negotiation during the 1980s.

Most important, the people at Magma experienced the link between their new skills, behaviors, and working relationships and how both the company and themselves performed. The gainsharing payouts made this tangible. But for many, the intangible rewards of setting a new course for themselves and their company were greater. As Don Shelton puts it, "Each night I think about how much distance there is between that other life that we had and this cooperative relationship we've developed here. I've been through thousands of grievance hearings over thousands of issues for thirty years, and today, you know, that's like a piece of something passing through my head. Like a lifetime that didn't produce anything. Today we're producing a lot for the future and for the present. So it makes it all worthwhile. I am thrilled to be a part of it."

COORDINATING THE REENGINEERING OF BANCA DI AMERICA E DI ITALIA (BAI)

Long-standing managerial perspective induces many leaders to overestimate the importance of control and coordination to their change initiatives. Without much reflection, they equate getting hundreds or thousands of people to change behaviors with, say, building a new jetliner. How else, they assume, but tight coordination and control to deal with so many moving parts? Mike Berkin's Quality Assurance Committee, for example, initially considered heavy control a requirement for ensuring that hundreds of customers were surveyed, thousands of employees were trained, the activities of scores of "quality teams" coalesced, dozens of budgets added up, and so forth.

The bias is understandable. It is, after all, part of the command-and-control philosophy to consider organizations as big, complex machines in need of careful blueprinting, construction, and modification. When an initiative (e.g., total quality, a new strategy, reengineering) is really important to the organization, our managerial reflex is to rush for the organization charts, compensation and information systems, planning and budgeting processes, committees, and other tools needed to take care of the "machine."

Before doing that, however, take a step back. You already know that the high-performance organization demands fast and flexible networks of committed people instead of rigid, mechanistic routines efficiently executed by people who are cogs. In such organizations, information is the lifeblood for engaged and empowered people, not the whip used by overseeing managers to keep adversarial employees under control. The best control comes from people who take responsibility for doing the right things right; the best coordination comes from everyone understanding the big picture and their contribution to it. Few would disagree with the advantages of such new ways. Why, then, would you build your *change* initiative on the old ways? Remember, change is as change does.

The vast majority of today's behavior-driven performance initiatives do not require tight coordination and control. Typically, in fact, the number of people taking responsibility for change matters far more than whether their efforts are carefully controlled and aligned. Mike Berkin's performance quality initiative actually thrived in the absence of control. Yes, he did avoid "bastard breakthroughs" and encourage (although not require) breakthrough teams to pick goals central to the mission and strategic objectives of DBIS. With time, he also staged an annual Team Day to celebrate and share the most innovative accomplishments. These modest coordinating devices, however, were far less intrusive, burdensome, and costly than the committee's original plans for committees, budgets, "performance contracts", and other devices to ensure linkages across goals, information flows, decision flows, and total quality oversight.

Sometimes, of course, careful control and coordination are necessary. Between 1988 and 1992, for example, tight coordination helped Banca di America e di Italia (BAI) transform its approach to retail banking in Italy. BAI's CEO believed paperless banking could produce dramatic performance improvements. And he was right. By 1992, BAI had more than doubled productivity in its retail branches, increased customers accounts by half, reduced the cost of introducing new products by up to 80 percent, and doubled revenues—all while reducing its payroll and holding total computer capacity constant.

BAI's performance aspirations demanded a cautious approach to reengineering. The bank asked two cross-functional and cross-hierarchical teams to spend a year redesigning all three hundred transactions that make up retail banking. One team concentrated on how best to employ technology; the other, how best to employ people. In effect, the two teams aspired to nothing less than building a new bank from scratch—withdrawal, deposit, credit and other forms, accounting, reporting, control and other software systems, branch interior design, job descriptions. Everything.

BAI's change leaders could not have succeeded through pursuing a loose, hands-off strategy like the one Mike Berkin used. Unlike DBIS's performance quality, reengineering BAI into a paperless bank met each of the major criteria that determine when you need to closely coordinate and control a change initiative:

▶ *Asset/technology investment.* BAI was making a major technology investment that deserved cautious managerial deliberation and judgment. Put simply, the new system *had* to work. The integrity of customer accounts and funds, the compliance with regulatory controls, and the quality of the bank's balance sheet were all at stake. By contrast, the DBIS performance quality initiative demanded no special or sizable investment in technology, machinery, or other assets.

♦ *Interdependent activities spanning the organization.* Without conscientiously attending to how work was done across organization boundaries, BAI could not succeed. Dramatic performance improvements in speed, zero defects, accuracy, and customer service for three hundred transactions required coordination among such back-office activities as credit, audit, accounting, systems, and operations and the front-office efforts of relationship managers, product and service directors, tellers, and others. DBIS was not reengineering any process as broad or deep as retail banking. The performance aspirations of any single breakthrough team were far less sensitive to interdependency.

♦ *Time pressure.* BAI would do something of this magnitude only once, or at least once in a great while. The bank had to get it right. By contrast, most change initiatives do not require getting it right the first time. Indeed, they benefit from the experimentation and modification associated with less concern for perfection, not more.

♦ *Brand/goodwill vulnerability.* When BAI rolled out its new retail bank, it put the brand name and goodwill of the bank on the line. The bank had to manage against the risk of numerous customer defections. This does not mean that the mere fact of customer contact calls for heavy control. For example, several of DBIS's performance quality breakthroughs involved customers. But none of them—individually or collectively—had the scope and reach of paperless retail banking. In that respect, the BAI initiative *was* the bank.

In light of the size of BAI's investment, the complexity of both its technical and human aspects, and the risk it incurred with customers, its reengineering initiative did parallel building a new jetliner. To ensure the appropriate control and coordination, the two teams worked hard to complete the design of the new bank before asking others to join the effort. They communicated with people throughout, but asked them to take responsibility for performance and change only after the teams had an approach they knew would perform. By that time, of course, the CEO and other senior executives at BAI were literally invested in the success of the initiative. There was little chance that hierarchical demands would be made by people who themselves were not prepared to live the change.

You need to reach your own conclusion about how much control and coordination your specific initiative requires. Pay attention to the performance implications of the four criteria described above instead of traditional concerns for planning and decision-making infrastructure. You will discover that the BAI initiative is the exception, not the rule. Unlike it, most behavior-driven initiatives do not entail multi-million-dollar asset or technology investments, complex redesigns of interdependent work flows across the entire organization, "one strike or you're out" pressure, or risking the enterprise's entire brand and goodwill. Instead, the more typical total quality, customer service, strategic innovation, empowerment, self-directed teams, core competency, and other initiatives depend mostly on people taking responsibility for new ways of working.

Indeed, not even all reengineering initiatives put as much at stake as BAI did. The Magma Metals change, for example, included redesigning work with the whole picture in view. Consequently, part of John and Bob's initiative turned on how well people coordinated across interdependent activities that spanned parts of the organization. Magma's leaders, however, were not making a major investment in technology or other assets, subjecting the company's goodwill to extensive risk, or setting down a one-time path that precluded experimentation. In fact, part of John and Bob's team purpose was to get Magma's employees to coordinate for themselves as opposed to depend on senior management. When viewed against the four basic factors, then, it made sense for Magma's leaders to worry more about coordination and control than did Mike Berkin of DBIS, but far less than the two BAI reengineering teams.

CONCLUSION: CONSIDER YOUR OPTIONS AND USE WHATEVER WORKS

You can create several options for leading your change initiative by thinking through your performance and change task, the mix of readiness and reluctance among the people who matter, and the sources of influence leverage in your position and resources. In teaming up, John Champagne and Bob Guadiana employed mutuality to revitalize their combined hierarchical authority for leading change at Magma. Both Terry Murphy at Tandem and Mike Berkin of Dun & Bradstreet blended hierarchy, exchange, and mutuality with a minimum of control and coordination. Steve Frangos and his Kodak Black & White leadership colleagues used hierarchy and mutuality with modest coordination. The change managers at BAI also used hierarchy and mutuality, but relied on extensive coordination and control because of the size and nature of the bet they were making.

Ultimately, your strategy should include whatever works. Take full advantage of the hierarchical authority directly exercisable by you and those of your colleagues prepared to live the change. Use team performance wherever possible. Real teams are the best available vehicle for small groups of people who must deliver both performance and behavior change. But teams and teamwork are not the same thing. For example, a compelling and specific performance challenge is the mainspring of a team, not the desire to be a team. Mutuality, then, requires adhering to the discipline of teams if, like John Champagne and Bob Guadiana, you hope to use it effectively.

There is a discipline behind exchange as well, and you understand it: it is the discipline of the marketplace. By submitting yourself and your resources to it, you force yourself to consider the benefits of change from the perspective of the people you hope to enlist. The Tandem district sales managers and account representatives who agreed to experience solution selling were not primarily concerned with behavior change, although they knew that was part of the "price." Performance was their principal objective. They were persuaded that Terry Murphy's products and services could help them achieve their goals.

Whatever blend of approaches you adopt, remember to stick to the ten new management principles. Focus relentlessly on getting people to experience change (trial and repurchase) instead of naively building awareness alone. Start small and continually enlist more and more people to join you in taking responsibility for performance and change. Prudently deploy and grow your resources to provide the just-in-time training, information, help, and reinforcement that people need to succeed. If performance involves major asset investments and interdependent changes across the organization, then take the control and coordination steps necessary. Without a compelling performance reason for control, however, avoid repeating the very behaviors you may well be trying to change. In this as in all other aspects of your strategy, bear in mind that change is as change does.

Chapter Eight

Shaping and Improvising Strategies That Work

Improvisation guides performance and change. The fact that your initiative depends on many people learning to do things differently means that neither you nor others have mastered the skills, behaviors, and working relationships required for performance. You cannot rely on what you already know. You must make stuff up, try things out, see what works and what does not. Only performance as your objective and the new principles as your discipline should remain constant.

You can use the following questions to improvise a pragmatic strategy for getting started:

1. Who are the people whose performance and behavior change matter most to your initiative?

- What are the performance objectives of your initiative?
- What jobs are held by the people who matter to that performance objective?
- How much of the organization do they span?
- What are the specific performance results each of those jobholders must contribute to your initiative?

- What are the from/to changes in skills, behaviors, and working relationships that they must learn in order to perform?

2. Who among them is ready to join you in living the change?

   - Who, besides yourself, is ready to live the change you want to bring about?

   - Have you and each of those people set specific performance and change objectives to which you hold yourselves accountable?

   - Who has already experienced the change and is looking for more?

   - Who is an early adopter and change seeker you can depend on to experiment with new ways of doing things?

   - Who faces performance consequences so acute and so threatening that he or she is ready to "try anything"?

   - Who already believes that he or she *must* change?

3. Who remains reluctant, and why?

   - Who still does not understand the link between his or her own specific changes and performance contributions and the big picture of the organization's performance?

   - Who still does not understand the specific from/to changes in skills, behaviors, and working relationships that matter most?

   - Who doesn't yet desire making the effort to change?

   - Who has yet to experience change or to make plans for doing so?

   - What are the sources of negative and positive reinforcement people might expect from organizational arrangements?

4. With whom can you use *hierarchy* to directly gain personal commitments to performance goals?

   - Can you specifically articulate the performance goals you wish to command from others? For example, can you distinguish between commanding a broad purpose ("faster product development") and the goals that will make it happen ("cut the current cycle time in half")?

- Do you have the hierarchical authority to directly command ("tell") specific performance goals from any of the people who matter?

- Do colleagues of yours who are ready to live the change have the hierarchical authority to directly command specific performance goals from any of the people who matter?

- Can you gain hierarchical authority for commanding performance, either directly or indirectly, without sinking into the quicksand of decisions, abstractions, and designs?

5. With whom can you use *exchange* to directly gain personal commitments to performance goals?

- Do you have resources and/or opportunities that other people need for success?

- Can you shape those resources and opportunities into a set of products and services that meet specific needs of people from their perspective?

- Have you assured yourself that you can deliver whatever value is promised in your set of products and services?

- Can you articulate the specific, personal performance demands you wish to make as the "price" for providing your set of products and services?

- Are you prepared to walk away from people who do not commit to your "price"?

- Have you thought through the messages, vehicles, and timing for promoting the "sales" and growth of your "business"?

6. With whom can you use *mutuality* to directly gain personal commitments to performance goals?

- Are there specific performance goals that matter to your initiative that demand the real-time contributions of a small number of people working as a team?

- Who are the people you wish to influence who might contribute to those goals?

- What capacity do you and they have for teaming up?

- Are you prepared to apply the six basic aspects of the team performance discipline to your efforts? That is, are you prepared to work hard at becoming a small team of people with complementary skills who hold yourselves mutually accountable for a common purpose, set of performance goals, and working approach?

- Can others besides you use the team discipline to make a contribution to your inititiative?

- How might you team up with other people, and thereby extend the hierarchical and exchange leverage available to your initiative?

7. What is your time and other resource capacity for providing just-in-time help and reinforcement?

- Have you mapped out a trial and repurchase curve like that in the bottom graph on page 160?

- How can you get early adopters to help you in the beginning stages of that curve?

- What will be your approach to building awareness? How soon and how broadly will you communicate that the changes at hand are of the utmost importance?

- What information, training, and other resources do people need to succeed?

- Who among the people who must change will need personal reinforcement for their efforts and how will you make sure they get it?

- What specific approaches will you use to deploy help and reinforcement just in time?

- How many specific performance and change efforts involving how many people do you have the capacity to support?

- How will you grow that capacity over time?

8. How much or how little *coordination and control* is demanded by the performance objective at hand?

- How sizable is the investment in technology or other assets associated with your initiative?

- How seriously and over what time frame will your initiative put the brand or goodwill of your organization at risk, especially with customers or clients?

- Does the performance of your initiative depend on specific and numerous interconnections of many people spanning the organization? Or does performance depend on cumulative but not necessarily interdependent efforts?

- What pressure exists for getting the performance and change right the first time?

- When coordination and control are needed, who should exercise it? For example, should the people who matter to your initiative coordinate among themselves as a critical aspect of their own behavior and skill change? Or does performance require a small set of individuals coordinating and controlling the activities of larger numbers of other people?

As we have seen, these questions can help you generate a variety of options in addition to the decision/awareness/design approach. Whatever strategy for change you begin with, however, do not expect it to remain unmodified throughout the period ahead. Managing behavior change is too hard for that. Changing "the way we do things around here" threatens job security, friendships, affiliations, and many people's sense of purpose and meaning. With both economics and emotions stirred up, you must anticipate as many surprises, obstacles, and failures as successes along the way. Your constant concern should be *"What can we do now* to continue making performance and change happen?"

In other words, you must improvise. Change leaders who continue to improvise grow confident in the face of whatever wins and woes they encounter. Those who do not improvise reap confusion and disappointment. Initiatives that are going sour have their own look and feel. Instead of observable performance gains and increasing numbers of people joining the "we" who will make change happen, failing initiatives betray confused leadership, a lost sense of purpose, flagging energy and enthusiasm, flavor-of-the-month criticisms, and complaints about unmade big decisions, missing top management commitment, and insurmountable resistance.

The story of this chapter explores the indicators of success and failure and what you can do about them. It recounts the efforts of the leaders of the Organization Performance Practice (OPP) at the management consulting firm of McKinsey & Company during the five-year period in which they took on a critical behavior-driven initiative. The description of OPP's initial change strategy will help you review Part 2's insights about getting started. How OPP's leaders improvised their way through a series of successes, obstacles, failures, and surprises will give you perspective for keeping your own change initiative fresh and vital to the purpose at hand.

IMPROVISING A STRATEGY FOR MCKINSEY'S ORGANIZATION PERFORMANCE PRACTICE

For most of the 1980s, McKinsey & Company did not have a unified practice that focused on organization matters. Instead, separate Centers of Competence explored issues of interest to the consultants who participated in them. The Building Institutional Skills Center and the Change Management Center, for example, pioneered much of McKinsey's early thinking on how to help clients with fundamental skill and behavior change. When the leaders of those two Centers decided to merge into a single Organization Performance Practice (OPP) in mid-1989, they realized they faced a critical and ironic challenge: How could they lead fundamental skill and behavior change in McKinsey itself?

For most of the previous two decades, McKinsey consultants had concentrated on matters of strategy. Over that period, clients asked for help with such performance challenges as how to identify the best new opportunities, how to reorganize in response to competitive pressures, what major asset decisions to make, or how to reduce costs with minimum damage to morale and maximum advantage to competitiveness. McKinsey's recommendations nearly always focused on providing the facts, analyses, and insights senior client executives needed to make decisions about strategy. By 1989, however, forces at work in the world had produced new dilemmas for clients.

As one of OPP's leaders put it, "Bad things kept happening to good strategies." Unlike most McKinsey consultants, he and his colleagues deeply appreciated that, increasingly, existing people from top to bottom and all across the client organization did not have the capabilities required to implement McKinsey's strategic recommendations. In such cases, neither McKinsey's analytical rigor nor its insightful answers were enough to make a difference to client results. Instead, performance depended on lots of existing client people learning new skills, behaviors, and working relationships—or what OPP's leaders called "major change."

OPP's leaders were convinced that the value of McKinsey's work to clients in the 1990s and beyond would turn more often than not on how well McKinsey consultants *themselves* learned to use the fundamentally new set of skills, behaviors, and working relationships demanded by major change. This implied a number of from/to shifts, including the following:

1. *FROM* assuming that client performance would automatically respond to the strategic decisions that McKinsey recommended *TO* recognizing those occasions when client performance depended on *both* sound decisions *and* broad-based behavior change

2. *FROM* adhering to the dictate that "structure follows strategy" and "implementation follows structure" *TO* learning when and how implementation depended more on getting people to *experience* behavior change than on refining descriptions of strategies and organization designs

3. *FROM* considering process and facilitation skills as secondary *TO* embracing *both* expert-based *and* facilitation-based consulting skills

4. FROM restricting working relationships to senior client executives and client members of McKinsey project teams **TO** working with all the people in the client organization whose skills and behaviors mattered to the performance challenge at hand

5. FROM relying solely on new intellectual concepts and frameworks to drive learning in clients and consultants alike **TO** relying on *both* intellectual concepts *and* experience-based, learn-by-doing approaches to change

The forty or so consultants who had been active in the Building Institutional Skills Center and the Change Management Center had learned many of these from/to changes. But, as OPP's leaders knew well, thousands of McKinsey strategy-oriented consultants had not. Somehow, the leaders had to figure out a strategy to get an increasing number of consultants throughout the firm to take responsibility for change. To better understand that challenge, they put together a Change Board. It revealed the following picture:

People. McKinsey consultants had the minimum capability to successfully learn the new skills and behaviors. The majority of them, however, would be reluctant to change for a variety of reasons, including the following:

▶ ***Understanding.*** Too few consultants could articulate the specific from/to challenges that lay ahead of them. In 1989, for example, most made no distinction between performance-only client challenges versus performance-and-change challenges. In addition, the majority mistakenly equated new organization designs with strategic implementation and change. And because of the success of the McKinsey 7S Model* introduced in *In Search of Excellence*, most mid-to-senior consultants believed they were masters of organization design.

---

*The McKinsey 7S Model breaks organization design into seven elements: *strategy* (where and how an organization competes); *structure* (reporting relationships); *skills* (core competencies); *systems* (planning, budgeting, compensation, information, etc.); *staff* (people); *style* (how leaders use time, attention, and symbolic behavior); and, *shared values* (what the organization believes is important, i.e., "how we do things around here"). The model suggests that organizational effectiveness depends on all seven of these elements being in alignment.

As applied, however, the 7S Model focused more on *describing* organizational attributes than on making those attributes a reality. Description worked well for dividing up a client's decision-making responsibilities, but it alone was not enough to foster real change in the underlying skills, behaviors, and work by which client organizations deliver value to their customers. Moreover, the 7S Model's emphasis on alignment was more appropriate to performance-only challenges than to turbulent periods of performance and change. Consequently, 7S inspired recommendations that too easily fell victim to the top management decisions and designs trap—a phenomenon too few consultants understood.

Finally, the popularity of 7S, like other McKinsey originated constructs, had reinforced a deep-seated bias favoring new intellectual concepts and frameworks as the only path for advancing knowledge and capability. Most McKinsey consultants, for example, expected OPP to work exclusively on knowledge development, which meant finding "the next big idea after 7S" as opposed to emphasizing experience-based, learn-by-doing approaches. In contrast, OPP's leaders believed the concept-only approach was necessary but insufficient. They held out little hope, for example, that intellectual constructs could replace experience as a source for the emotion, desire, and irrationality critical to adult learning and change.

▶ *Desire.* Many McKinsey consultants, especially at the senior levels, felt little need to change their own skills, behaviors, or working relationships. There were warning signs on the horizon, but only the early adopters among the seniors were heeding them. McKinsey's focus on strategy, for example, had left it on the sidelines throughout the first decade of the total quality movement. Moreover, the "bad things" that kept happening to McKinsey strategies had spawned a growing industry for other consultants who helped clients implement recommended changes. Interestingly, the consulting firms taking advantage of this opportunity called it "the McKinsey after-market."

Nevertheless, client demand for strategy work was at record levels. So were firm economics and partner pay. Sticking to the "way we do things around here" had made senior McKinsey partners very wealthy. Moreover, in 1989, most people considered McKinsey the preeminent consulting firm in the world. Finally, senior McKinsey consultants had their deepest professional ties with equally senior client executives. Both groups reinforced a mutual worldview that equated leadership with brilliant, tough-minded, and decisive strategic insight and decision making. Learning how to help clients manage change, therefore, was at best an opportunity, not a threat, for the senior consultants who dominated the firm.

More desire to learn new ways of consulting was seen among the junior-to-mid-level consultants working with the client managers who had to implement the strategies and other decisions emerging from McKinsey's work. And, as in most organizations, a group of early adopters existed at every level of seniority who would help experiment with and champion new ways of consulting.

▶ *Planning/action.* Few McKinsey consultants had either experienced the changes at hand or had crafted plans for doing so. Consultants, for example, regularly put together plans for their own skill and career development. Only a minority included proactive steps for learning the skills, behaviors, and working relationships critical to clients facing behavior-driven change. Far more career plans reflected concerns for acquiring the strategy and related client skills so essential to advancement within the firm.

▶ *Reinforcement.* The 1980s had been the "strategy decade" at McKinsey. The firm's professionals respected organization issues but considered them secondary to strategy. Career advancement and annual bonuses depended more on developing and deploying strategy skills than change management skills. The most powerful committee and office management assignments went to strategists. Even the firm's 1988 election of managing director reflected this orientation. In a choice between Fred Gluck, who had galvanized McKinsey's strategy efforts in the late 1970s and early 1980s, and Jon Katzenbach, an organization consultant, McKinsey partners chose Gluck.

▶ *Position/Resources.* OPP's leaders hoped an increasing number of consultants would take responsibility for learning when and how to help clients confronted by behavior-driven change. This meant challenging consultants to risk new behaviors and approaches in their actual client work—that is, in the performance context that mattered most. Influencing the client agendas of other McKinsey consultants, however, is difficult. OPP's leaders would have to employ both the limited hierarchical leverage available to them as well as the nonhierarchical means of exchange and mutuality.

Partnership prevails over hierarchy in most professional service firms like McKinsey. Of course, there is a hierarchy. At McKinsey, it starts with the managing director and the Shareholders Committee and expands through a variety of geographic office managers, administrative functions, other committees, and, finally, various practice groups like OPP. But this hierarchy focuses mainly on building and sustaining McKinsey as an institution.

The conduct of client work, by contrast, is entirely in the hands of the partners and associates doing that work. At any given time, hundreds of different McKinsey project teams are assisting clients. And, for the most part, the senior-to-junior hierarchy within these projects gives way to the team discipline necessary to performance. When it comes to influencing work at the client interface, therefore, the wiser appeal within McKinsey is to the partnership's shared values instead of to its hierarchy.

Consequently, OPP's leaders had only two limited sources of direct hierarchical authority. First, they could direct the consultants working with them in their own client efforts. That, however, represented less than half of 1 percent of McKinsey's total client work. Second, they could command specific contributions to OPP from those professionals who were members of the practice. But OPP, like most practice groups, was chartered to advance knowledge, not do client work. Accordingly, the OPP strategy would need to improvise ways of using contributions to the practice to put people in client-related performance contexts that mattered.

OPP's leaders did control the resources and opportunities associated with McKinsey's organization practice. They also deeply believed that client demand for change-oriented consulting would rise dramatically and, as a result, cause increasing numbers of consultants to turn to OPP for help. Thus, by devising a series of exchange strategies to package and deploy resources in a just-in-time-to-perform fashion, the leaders hoped to influence the performance context of others. Finally, professional service firms are, by nature, team-based cultures. The leaders knew they could employ the team discipline to promote the success of their initiative.

▶ *Performance/Coordination.* The most interesting coordination-and-control issue imposed by OPP's challenge concerned language and energy. Unlike the BAI reengineering initiative, OPP's success did not require any significant asset or technology investments, complex interdependent activities of hundreds of people, unique one-try-only time pressures, or comprehensive brand/goodwill risks at the client interface. Accordingly, OPP would have no need for control-heavy budgeting, planning, reviews, ad hoc committee structures, and so on.

However, OPP had to speak coherently to their McKinsey colleagues. Much reluctance to change arose from the misunderstanding generated by a babel of concepts, frameworks, and messages that had emerged during the "Center"-based years. Moreover, given the centrality of the exchange strategy, OPP's leaders had to find a way to manage the resources and energies of the practice as productively as possible. Indeed, the need to coordinate language and energy lay behind the leaders' choice to abandon the "Centers" in favor of a single practice.

▶ *OPP's Strategy.* In light of this picture, OPP's leaders chose capability building instead of knowledge building as their top priority. They also decided to focus most on mid-level associates and young partners. And they crafted a blend of hierarchy, exchange, mutuality, and coordinating approaches to influence the performance contexts of the consultants in their target market, including the following:

▶ *Joint client/consultant workshops.* Before the formation of OPP, three of its leaders had innovated a new approach to capability building by inviting consultants to bring their client executives to workshops to focus on client work already under way. This required consultants to risk a different working relationship with their clients in a performance context that mattered. In the workshops, for example, consultant and client alike were nonexperts, jointly searching for new approaches to the specific challenge at hand. In exchange for exposing themselves to that risk, consultants could introduce themselves and their clients to the power of experience-based, performance-focused learning. Because of its success, OPP's leaders decided to grow the "workshop business."

▶ *The Client Service Center.* The mid-level McKinsey associates who manage day-to-day client work are called engagement managers (EMs). Typically, geographic office managers, in consultation with their office colleagues, deploy EMs. OPP's leaders decided to offer the following exchange. For EMs selected to join the Client Service Center, the OPP leaders promised to deploy and support EMs in change management client work in exchange for office managers transferring their authority to make work assignments for a period of one to two years.

▶ *The Rapid Response Network.* The traditional approach to disseminating information and help among McKinsey practices included training sessions, broadly distributed written documents, and informal word-of-mouth personal networks. None was aimed at delivering the most relevant new approaches and consulting assistance to people spread across dozens of offices on five continents just in time to meet their unique client needs. OPP's leaders asked a team to design and operate the Rapid Response Network to do that. It promised any consultant who called a centralized telephone number prompt access to the most experienced consultants and best current practices in the firm. By monitoring common questions, issues, and approaches around the world, Rapid Response also offered OPP the chance to manage the priority and coherency of the consulting practices it believed most useful to managing behavior-driven change.

In addition to asking specific teams to drive Rapid Response, the workshop business, and the Client Service Center, OPP's leaders also chose to apply the team discipline of mutuality to themselves. They suspected that driving change within McKinsey would demand a non-traditional approach to practice leadership. Most practice leaders, for example, made knowledge building instead of capability building their top priority, which made sense when new concepts and frameworks quickly translated into new consulting skills. But OPP faced a different challenge. To build capabilities, they had to get other consultants to experience change, not just read and think about it.

Their agenda would demand an extraordinary time commitment. Instead of the 10 to 15 percent typical of most practice leaders, the OPP leaders agreed to spend a minimum of 20 percent, and in some cases more than 50 percent, of their efforts on OPP's objectives. Both the capability-building priority and the unusual time commitments bore serious risks to their professional advancement and reward. But as they wrapped up their strategic planning effort in mid-1989, the leaders of OPP agreed they were doing the right thing and looked forward to making a difference.

IMPROVISING THROUGH OBSTACLES, FAILURES, AND SUCCESSES

Sixteen months later, when OPP's leaders gathered at McKinsey's biennial worldwide partners conference, their strategy had begun to pay off. More and more consultants were distinguishing between performance-only versus performance-and-change assignments. An increasing number of mid-level consultants had learned new skills. Most important, more clients were making progress against their behavior-driven performance challenges.

All that was good news. But many difficulties and frustrations also emerged because of flaws within OPP's own efforts and because of still-reluctant colleagues beyond the practice. The Client Service Center, for example, had gained a more enthusiastic reception from the EMs asked to join it than the office managers asked to give over assignment power. People within and beyond OPP pressured the practice to reinstate concept and framework development as the top priority. OPP's positive influence extended more to North America than to Europe or Asia. And the team discipline among OPP's leaders had faltered, threatening not only their team performance but the purpose and direction of OPP itself.

As OPP's leaders reviewed the progress and pitfalls, they observed all the major factors that distinguish change initiatives that are working from those that are not:

▶ *Performance focus and results.* In preparing for the biennial conference, OPP's leaders had carefully assessed the performance focus and outcomes from their various efforts. They were gratified to find specific performance and change impacts in their own client work as well as that of early adopters. They discovered that the Rapid Response Network had contributed to one-fifth of the firm's projects in its first full year of operation. The number of joint client/consultant project teams attending OPP workshops had grown. The Client Service Center, however, had gotten off to a bumpy start. The EMs in it were not getting assigned to change management projects as easily as planned. And OPP was not responding enough to opportunities in Europe and Asia.

▶ *Clarity of purpose and language.* Discussions with internal customers as well as analysis of Rapid Response phone calls indicated that consultants understood OPP's determination to focus on behavior-driven change. A more coherent language about change was developing within McKinsey that included terms like the "Change Board," "skill-based sources of competitive advantage," "major change," and "vision." And OPP had begun influencing the shared values at the heart of McKinsey's big picture—more and more consultants now talked about "managing change" as part of the top management agenda.

The most difficult issue concerned a growing debate over how best to drive change within McKinsey. Some of OPP's leaders, several OPP participants, and many consultants beyond OPP questioned the capability-building priority that had been established. Some, like those in OPP, did this out of a both/and conviction seeking to rebalance knowledge and capability building. Others, particularly among senior consultants who remained reluctant to change, promoted a return to knowledge development out of the traditional, although here misguided, belief equating new concepts with new capability.

▶ *The number of people taking responsibility for change.* By the end of 1990, McKinsey consultants had observed a striking growth in demand from clients needing help with behavior-driven change. The biennial conference, for example, was organized around McKinsey's practices, and significantly more partners had signed up for the OPP sessions than for the strategy and operations alternatives. The results from the client work of OPP leaders and early adopters, Rapid Response, the workshops, and even the Client Service Center indicated a steady increase in the number of people taking responsibility for change, especially at the mid-tenure levels. However, OPP had not gotten close to moving up the steep part of the trial and repurchase curve reviewed in Chapter Six. And reluctance among the most senior consultants remained a difficult challenge for all the same reasons OPP had identified sixteen months earlier.

▶ *Resource capacity and just-in-time deployment.* Rapid Response had established a clear "best practice" in how to galvanize and deploy resources in a just-in-time fashion. Although off to a slow start, the Client Service Center still promised to build deep capabilities in a growing number of EMs over time, thereby expanding McKinsey's capacity to do change management work. However, OPP's leaders recognized the need to respond to the growing demand for new concepts and frameworks without jeopardizing resources needed to build capabilities.

▶ *Leaders who are living the change.* Individually, OPP's leaders were living the change. They practiced the new behaviors and skills in their own client work. They volunteered to help early adopters and other consultants as often as possible. They each had delivered on the specific time and performance commitments made sixteen months earlier. In terms of team performance, however, their discipline had broken down. Unlike the teams driving Rapid Response, workshops, and the Client Service Center, the leadership group lacked a common purpose, common set of goals, and commonly agreed upon working approach to which they would hold themselves mutually accountable. The debate over the role and priority of knowledge building contributed to that. So did the tensions caused when extraordinary time commitments conflicted with individual client work and career expectations.

The reality of improvising your way through change demands revising specific strategies *over time*. OPP's leaders, for example, "made stuff up" in response to successes and frustrations before, during and after the biennial conference. By mid-1991, however, their improvisations had framed a variety of modified and new strategies for moving forward, including:

▶ *Sponsoring a knowledge integration project.* OPP leaders put knowledge building back on their agenda by sponsoring three teams of predominantly non-OPP consultants—one each in Asia, Europe, and North America—to investigate and report on the best current thinking and practice regarding change management. In addition to answering the call for concept development, this project offered the chance to grow the "we" behind OPP's initiative as well as to continue eliminating confusion among the concepts and approaches used to help clients. A handful of non-OPP senior partners agreed to lead the work of those teams.

▶ *Repackaging the workshops.* The original design of the workshops dated back to the mid-1980s. Given their effectiveness, OPP decided to incorporate a variety of new approaches and lessons learned that included refocusing the workshops from pure skill building to "making change happen."

▶ *Expanding Rapid Response.* OPP's leaders challenged the Rapid Response team to dramatically grow their "business." And the team itself decided to take advantage of unexpected interest from other McKinsey practice groups as well as the firm's central office of information and technology management.

▶ *Getting tougher in the Client Service Center.* The team running the Client Service Center resolved to communicate more clearly and creatively about the importance of gaining assignment authority for the EMs admitted to the program.

▶ *Joint venturing with other practices.* Unsurprisingly, a number of practices beyond OPP found their own new and exciting concepts increasingly subject to the ability of client management to drive behavior-driven change. The information technology practice, for example, was discovering that dealing with change was, as Michael Hammer, James Champy, and others would later comment, the single major obstacle to reengineering. OPP decided to use mutuality in reaching out to other practices, hoping that joint practice teams could find additional opportunities to integrate new consulting skills in client work.

▶ *Collaborating with non-McKinsey consultants.* A few successful experiments at client collaboration between OPP partners and non-McKinsey consultants encouraged OPP's leaders to try to promote that idea more widely. The key challenge, they believed, would be to persuade McKinsey and non-McKinsey professionals alike that a consultant did not have to be part of the firm to practice McKinsey values.

▶ *Adopting a guerrilla strategy for senior consultants.* As in most organizations facing change, the senior ranks at McKinsey are limited in size and each individual is a target market segment of one. Accordingly, OPP's leaders planned to look for chances to influence senior McKinsey consultants on a one-by-one ("guerrilla") basis.

▶ *Taking advantage of champions beyond North America.* A few dozen mid-tenure associates and partners had emerged in Australia, Japan, England, and Germany as real champions of major change. All had their own ideas and enthusiasms for moving OPP's agenda forward. OPP's leaders recognized that no control-oriented requirements prevented them from embracing those champions in the big tent OPP hoped to build.

▶ *Building external, client pull on consultant behavior.* Among
other things, in deciding to write *The Wisdom of Teams*, Jon
Katzenbach and I (who were both members of OPP at the time)
hoped to create specific demand from clients for new consulting
approaches, including paying attention to all of the people at a client
organization whose performance and change mattered to the challenge at hand.

▶ *Abandoning the team approach to leadership.* OPP's leaders
spent months trying to reinvigorate the team discipline among
themselves in a variety of ways, including inviting two additional
partners to join the team. Nothing worked. They failed to find
specific purposes, goals, and working approaches to which they would
hold themselves mutually accountable. Instead, by mid-1991, they
admitted to themselves that to act as a traditional working group
of individuals would make more sense than to fall into the trap of
becoming a pseudoteam.

IMPROVISING, AGAIN

Some modifications worked, others failed, and still others generated
unexpected surprises. Throughout it all, an expanding group of change
leaders at McKinsey continued to improvise. The Knowledge
Integration Project, for example, successfully increased the understanding, desire, and experiences of change management consulting
among people previously unassociated with OPP. It did not produce
new concepts or frameworks, although it did prevent unneeded competition among essentially identical approaches bearing different names.

Unexpectedly, the joint venture with the information technology
practice triggered the chance to develop a new concept called the
"horizontal organization," a pragmatic series of steps for reconnecting
organization design to real work (see Chapter Ten). Work on *The
Wisdom of Teams* led to important distinctions between the concepts
of "real teams" versus "working groups" that, as mentioned, OPP's
leaders were able to apply to themselves. Meanwhile, Robert

Schaffer's breakthrough strategy—not a new concept but one new to McKinsey—made tremendous performance and change impacts after a series of McKinsey partners collaborated with an outside consultant in a handful of client assignments.

In another surprise, the assignment dilemma troubling the Client Service Center largely disappeared. So many clients were confronting behavior-driven change that it became easy to coordinate assignments with office managers to ensure that EMs were working on relevant projects. With this aspect behind it, applications shot up, nearly doubling the number of EMs in the program. This effort too produced a critical new framework that promoted harmonization of top-down, bottom-up, and cross-functional change initiatives as more important than worrying over the alignment of organization design elements. Finally, growing client demand combined with the Rapid Response team's extraordinary service standards to double their business over the next two years. When phone calls continued to come disproportionately from North America, the Rapid Response team improvised by setting up a European desk that could provide better service to consultants living in the relevant time zones.

Several of OPP's new creations, of course, crumbled. Apart from the example of the breakthrough strategy mentioned above, the attempt to syndicate collaboration with non-McKinsey consultants was victimized by the closed aspect of McKinsey's strong culture. Not every attempt at collaborating with other practices produced results. An opportunistic OPP offer to help managing director Fred Gluck integrate a major McKinsey acquisition was rejected. And the guerrilla strategy for influencing senior partners never got off the ground. Because of the time commitments and career risks involved, it could not be accomplished without a team discipline among OPP's leaders.

By 1993, a new set of leaders took over OPP and the practice once again balkanized. Unlike the Center-based period before 1989, however, the separate OPP leadership groups in Europe, Asia, Australia, and North America formed around geographic convenience instead of widely varying sets of purposes and issues. Managing behavior–driven change was central to the agendas of all of them. And the skill and behavior changes wrought by OPP's continuing stream of improvisations over the previous five years provided major momentum on which all could continue to build.

Conclusion: Prepare to Improvise Often

No single change initiative transforms an entire organization. The Minnesota state government, for example, was not entirely reinvented because of the successful initiative within its Department of Administration. Nor did all of Kodak change as a result of the new skills, behaviors, and performance in the Black & White film flow. Terry Murphy's contributions did not transform Tandem. And five years of OPP efforts did not dislodge strategy as the primary competency in McKinsey.

Still, by 1993, fewer "bad things" were happening to McKinsey's recommendations. Most consultants could distinguish performance-only from performance-and-change client challenges. Few continued to believe naively in the power of decisions and descriptions to drive change. Hundreds had taken responsibility for learning the skills, behaviors, and working relationships needed to put experience-based methodologies to work. None of that would have happened without a strategy for leading change and a continuing commitment to improvisation.

Armed with the ten new management principles, you, too, must craft the most pragmatic blend of hierarchy, exchange, mutuality, and coordination to make your initiative a success. Change, however, is a dynamic phenomenon. From the moment you begin, therefore, prepare yourself to improvise:

▶ *Build on successes.* In taking advantage of successes in the workshops, Rapid Response, and their own client work, OPP's leaders consistently asked, "How can we expand from here? How can we syndicate this to a larger audience who must change?" Their approach resembled that of Mike Berkin, who grew his DBIS Quality Shop by building on successes instead of despairing over frustrations. Parts of DBIS, for example, remained reluctant well into the period of change. Instead of forcing high-noon showdowns, however, Mike and his colleagues celebrated and expanded on the positive contributions of people who were joining in institutionalizing total quality. Ultimately, most of those who were reluctant joined the party.

▶ *Take advantage of the unexpected, whether positive or negative.* Steve Frangos and his gang used the Kodak worldwide manufacturing proposal to gut the Black & White film flow as a platform for building understanding, desire, plans of action, and reinforcement. Indeed, that event more than any other produced a powerful vision for Black & White. Similarly, Rapid Response expanded both its presence and its impact by embracing unexpected interest from McKinsey's central information and technology office. And the principles for designing a horizontal organization emerged from an unexpected effort within the firm's information technology practice.

▶ *Continue to seize readiness wherever you find it.* When John Champagne reached out to Bob Guadiana after eighteen months of frustrating dialogue at Magma Metals, he found a partner where few executives would have even looked—namely, a high-ranking union official. By persistently asking others "What can you do to make a difference?" the team of John Champagne and Bob Guadiana empowered a steady stream of people who were ready to reinvent Magma. In asking interested non-OPP senior partners to take the lead in the Knowledge Integration Project, OPP went with the positive flow where it existed. As a result, they gained leadership from consultants not previously thought to be "organization types."

▶ *Never give up on those who remain reluctant.* Contests, focus groups, surveys, newsletters, teams, and new language were only some of the continuing stream of inventions employed by the Minnesota state government's change leaders to induce reluctant state employees to embrace a different paradigm and level of performance in that state's Department of Administration. Similarly, OPP remained in a selling mode throughout the five-year period of change. Of course, people who "got in the way" were frustrating. But no one in OPP doubted for a moment that their McKinsey colleagues believed strongly in client service. The challenge, therefore, was not to quit on people, but to keep searching for a way to help them experience the advantages of different approaches to consulting.

‣ *Look to performance and the art of the possible to inspire your inventiveness.* In using the Client Service Center, Rapid Response, workshops, and other means to shift OPP's resources as much as possible toward doing specific client work, its leaders seized the high ground of performance—the surest context in any organization for staying focused on *what is possible*. Similarly, for example, Terry Murphy's efforts faced severe budget pressures because of Tandem's financial difficulties. A few executives always actively hoped to eliminate Terry's solution sales division entirely. Terry and his colleagues couldn't do much about that. By staying focused on *what they could do* to drive new skills, behaviors, and performance, they gave themselves the best chance for survival.

‣ *Constantly revisit the disciplines and impact of your specific strategies.* Black & White's leaders at Kodak grew continually better at hierarchy and mutuality. Mike Berkin added hierarchy and mutuality to exchange once he found the opportunity to do so. Terry Murphy and his colleagues continued to work hard at getting each of the key elements in their exchange strategy right. And John Champagne and Bob Guadiana used the elements of team performance as a discipline for continuing to improve their performance. Likewise, OPP's leaders never stopped assessing themselves and others against the underlying principles and disciplines of their strategies.

Behavior-driven change within organizations is a human movement. As a leader, your job is to expand that movement, to build the "we" who will make performance and change happen. If you will make the effort, you *can* understand who is ready and who remains reluctant. And regardless of who you are or what position you hold, you *can* improvise ways to influence the performance agendas of the people you hope to enlist. Can you be assured of total success? Of transforming your organization entirely and forever? No. But if you seize the opportunity to lead a single change initiative, you *can* make a lasting difference to yourself and to everyone who joins you.

PART 3

VISIONS

THE MANAGEMENT PRINCIPLES

1. *Keep performance results the primary objective of behavior and skill change.*

2. *Continually increase the number of individuals taking responsibility for their own change.*

3. *Ensure each person always knows why his or her performance and change matters to the purpose and results of the whole organization.*

4. *Put people in a position to learn by doing and provide them the information and support needed just in time to perform.*

5. *Embrace improvisation as the best path to both performance and change.*

6. *Use team performance to drive change whenever demanded.*

7. *Concentrate organization designs on the work people do, not the decision-making authority they have.*

8. *Create and focus energy and meaningful language because they are the scarcest resources during periods of change.*

9. *Stimulate and sustain behavior-driven change by harmonizing initiatives throughout the organization.*

10. *Practice leadership based on the courage to live the change you wish to bring about.*

*Y*ou cannot rely on any single initiative to transform your entire enterprise. Nor can you personally lead every initiative needed. Instead, you must use vision to orchestrate change. More than a decade of experience with change has schooled you in the importance of articulating a vision of what you want your organization to become and why. But visions of what and why are not enough. You must also shape a vision of how the organization will get through the period of change itself.

Words, pictures, initiatives, and personal actions provide the buildings blocks for vision. When combined, they generate the energy and meaningful language that are the scarcest resources of change. For people to master behavior change takes a lot of hard work. Without creating and focusing such energy and effort, no organization can succeed. The meaningful aspirations and insights so often embodied within special words and phrases help people make and focus their efforts. Language—for example, "Six Sigma" at Motorola, "quality" at Ford, "innovation" at 3M, "boundarylessness" at General Electric—can become an immensely valuable asset to those of you who pay attention to the link among meaning, performance, and effort.

Organizations have only so much capacity for change at any given time. You can shape effective visions of how by choosing a set of specific initiatives—some behavior driven, some not—that emotionally and rationally inspire confidence in the people who must take responsibility for change. Often, those initiatives must include new organization designs. Unlike performance-only challenges that benefit from already capable people, however, performance-and-change challenges do not yield automatically to new organization designs. You should not rely on the illusion of alignment among strategy, structure, and compensation and information systems as sufficient to make change happen. Indeed, the most powerful new organization designs—team- and process-based approaches—demand behavior changes to succeed. So, although new designs and reorganizations play a role, they are never enough to shape a complete vision of how.

Nothing is more powerful than your personal vision of how. In asking people to take charge of change, you must practice the golden rule of managing change: Do unto yourself what you would have others do unto themselves. *Only leaders who demonstrate the courage to live the change they wish to bring about inspire confidence among people who choose to follow. Tapping into that courage demands more than intellectual commitment and tough decision making. Leaders must themselves seek out the specific performance opportunities and personal experiences needed to learn the new disciplines and behaviors demanded by change. Only then can you—like all other people—truly join the "we" who will make performance and change happen.*

Chapter Nine

Energy and Meaningful Language: The *How* Part of Vision

"The last thing IBM needs right now is a vision," announced Lou Gerstner four months into one of the most complex change challenges in history. His words join President George Bush's famous gaffe about the "vision thing" as among the strangest remarks ever uttered by otherwise talented leaders. In each case, thousands of affected people instantly winced. They sensed something profoundly wrong, and they were right. In badmouthing vision, Gerstner unintentionally *depersonalized* a thoroughly human challenge—guiding people to create and focus the energy and meaningful language necessary to transform themselves.

People must take responsibility for their own behavior change. Not even chief executives—however brilliant, incisive and tough-minded—can do it for them. CEOs *can* take responsibility for making strategic, organizational, or operational decisions. Recognizing, for example, that IBM's cost structure was bloated, Gerstner could and did eliminate several billion dollars of expenses and tens of thousands of jobs. But when the dust settled from the downsizing, the reality of behavior-driven change remained—the only behavior and skill change Lou Gerstner could take responsibility for at IBM was his own.

Leading an entire organization of people to embrace behavior change requires more than making decisions. It also stands apart from leading a single initiative. As an initiative leader, you can use the principles and strategies to engage people directly in making the personal performance commitments that trigger change. You can live the change together with the specific people you hope to enlist. Of course, any CEO might choose to lead a single behavior-driven initiative. But that will not suffice. No single initiative has enough scope to encompass all the people who matter to an entire organization's transformation. And chief executives rarely have the time to lead more than a single initiative, if that.

Transformational leadership at the whole-organization level, then, involves more than engaging in the daily fray. It requires you to orchestrate change from a distance. Only you can define and manage the entire performance and change agenda. Only you can provide the possibility of purpose to the whole organization. Only you can give all the people the opportunity to follow your lead. At your remove, your challenge is to convert distance into perspective and perspective into *vision.*

"Without a vision," goes the biblical adage, "the people shall perish." Perish or not, visionless people do not change. Who among you will overcome economic and emotional reluctance to embrace behavior change without some notion of *why* you should, *what* results your efforts will produce, and *how* you can succeed? Without a vision of why, what, and how, you would have no part of behavior change in your personal life. You would not create and focus the energy to quit smoking, diet successfully, learn the piano, or revitalize a relationship. Why should it be any different inside an organization where you and others face so many economic and social complexities? It isn't.

But what makes a good vision? More than a decade of visioning experience has taught leaders much about the purpose and performance part of visionary aspirations. Effective visions of what and why are as follows:

▶ *Simple.* They contain a small number of clear, easily remembered aspirations. Visions with too many thoughts, sentences, and paragraphs never survive long in people's minds. The completeness in such lengthy expositions might provide useful checklists for managerial reviews. But when leaders shape visions that are too wordy, people edit out all but the most meaningful aspirations. Those few thoughts and expressions become the real vision. Why not, as leaders, make the editing choices yourselves?

▶ *Sound.* Visions must be grounded in strategy. People need tremendous energy to get through periods of change; they need inspiration. But no one adheres long to lofty visions that are not credible. Instead, visions must include strategies that make sense in light of customers, competition, suppliers, governments and other third parties, and how you can best deploy your organization's unique combination of competencies, advantages, and disadvantages.

▶ *Purposeful.* In using vision to articulate the what and why of performance and change, remember you must speak to people's hearts as well as their minds. You must address desire, emotion, experience, and risk. Vision must have a higher, nobler, even irrational purpose that will inspire people to make it happen. Superlatives such as "first," "best," "world class"—so long as they too are credible—can help you name and capture the possibilities within the human spirit.

▶ *Performance driven.* Nothing answers the question "Why are we doing this?" more concretely than a clear, measurable performance aspiration. Strategic intent, a popular notion a few years back, captured this well. When Pepsi declares a vision to "Beat Coke" (or vice versa), any number of specific performance objectives jump out to be set, calibrated, and achieved.

▶ *Meaningful.* Powerful visions include words or concepts that have the potential to generate meaningful interpretations that can guide the choice of what to do—and what not to do—in the thousands of different performance contexts that make up organizations. As such meanings take hold, a consistent language emerges that helps people trust each other and their leaders throughout the period of change.

▶ *Inclusive.* Everyone you hope will contribute to and benefit from the organization's vision must find themselves within it. This

certainly includes the people who work for the organization. But as
events, technology, and economics continue to force the rights and
responsibilities of *community* on organizations, visions must also
encompass customers, suppliers, strategic partners, shareholders,
and other people who matter to an organization's future.

Most leaders are not as familiar with constructing the *how* part of
vision. As you tackle that challenge, remember a key lesson you have
learned from visions of what and why—aspirations must be more
than platitudes. In that sense, Lou Gerstner was right. The last thing
IBM needed was a new set of wall plaques. Leaders who confuse
vision with cliché, however, betray their own ignorance of the human
part of performance and change challenges. Vision is not about slo-
ganeering. It is about stimulating and managing the dynamic flow of
energy and meaning that people use to take charge of change.

Visions must be alive. Using an analogy from finance, visions are
more like cash-flow statements than balance sheets. Balance sheets
depict the financial strength of an enterprise at any single point in time.
They show an X-ray of the skeleton. Cash flow, by contrast, goes
beyond a single snapshot to portray how cash, the financial lifeblood of
organizations, courses through the enterprise. How much and from
what sources does the enterprise generate cash, and to what uses
must that cash be put to keep the body healthy? Do cash-flow statements have a bottom line? Yes. But making any difference to it requires
managers to understand and continuously improve the flows. When
leaders manage cash flow, they manage organizational vitality.

Similarly, when leaders use a vision of *how* to manage through a
period of change, they attend to the energy and meaningful language
that are the lifeblood of behavior-driven transformation. The sources
of vision are words, pictures, initiatives, and personal actions. The uses
are energy, meaning, change, and performance. Like cash-flow statements, visions have a bottom line. General Electric, for example,
"seeks to be number 1 or 2 in its chosen industries through speed, simplicity, and boundarylessness." That vision of what and why meets all
the above criteria. But making those words come alive with energy
and meaning is the *how* part of vision.

This chapter explores the connection among vision, energy, and meaning. As the story of Educational Alternatives' first three years of running nine Baltimore public schools illustrates, leaders who ignore the *how* part of vision fall short of translating compelling ideas into the energy and language that people need to get through a period of behavior-driven change.

EDUCATIONAL ALTERNATIVES IN BALTIMORE

In June 1992, the *Baltimore Sun* enthusiastically reported its city's decision to hire Educational Alternatives, Inc. (EAI), to run nine schools for five years. The paper applauded the superintendent, mayor, school board, and union for boldly choosing to put private/public education partnerships to a real test. And it noted that everyone—city and union officials, school board members, principals, teachers, reporters—who had visited EAI's model elementary school in South Pointe, Florida, had come away impressed with the company's vision, philosophy, and practice.

At South Pointe, EAI demonstrated that it could combine best practices from education and business to fulfill its vision of "finding and nurturing the gifts and talents of each child." Four major themes characterized its approach:

1. *Maintain a clean and safe environment for learning.* Through its alliance with Johnson Controls, EAI provides attractive, clean, safe, and well-managed school facilities. This promised major benefits to the nine Baltimore schools, some of which suffered from inner-city blight. It is hard for principals, teachers, parents, and students to focus on learning when distracted by poor heating and lighting, crumbling walls, leaky faucets, wet and soiled washrooms, broken glass, cockroaches, and crime.

2. *Engage each child's own gifts and talents.* No two children are alike; each has a best way to learn. EAI's teaching method, which it has dubbed "Tesseract," finds that best way by working from the child out instead of from the teacher or system in. Guided by Tesseract, teachers discover and adjust their teaching styles to

respond to each child's learning style. EAI's confidence in Tesseract extends to children with special needs. It promotes mainstreaming special education children faced with handicaps, learning disabilities, or other challenges into regular classrooms instead of keeping them separate.

EAI emphasizes an integrated curriculum to nurture the whole person. Art, music, and physical education are blended with what EAI describes as "whole math" and "whole language." The company floods teachers with the new ideas, approaches, materials, supplies, and books needed to customize a rich, challenging education that inspires children. Finally, through its alliance with Computer Curriculum Corporation, EAI puts computers and software in classrooms to support an individualized development and monitoring program for every child.

3. *Build child-focused partnerships.* EAI asks parents and teachers to collaborate on "personal education plans" for children. In addition, EAI asks two adults—teacher plus instructional intern—to team up in each classroom. And, as mentioned, it forms partnerships with companies such as Johnson Controls and Computer Curriculum Corporation to deliver essential services.

4. *Manage for results.* Through combining best business and education practices, EAI seeks to spend a higher percentage of budget directly on education while simultaneously earning a profit for itself. Most important, it promises both qualitative (safety, trust, fulfillment, preparedness) and quantitative (attendance, test scores) results from a superior education.

The rationale and innovation of EAI's program generated much of the excitement that Baltimore visitors observed at South Pointe elementary school. But a good deal of enthusiasm also arose because the teachers, principal, and parents at South Pointe were all there voluntarily. Backed by the Dade County School Board and Teachers Union, EAI had built a brand new school, provided a full year of background and training to the handpicked principal, selected teachers who applied from around the nation, and accepted—"magnet" style—

children from across Dade County to attend. Everyone at South Pointe wanted to be at South Pointe.

The voluntary aspect of the South Pointe story triggered the lone cautionary remark in the *Baltimore Sun*'s celebratory story about the nine-school program. "EAI will not have the luxury of hiring only teachers who are enthusiastic about teaching the Tesseract way," the *Sun* commented toward the end of the article. "They will have to give them training and handholding as the school year unfolds." The *Sun* might also have mentioned other adults who had not volunteered to be part of Baltimore's nine-school experiment: principals, paraprofessionals (teacher's aides), and parents.

Three years later, the *Sun*'s minor concern—and EAI's inadequate response to its implications—marked the difference between an extraordinary success that might have been versus an educational improvement beset by controversy. The description of the company's basic program was as convincing as ever. Where behavior-change mattered little, its initiatives excelled. Schools were clean, attractive, safe, and well run. Hundreds of computers were in place. Teachers enjoyed hassle-free access to materials, supplies, and books. Some parents took the chance to become more involved in their children's education. The children undoubtedly were better off than they had been before 1992.

Yet, although attendance and some students' test scores rose, the promise of EAI's mission had not materialized three years into the five-year contract. Most parents showed up for the initial "personal education plan" sessions each school year, but few stuck with the effort needed to collaborate with teachers. Teachers were inundated with ideas, training, materials, supplies, and books. But just how many translated EAI's wonderful programs into classroom practice remained unclear. The principals believed in Tesseract; they applauded EAI's financial and business services. But several despaired over the inadequate time and reinforcement EAI provided to themselves and their professional staffs.

Meanwhile, the teachers' union had gone from supportive to resistant. Communities surrounding the nine schools remained confused, especially over the "profit motive" that EAI's detractors criticized. And some among the press and the politicians did what any shark does when it smells blood: attack, attack, attack. As one Baltimore citizen commented, "There is a growing sense that EAI has had an extraordinary opportunity that, for any number of reasons, may have been squandered." Three years after celebrating EAI's arrival, the *Baltimore Sun* now reported, "The project is in peril."

ENERGY AND MEANINGFUL LANGUAGE: THE SCARCE RESOURCES OF CHANGE

Unlike at South Pointe, EAI confronted broad-based behavior-driven change in the nine Baltimore schools. Performance results depended on hundreds of existing employees and thousands of existing parents learning new skills, behaviors, and working relationships. At an abstract level, none of the affected adults disagreed with EAI's vision of "finding and nurturing the gifts and talents of each child." Who could? But the toughest issue was not the what or the why part of EAI's vision. It was *how.* To prevent its vision from becoming a mere slogan, EAI had to show the adults how they could translate abstraction into the specific energy and meaningful language they needed to get through the period of change ahead.

Energy and meaningful language, not money or ideas, are the scarce resources of behavior-driven change. Consider energy (or, if you prefer, effort). It takes extra energy for an individual to work through the sources of reluctance we reviewed in Chapter Two. Neither understanding nor desire nor planning nor action come without effort. And people rarely progress without setbacks. Instead, they must work hard throughout the period of change until they have integrated new behaviors into daily routines.

In a real sense, people confronting behavior and skill change at work have two jobs—a "from" job and a "to" job. People know the "from" job well—completing the variety of tasks and goals assigned to them. The second job is learning how to work differently. Ultimately, the individuals must integrate new behaviors and skills into daily routines so that only one job remains. But until then, that second job weighs on their mind and their time every day when they arrive at work.

In addition to the job they knew, for example, each Baltimore teacher faced the challenge of learning Tesseract. EAI wanted them to move from being "a sage on stage" (teacher-centered) to being "a guide on the side" (student-centered), which required them to

▶ handle a class that jumped in size from twenty-five to thirty-five

▶ integrate art, music, and physical education previously taught by other teachers

▶ apply curricular concepts such as whole math and whole language

▶ respond to the needs of special education children, including how to maintain discipline among some of those children and their new classmates

▶ spend time collaborating with parents on personal education plans

▶ team up with the new instructional intern in their classroom

None of that was impossible; Baltimore's teachers had the minimum capabilities required. But no one should underestimate the amount of hard work it would take. EAI's leadership task was to create, focus, and harmonize the energy and effort that people needed to get through the period of change.

Furthermore, nobody changes in a vacuum; behavior struggles happen in the presence of other people. In addition to two jobs, then, existing employees belong to two organizations—a "from" organization and a "to" organization. Each has a formal and informal aspect. Often, the formal arrangements in the "from" organization do not change dramatically until well into the period of change. Reporting structures and planning, budgeting, and compensation systems, for example, remain wholly or significantly the same. Meanwhile, the informal attributes of the "from" organization—the shared habits and beliefs of "how we do things around here"—pervade much of the period of change.

The formal part of the "to" organization includes the full array of initiatives under way. In Baltimore, the new Tesseract organization encompassed

- morning meetings where kids of all ages discussed the day and their lives together
- Wednesday afternoon staff development sessions
- personal education plans
- instructional interns
- new computers
- lead teachers who acted as liaisons between EAI and the schools
- the professional staff of EAI and its business partners, such as Johnson Controls

People faced with change must take responsibility for living the informal aspects of the "to" organization. At any given moment, some people do, some don't. Depending on the situation, the same individual might sometimes continue the old habits of the "from" organization and at other times try to live the change of the "to" organization. The quality of personal reinforcement anyone receives depends on which organization—which group of people—surrounds him or her. The teachers at one school, for example, leaped ahead of their colleagues in using Tesseract. Sometimes teachers from the other eight schools viewed that group with admiration, at other times they referred to them as "suckers." It all depended on the organizational context.

Throughout the period of change, the "to" organization contends with the "from" organization for the allegiance and energy of people. Like it or not, transformational leaders must manage through such complexities. Change does not proceed by description alone, even when a description is as powerful as EAI's Tesseract program. Instead, change requires risking experience, and experience is messy. At any moment following the opening of school in 1992, for example, the description of EAI's four-part program mattered far less than how much energy and effort thousands of existing professionals and parents were investing in making performance and change happen.

Getting beyond descriptions also pertains to the second scarce resource of change: meaningful language. The description of EAI's program made sense on paper. Like other contemporary behavior and skill challenges, however, the performance of the Tesseract model depended on making sense—creating enduring intellectual, emotional, and experiential *meaning*—to people. "Child-centered education" brings to mind a variety of possibilities. So do the terms "customer driven," "total quality," "reengineering," "core competency," "time-based competition," "reinventing government," "teams," "empowerment," "continuous improvement," and "learning organization." But what do they mean for how specific people in real organizations do work?

Think for a moment about the rich and practical variety of meanings that "innovation" has at 3M or "boundarylessness" at General Electric or "performance quality" at Dun & Bradstreet. In each case, what were mere words at the beginning of a period of change became, by the end, assets. Once armed with intellectual, emotional, and experiential meaning, people in those organizations could respond to scores of different situations with an economy of effort and energy. Indeed, once meanings become assets, the period of change—and the need for extra energy to get through it—is drawing to a close. Two jobs are becoming one; the "from" organization fades away.

Managers of performance-only challenges are masters at attending to the value of assets. Having invested millions of dollars in new plant and equipment, for example, no responsible manager abandons the asset after the party celebrating its opening. To make assets of meaning, managers of performance-and-change challenges must be equally attentive. They cannot succeed by simplistically equating the introduction of new words with the assets they hope to develop and exploit. If they do, as you know from experience, the intended, useful meaning of new language (e.g., "total quality" or "reengineering") will easily evaporate. Instead, managers must work hard to instill and preserve new language throughout the organization. They must manage language to create meaning. At Dun & Bradstreet, for example, Mike Berkin paid a lot of attention to the difference between the performance quality breakthroughs he desired and the "bastard breakthroughs" to be avoided. EAI's leaders faced the same challenge in converting "Tesseract" into a language of change filled with meaning.

In contrast to energy and meaning, money is less scarce during periods of change. More than a decade of performance and change has demonstrated a remarkably consistent, if counterintuitive, phenomenon. Because so many of today's challenges seek improvement in both value and cost, enough savings are available to invest in change. Nearly always, the "way we do things around here" is unnecessarily expensive; the cost of quality, we have learned, is free. That applied to EAI. Even though Baltimore would pay EAI the citywide average cost per pupil, the company knew it could find the savings required to fund both greater educational expenditure and profit.

Money is also less critical for a second reason—its relationship to behavior change. Throwing money at behavior issues has modest impacts, at best. Sure, more money is better than less if properly employed to facilitate change. But think back to the stories in this book as well as your experience. Whether people embrace the experience of change rarely turns on money. Neither the presence nor absence of money prevented Joan Yancey of Tandem from making a solution sales call on an existing client. Nor did it determine whether people at Kodak's Black & White, the Minnesota Department of Administration, Magma Metals, Dun & Bradstreet, Wireboard, Iberian Motors, Clean Keepers, or Baltimore's nine schools would take responsibility for change. The decision to take charge of change is far more personal than monetary.

THE VISION OF *HOW:* ASSEMBLING INITIATIVES THAT CREATE, FOCUS, AND HARMONIZE ENERGY

In addition to why and what, transformational leaders must have a vision of *how* their organization will proceed through the period of

change. If you are at the top, you must help people see the combination of initiatives that can create, focus, and harmonize the energy
they collectively need to take charge of change. Creating energy is
straightforward; anything that unfreezes people creates energy. The
decision by Baltimore officials to sign the EAI contract, for example,
certainly stirred up teachers, principals, parents, and others.

But stirring up people leads as easily to anxiety as to enthusiasm.
Once created, energy must be focused. Initiatives that marry purpose
and change to performance outcomes focus people on what matters
most. Had EAI, for example, used the ten new management principles
to manage personal education plans as a behavior-driven change initiative, they would have done a better of job of continually increasing
the number of teachers and parents taking responsibility for collaborating on each child's education.

Finally, initiatives must harmonize with one another to help people
see how change can happen across an entire organization. Visions of
how always include both behavior-driven and nonbehavior-driven
initiatives. Outsourcing the management of facilities to Johnson
Controls, for example, did not depend on many existing school employees learning new behaviors. But in liberating principals and teachers
to concentrate on education instead of heating, lighting, plumbing, and
security, it reinforced other initiatives, such as personal education
plans and mainstreaming special education kids, that did require
existing employees to change behaviors.

Over the past decade, a debate has emerged over the sequencing
of change initiatives. Some argue change must proceed top-down
from a detailed, confident view among executives about the complete
strategy, operations, and organization desired. Others contend change
must proceed from the bottom of the organization up. And still
others suggest enterprises should start with initiatives that cut across
existing organizational boundaries.

Experience shows, however, that sequence matters far less than
reinforcement. Any initiative—top-down, bottom-up, or cross-boundary—can create and focus the energy needed to begin a period of
behavior-driven change. But the period of change draws to a close only

when enough existing people have incorporated into their daily routines the new skills, behaviors, and working relationships needed to sustain organization performance. No organization has ever gained traction against that outcome until a combination of top-down, bottom-up, and cross-boundary initiatives that reinforced one another was in place. Thus, you should worry more about harmonizing initiatives to reinforce each other than their sequence of appearance.

Mike Berkin's Quality Shop, for example, was only one of several initiatives that Ron Glover and his senior colleagues set in motion at Dun & Bradstreet's Information Services division. Their vision of what and why was to transform DBIS into "a trusted business partner that earned the right to be our customers' preferred provider of information solutions." To achieve it, DBIS's leaders also put together a vision of *how* (illustrated in the diagram on page 243) that included the following behavior-driven and non-behavior-driven initiatives:

1. Top-down

   ‣ Building and communicating a cohesive leadership vision of *what* and *how* (behavior driven)

   ‣ Defining the best pricing strategy (not behavior driven)

   ‣ Investing in advertising and promotion (not behavior driven)

2. Bottom-up

   ‣ Total quality and continuous improvement through "performance quality" (behavior driven)

3. Cross-boundary

   ‣ Reengineering the new product development process (behavior driven)
   ‣ Reengineering the sales and service process (behavior driven)

Not all the initiatives worked. Unlike performance quality, for example, the leaders of the sales and service initiative failed to use the management principles and strategies required for behavior-driven change. Furthermore, with events and progress, Ron Glover's leadership group improvised and added initiatives to their vision of *how*. But at all times, Ron recognized the responsibility of a transformational leader to communicate to everyone in DBIS *how* they could get through the period of change.

Had they understood their challenge better, EAI's leaders might have created a vision of *how* to achieve greater performance and

A "Vision of How"

(from Dun & Bradstreet Information Services)

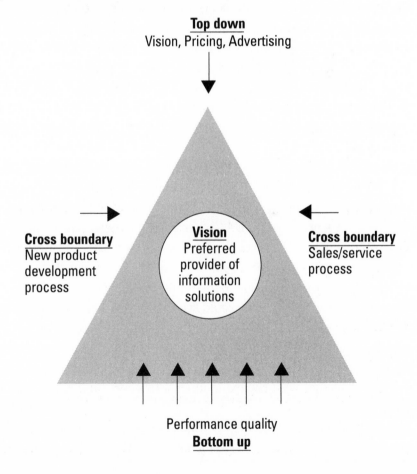

behavior change over the first three years they managed the nine Baltimore schools. Instead, EAI faltered in creating, focusing, and harmonizing energy. To avoid their mistakes, you must respect the following challenges:

▶ *Establish and sustain a tight link between vision and performance.* As the diagram on the opposite page illustrates, visions must link purpose to performance so that all key constituencies see how they can contribute to as well as benefit from the enterprise. In theory, satisfying any single constituency satisfies all. Throughout much of the 1970s and 1980s, for example, executives worshiped shareholder value in the misguided belief that everyone else would understand the benefit of keeping the owners happy. The theory, however, broke down; both customers and employees got lost in the shuffle. Today's new altar suggests that the customer is king. But it too will fail if employees and shareholders do not explicitly see how they benefit from organization performance. Leaders must ensure a *balanced* focus on all the constituencies who matter to the health of the enterprise.

People who participate only in theory lose heart. Many constituencies, for example, needed to participate in making Baltimore's nine schools better: students, parents, school professionals, unions, taxpayers, EAI's employees, EAI's business partners (e.g., Johnson Controls), and EAI's shareholders. But EAI's vision and program were exclusively child centered. None of the other constituencies would question the aspiration to give children the best education possible. And, theoretically, they could see their role and benefit in making that happen. But in shifting from its vision of *what* to a vision of *how,* EAI needed to demonstrate how performance explicitly benefited *everyone* involved, not just the children. The company particularly failed at that with regard to unions, teachers, and other school professionals.

Once established, initiatives in the vision of *how* must sustain a clear and compelling link to performance. EAI had little difficulty connecting performance to its most successful initiative—outsourcing facilities management to Johnson Controls. Teachers and principals, for example, immediately grasped the benefit of freedom from depressing working conditions and bureaucratic processes for ordering materials and supplies. By contrast, EAI only fuzzily linked its many curricular changes to performance goals and results. There were broad goals (e.g., improved test scores) and conceptual curricular changes (e.g., whole language). But there was no *managed connection* ensuring that specific people took responsibility for monitoring what changes were being put to use in the classroom and with what effect on both student progress and teachers' skills. As one assistant superintendent put it, "There's no monitoring, there's no attempt to try an idea and to report on how well it worked."

Without tight, managed linkages, neither EAI nor anyone else could constructively comment on how much skill and behavior change had occurred. In year three, for example, some teachers still said,

Dimensions of a Balanced Vision

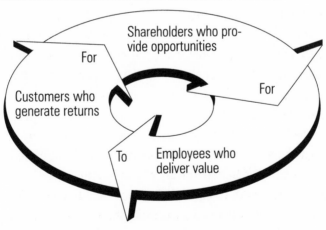

Shareholders who provide opportunities

For

Customers who generate returns

For

To Employees who deliver value

Leadership ensures balance and focus

"EAI's training is insulting and useless," whereas others maintained, "I am a better teacher today." Having failed to establish and sustain performance that would benefit teachers as a goal of its vision, EAI had no objective proof that either comment was correct.

▶ *Distinguish between behavior-driven and non-behavior-driven initiatives.* People who do not see the difference between non-behavior-driven and behavior-driven initiatives will mismanage change. EAI never developed strategies for its behavior-driven initiatives. None of the company's tactics aimed to build the kind of experience-based trial and repurchase curve that marks an increasing number of adults taking responsibility for their own behavior change. Instead, EAI assumed that decisions and awareness were enough.

EAI's version of awareness building relied heavily on classroom instruction of teachers and parents. The training was useful, but studies have shown that unless adults take action on new concepts within a week of hearing them, no real learning happens. "Use it or lose it" is a piece of common sense that must be commonly applied during the period of change. Without a managerial approach calling for personal performance commitments and follow-up, EAI appeared to naively equate instruction with results.

Moreover, notwithstanding its student-centered philosophy, EAI approached adult instruction from the company's, not the adults', point of view. Not until year three did EAI encourage teachers to set the agenda for their Wednesday afternoon development sessions, thereby belatedly gaining the benefit of a just-in-time approach. Even then, as noted above, EAI had yet to link the Wednesday afternoon sessions with specific follow-up and performance outcomes in classrooms. The difference between EAI's "talk" (student centered) and its "walk" (EAI centered) made itself felt. Said one teacher, "When EAI came in, it was like a takeover, a hatchet job. They just didn't take the time or have the patience to understand and prepare people. Instead, they just said to us, 'You *must* teach this way!'" EAI could not have intended this dispiriting impression. Their failure to manage change, however, created it.

▶ *Concentrate cross-boundary initiatives on work.* The quicker that managers guide cross-boundary initiatives away from decisions and decision-making authority to *how people do work,* the better. EAI's mainstreaming initiative, for example, sought to eliminate the boundary between regular and special education. On the whole, it made sense. Baltimore has twice as many students classified "special ed" as the Maryland state average; many would benefit from regular classroom instruction. *But not all.*

EAI did not aggressively take a leadership role in getting parents (many of whom had struggled for years to get their children classified "special") and teachers (who faced the daunting challenge of maintaining discipline among children who viewed each other as different) to focus on the *work* of mainstreaming. Had they focused on work, EAI, teachers, and parents would have discovered through experience which children could be mainstreamed and which could not. Instead, debate continued for a long time over decisions instead of work and performance outcomes. And because EAI was perceived as strident in its position, the question of its profit motive was raised unfairly.

▶ *Recognize that leaders, too, may need to learn new skills and behaviors.* Visionaries are not immune from behavior and skill change. Leaders should not assume that direction setting is their sole challenge. Indeed, as we will discuss in Chapter Eleven, the personal actions of leaders—including the courage to take responsibility for their own behavior and skill change—put a stamp on their vision of what, why, and how. Three years of the Baltimore experiment suggested at least the following behavior and skill challenges for EAI's own executives and employees: communicating and leading in an urban setting; learning the discipline of team performance; working with unions; and managing broad-based behavior-driven change.

▶ *Pace change by operating at, but not beyond, the organization's capacity to learn.* People do have limits. To keep your vision of *how* credible, you must find and respect them. Keep in mind that successful performance and change increases the energy and capacity for further change. Do not, as EAI did, throw everything at people all at once. Give them a chance to take responsibility for change. Leaders who do not pace initiatives find that pacing happens anyway. But instead of reflecting the choices of leaders, the rate of change mirrors the uncoordinated and random limits of exhausted and anxious people.

▶ *Communicating the vision of* how *to the "we" who will make it happen.* Leaders must communicate, communicate, communicate. Transformational leaders are like actors and teachers. They repeat their lines to any audience they can find; they interpret their vision for any who will listen. In the past several years, many leaders have learned to communicate the what and why parts of vision. But they must also communicate their vision of *how.*

Only in year three, for example, did EAI executives begin actively to reach out to the local communities surrounding the nine schools. Before then, they maintained, "we wished to let our results speak for themselves." Most people, however, are not stoics. They want to *hear* from those who would lead them. They want leaders to spend time helping them understand how change can happen.

Moreover, they want to hear from leaders who are guided by a philosophy of both/and and "we" instead of either/or and we/they. Leaders must always look for readiness and never give up on people as resistors. It is far more important to get people to participate in the experience of change than to win a debate over the terms of their participation.

EAI confronted a much more difficult behavior-driven challenge than most private-sector businesses. Because education is an essential, much discussed, and much debated government service, Baltimore's decision had to involve politics and the media. EAI could expect controversy and publicity—which was all the more reason the company should have seized the high ground of both/and and "we." Unfortunately, EAI soon betrayed an either/or, we/they attitude. At the time of signing the contract, for example, EAI indicated that the paraprofessional teacher's aides in the nine schools would have a role. Within a few months, EAI changed the rules. Instead of finding a way for a key constituency to become part of the "we" making education work in Baltimore, EAI chose to exclude "them" and hire only new instructional interns to team up with teachers in the classrooms.

That we/they tactic backfired. Many paraprofessionals were longstanding members of local communities. When they cried "foul," as one observer notes, "it poisoned the atmosphere." The teacher's aides were also part of the union and, before the first school year was finished, the union was actively opposing EAI. Finally, even by year three, EAI had yet to figure out how best to hire, train, support, and retain instructional interns. Varying quality, attitude, and turnover among the interns plagued the many aspects of EAI's program—increased class size, mainstreaming, integrated curriculum, computers—that depended on two adults in the classroom. Because paraprofessionals earned $11 an hour versus $8 for instructional interns, the profit motive also got mixed up in the controversy.

THE LANGUAGE OF CHANGE: MAKING ASSETS OUT OF MEANING

"By the way," said Mrs. Whatsit, the weird visitor about to leave the Murry house in Madeleine L'Engle's children's story *A Wrinkle In Time*, "there is such a thing as a tesseract." Mrs. Whatsit appears first as tramp, then goddess to help Meg Murry, a young girl who doesn't fit in at school, find her missing father and, in the process, find herself. Tesseract is defined by Mrs. Whatsit as "a fifth-dimensional corridor leading to destinations otherwise beyond reach." Meg's father managed to "tesser" his way to the fifth dimension, but could not get back. By the time Meg, her brother, and her friend retrieve Mr. Murry, all have learned that each individual has a unique set of gifts and talents. No one should be expected to advance through life—or school—in quite the same way as anyone else.

EAI adopted "Tesseract" in the mid-1980s as the name for its child-centered education philosophy. Over the years, people at EAI have developed an entire language of intellectual, emotional, and experiential meanings attached to Tesseract—more, indeed, than even Mrs.

Whatsit imagined. Whole language, whole math, integrated curriculum, computer-based learning, mainstreaming, relationship building, self-esteem, problem-solving skills, personal education plans, instructional interns—all are part of what Tesseract means to EAI. In bringing Tesseract to Baltimore, however, EAI's challenge was not to carry on a conversation with itself. Rather, it had to open up that "fifth-dimensional corridor" to thousands of parents, students, and professionals so that they too could understand, develop, apply—even grow—the number of meanings that would help "nurture the gifts and talents of each child."

EAI's goal should have been to make assets out of the meanings of Tesseract through the slow, sure, and steady growth of a language of change. That "Tesseract" is an odd word is irrelevant. Motorola employees, for example, have transformed the equally mysterious statistical concept Six Sigma into a variety of meanings used to deliver customer satisfaction and continuous improvement every day. Six Sigma became a tremendously valuable asset to Motorola. So did performance quality at Dun & Bradstreet, zebra at Kodak's Black & White, and customer at the Minnesota Department of Administration.

But meanings do not become assets without hard work and managerial judgment. Leaders must prepare themselves for a struggle when they inject new words into organizations. New concepts trigger several reactions. Some people see the possibilities intended in the new words and seize the chance for change. Others, out of reluctance, wait on the sidelines, half hoping that "this too shall pass." Still others, perceiving top management's enthusiasm for new labels, rush to get preexisting agendas approved—sometimes appropriately, sometimes not. Ask yourself, for example, how many old habits and meanings currently parade under the banner of "reengineering," "quality" or "teams"?

Managers must steer a middle course between political correctness and political babble. On the one hand, leaders should avoid becoming language cops so insistent on word usage that people worry more about saying the right thing than meaning the best thing. Top executives in some organizations, for example, have policed the total quality language of Baldrige so punishingly that people jokingly refer to TQM as "totalitarian quality management."

On the other hand, a word cannot mean everything and something at the same time. Consider "reengineering." At one company I know, people have used reengineering to describe each of the following: downsizing, customer service, delayering, innovation, continuous improvement, total quality, reorganization, teams, benchmarking, empowerment, strategy, change—and reengineering. Instead of an asset, "reengineering" is a bankrupt concept at this company.

Reengineering concerns the radical improvement of business processes spanning all or major parts of an organization. Some people argue that no more than a handful of core processes such as new product development, order generation through fulfillment, and integrated logistics are properly the province of reengineering. Others say the number of processes range between fifteen and sixty. Either way, reengineering is about dramatically altering the major processes of an organization.

By contrast, total quality and continuous improvement concern themselves with improving performance in smaller chunks. When you think about it, a process is any combination of two or more tasks toward the same outcome. A flight attendant, for example, goes through several tasks to complete the process of demonstrating the safety features of an airplane. Viewed this way, as the illustration on page 252 shows, thousands of processes are contained within or across jobs or departments within organizations. But only a small number cross functions or span the entire enterprise.

Processes to the left of the double bar in the illustration are the bailiwick of total quality; those to the right, reengineering. As the stories of Dun & Bradstreet (total quality) and BAI (reengineering) indicate, knowing which side you are on makes a difference to the managerial approach you should take. Reengineering initiatives, for example, are far more likely to move across multiple organization boundaries than total quality or continuous improvement and, therefore, possibly demand (as in BAI) a more deliberate approach to coordination and control.

Such distinctions, then, matter a lot. You can make new words play a more meaningful role in your vision of *how* by doing the following:

▶ *Let performance, not false morality, drive the distinctions in meaning that you need.* Meaningful distinctions in language guide people to make choices about when and what to do versus when and what not to do. The from/to nature of most discussions about change *begins* to make important distinctions. Tandem, for example, sought to move from selling products alone to selling capabilities. Although it would take time for people at Tandem to understand what selling capabilities meant, they could make progress by distinguishing between the performance requirements and impacts of "product selling" versus "capability selling."

Making Sense of "Reengineering"

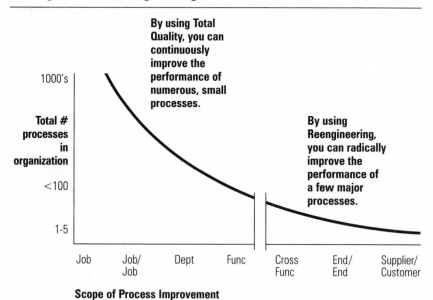

Scope of Process Improvement

Unfortunately, the from/to construct often combines with human nature to foster a false "good" versus "bad" morality with new words. This quickly gives way to either/or thinking at odds with performance and change. Don't let this happen. At Tandem, it should not be morally wrong to sell products; the company is, after all, a computer manufacturer. Instead, the challenge is to find a role for products in "capability selling." Similarly, too many people assume that teams are "good" and nonteams are "bad." Or hierarchy is "bad" and nonhierarchy is "good." But teams, nonteams, hierarchy, and nonhierarchy can each add value—depending on the performance challenge.

People who walk down the good/bad path avoid the responsibility to mean something productive when they use new language. When only "teams" are "good," everyone feels pressured to be part of a "team." People fail to learn much of anything new; "team" becomes no more than a new label for old arrangements. By contrast, people who focus on performance distinctions learn to differentiate between the team versus working group disciplines that Jon Katzenbach and I described in *The Wisdom of Teams*. If performance is achievable through the sum of individual contributions, a working group approach makes sense. If something more is needed, then the team discipline applies. The only "bad" choice we identified was to remain a pseudoteam—a group holding itself out as a team when in fact its members are not trying to apply any meaningful performance discipline at all.

▶ **Listen to the words and meanings people use.** Language is a collaborative activity. Meaning arises as much from what listeners hear as what speakers intend to say. Too many managers act as though language were more of a one-way phenomenon. Many also mistakenly reserve for themselves the right to coin new language and, thereby, miss the chance to discover powerful meanings that other people use. By contrast, leaders who listen closely to how words and phrases are being used in the organization can find rich meanings at work among people who are taking responsibility for change. At Magma Metals, for example, frontline employees described managers who delivered empty, useless directions as "visiposturing." Once this was known, everyone at Magma—union or nonunion, salaried or hourly employee —wanted to learn how to avoid doing it.

There is an additional objective to listening carefully: it helps you discover which words and meanings have become assets. Language and meaning are unpredictable. You cannot expect every special word or insight to take hold in the organization. Some will, some won't, and some, as mentioned above, will be added unexpectedly. Moreover, some will take on power and breadth that you never anticipated. Performance quality, for example, is far more central to Dun & Bradstreet's vision than originally expected. With purpose and performance as your guide, you want to listen hard. When you do hear those very special words, make sure you treat them with respect. They are, after all, vehicles that can carry you and the people of your organization through the period of change.

▶ *Pace the development of a language of change.* Single words do not become meaningful to adults overnight. Nor does an entire language of change develop instantly. Both take time. Just because one set of adults—people we call "experts"—have been through the period required to develop meaning for themselves does not preclude the need for other adults to have the same chance for experience, reflection, and insight.

Too many experts forget this sobering reality. Perhaps the best current example is the Baldrige. The Malcolm Baldrige National Quality Award has spawned a powerful and complex management framework that has quality at its core. That framework, however, is impenetrable to anybody unwilling to spend a tremendous amount of time and attention learning the language that explains it.

The complexity of Baldrige courts disaster among leaders who do not know how to manage broad-based behavior-driven change. Many leaders force their organizations through cram courses that, because they cannot possibly support the evolution of meaning at a human pace, cause people to worry more about jargon than either meaning or performance. Before long, people are pursuing change for the sake of change. Leaders must recognize that making the hundreds of established words within Baldrige into meaningful assets is extremely expensive and must be tied to purpose, performance, and change carefully. If they succeed, terrific! But, if unwisely managed, tens of millions of dollars will be spent before returns, if any, are reaped.

▶ ***Ensure that your personal actions build the meanings you seek to foster.*** Nothing vitiates the meaning of a new word or concept more quickly than leaders who do not "walk the talk." Most leaders understand this; few intentionally mislead people about meaning. Instead, a more difficult phenomenon is at work: very often, leaders themselves are just learning the meanings of new words and concepts. The challenge, then, is to put yourself as leader into a learning context. You must build in the experiences, discussions, and collective, self-conscious reflection that sustain the development of meaning for yourself as well as others. When Terry Murphy and others at Tandem, for example, led discussions aimed at locating the role of products in selling Tandem's capabilities, they went a long way toward building meanings that would make a difference for everyone.

Throughout the first three years in Baltimore, EAI worried more about definitions than meanings. Their approach to teacher training, for example, was a familiar one to most of us—sit in classrooms and listen to experts define words, and then go home and study them. That approach can work when the new concepts are strictly technical. The teachers, for example, could use classroom instruction and home study to learn about the computer hardware and software being placed in their classrooms. By contrast, teachers had to *experience* the words and concepts shaping the more important part of Tesseract. Hearing definitions of whole math, whole language, mainstreaming, integrated curriculum, problem-solving skills, and personal education plans would not suffice. As one frustrated teacher put it midway through year number two, "EAI told us to make the classroom exciting. But they didn't tell us *how.*"

Conclusion: Create a Vision of *How*

Like most leaders who aspire to visions of what and why, the people of EAI are committed to "finding and nurturing the gifts and talents of each child." Top management commitment, however, is not enough. Considering that learning was their business and being student centered was their vision, EAI's leaders should have been very good at managing the scarce resources of energy and meaning. They weren't. Instead, by applying traditional performance-only managerial practices, EAI violated every principle and possible strategy for managing performance and change.

They destroyed energy instead of creating it, they failed to focus energy that did emerge, and they created discord and exhaustion instead of harmony and capacity for change. They also fumbled away many chances to have Tesseract mean things that would enhance education. Worse still, they unintentionally fostered negative, adverse meanings that equated Tesseract with a profit motive that people did not trust. As one principal put it, "I just always felt they had a hidden agenda."

Without creating and improvising a vision of how teachers, para-professionals, instructional interns, parents, and EAI employees and partners could get through the period of change, EAI unintentionally made change more difficult, controversial, and unproductive than needed. What followed was three years of adults learning the hard way about performance and change.

Lessons, however, did emerge. By the end of year three, for example, EAI leaders were less arrogant. They began reaching out to teachers, adults, and other parents more as partners than as obstacles to change. They asked teachers to set the learning agenda for themselves. And, under the direction of Baltimore's mayor, EAI set about reconstructing its contract to focus more on performance results and outcomes.

One EAI executive said with resolve, "We can no longer be passive. It takes an entire village to raise a child. We must do a better job of preparing leadership and then hire, assess achievement, and demand accountability for success." The question, however, still remained: *How* would EAI do this? How would the company enlist a critical mass of people who mattered to take responsibility for making the Tesseract program work in the nine schools?

Much of the answer could be found in not repeating yet one more lesson learned in Baltimore. "We've missed," the EAI executive lamented, "the human piece."

Chapter Ten

Reconnecting Organization Designs to People, Performance, and Work

A picture *can* be worth a thousand words. New organization designs can portray powerful visions to guide people to work together in new ways needed to deliver performance and change. But design debates can also bewitch organizations. Too often, attachments to the classic hierarchy, overestimations of the power of decisions to cause change, and tendencies to get stuck in struggles for personal power contribute to an evil spell that dissipates energy and demoralizes people while producing, at best, the illusion of change. Therefore, you must attend to both the rewards and the risks in choosing to employ new designs if you hope to use pictures as visions that help people *see*.

Start by recognizing that, even when a new organization design might be constructive, it is only one of many initiatives needed to transform an enterprise. That role is more modest than the one design has traditionally played. Classic organization theory and practice is built on the "performance/conduct/design" model. In it, performance is determined by organization conduct which, in turn, is determined by organization design. Improvements in performance, then, entirely depend on shifts in design, as follows: DESIGN→

CONDUCT→ PERFORMANCE. This model, however, contemplates performance-only challenges concerned with such shareholder considerations as financial and market results. It also assumes that existing people are already capable and only need pointing in the right direction. And it suggests Pavlovian, mechanistic efficiency. Press any given design lever and expect the appropriate response. Because of its simplicity and power, this model supported the "structure follows strategy" mantra that guided senior executives for decades.

If, however, your organization faces performance challenges that depend on many existing people who are not already capable, the performance/conduct/design paradigm breaks down. In its place, you need to consider a more relevant approach: performance/purpose/behavior/initiatives. The illustration on pages 262 and 263 captures this people and performance driven model, along with a number of the most critical frameworks discussed in this book. Here performance is multidimensional. All key constituencies must benefit from your choice of specific performance goals that reflect the both/and challenges at hand. Moreover, do not act as though existing people have the needed competencies. Instead, you must identify whose behaviors and disciplines need to shift, articulate the from/to character of those changes, and assess the sources of readiness and reluctance among people throughout the organization. Finally, you must combine inspirational purpose (a vision of what and why) with a set of behavior-driven and non-behavior-driven initiatives (a vision of how) to make both performance and change happen.

In this approach, a design shift is only one of many choices available for leading change, not *the* choice. Moreover, if a new design itself depends on broad-based behavior change, you cannot assume Pavlovian responsiveness. Instead, you must use the new management principles and strategies necessary to enlist people into a "we" who will make the new design a reality.

This chapter explores both the promise and the pitfalls of considering organization design changes. The following basic beliefs underpin the discussion:

1. *Performance is the primary objective of design changes.* The expanding universe of performance challenges has enlarged the design choices available to you. The emergence of the team as an alternative to the classic working group of individuals offers a powerful choice. The new option of organizing horizontally instead of vertically can enable enterprises to become continuously better at process instead of function. But any design choice—individual, team, function, process, periodic, continuous, centralized, decentralized, structural, nonstructural—makes sense only if it contributes to performance. Different performance requirements in the same enterprise can require organizing some people around function and others around process; some people in teams, others in working groups. You must cobble together whatever both/and hybrid design will get the job done.

2. *Organization designs should concentrate on work.* You already know that everyone in winning organizations must both think and do. For example, superior designs integrate thinking and doing through, among other things, information and communications technology that informs and enables people. By contrast, designs that rigidly divide decision making from work fail to capture the day. Also, efforts that become struggles over authority risk ignoring the more pressing part of change: how will people do *work*? This does not mean that functional organizations are dead. If performance depends more on becoming continuously better at function instead of process, then functional designs make sense. But to make a contribution to performance results, functional designs too must concentrate on how people do work, not just make decisions.

3. *Organization designs should encompass all of the people whose performance and change matters.* Too often, management restricts design shifts to itself. For 90 percent of the people, the only change is in the boss's name or scope of responsibility. Modifications in compensation systems are the major exception; but even they tend to focus more on sales people than anyone else. This diet is too thin for broad-based behavior-driven challenges. If you hope to use design to provide a vision of how people can work together in new ways, you must paint that picture for all the people who matter.

4. *What gets measured gets done.* Broadly interpreted, measurement includes all nonstructural design considerations such as budgeting, planning, compensation, career paths, information systems, and operating reviews. Because they are nonstructural, each has more flexibility than big-picture organization designs. Yes, completely modifying the budgeting and planning system for a major enterprise is a huge undertaking. But you do not have to swim so deep to test those waters. Modest, informal, paper-based, "best you can do" approaches are always at hand for people who wish to measure and review the progress of individuals facing specific performance-and-change challenges.

5. *Alignment among multiple organization design elements can never fully precede change.* The 7S Model of organizations* correctly identifies strategy, skills, shared values, structure, systems, staff, and style as among the critical elements in any complete organization design. In addition, organizations that have all such elements in alignment are very good at delivering performance in the manner desired. That kind of alignment, however, emerges only after years of refining the organization's purpose and performance aspirations. By contrast, it is impossible to align the elements of organization design at the beginning of a period of behavior-driven change. No one, not even the leaders, knows enough. Too many variables depend on experiencing change. It is illusory, therefore, to pursue alignment first. People who do so condemn themselves to an endless round of debate over something they can never achieve. They unintentionally use design to defer the period of change instead of catalyzing it.

THE PERFORMANCE CHOICES BEHIND THE PICTURE

Countless studies have shown that the majority of people's daily communications and interactions happen within, not across, the structural boundaries of an organization. The pictorial part of vision speaks to this phenomenon. It is *structural.* Unlike visionary words that convey limitless possibilities (e.g., "boundarylessness"), visionary pictures must include lines and patterns to make any sense. They must

*See footnote on page 207

Performance ## Purpose

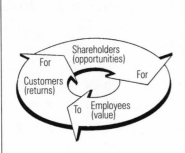

Translating broad purpose into specific goals

Vision of what and why that is:

- Simple
- Rational
- Inspirational
- Performance Driven
- Meaningful
- Inclusive

Behavior ◄► Initiatives

Which discipline?

	Function	Process
Team		
Individual/ working group		

Job Analysis	From	To
Time		
Objectives		
Skills		
Style		
Relationships		
Success Criteria		

Wheel of Change

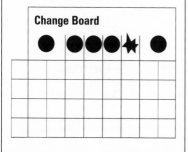

Change Board

Vision of "How"

Top down

Cross Boundary → ← Cross Boundary

Bottom up

For each initiative:
- Behavior-driven?
- If yes, what strategy for this curve, i.e. increasing number of people taking charge of change

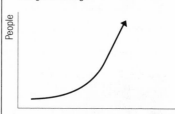

People / Time

Design: Which one?

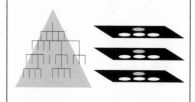

depict something meaningful to people about the boundaries within which they will spend most of their time and effort.

Indeed, the adverse consequences created by structural choices explains the need for verbal aspirations like "boundarylessness." But boundaries are also good. Consider the learning curve. Ever since the 1920s, we have understood that the more often people do the same thing, the better they become at it. And, as mentioned above, the structural boundaries in organizations determine what things people do repeatedly—that is, what they will become very good at. Therefore, if you wish to use pictures to communicate vision, you must decide what you believe the people in your organization ought to become *continuously* better at doing.

Think of a particular organization performance challenge you face as you look over the designs shown in the illustrations on page 266. Each picture communicates a vision with key skill and behavior messages. All are concerned with how best to structurally divide up and reintegrate work across an organization. Which makes the most sense for your performance challenge?

The vertical organization's classic hierarchy is suited to functionally driven, performance-only challenges. It is not likely to require behavior change because most existing employees already know it well. Work is divided into functions, then departments, then tasks. The chain of command goes up the function; the primary building block of performance is the individual; and, the manager's task is matching the right individuals with the right jobs and then measuring, evaluating, controlling, and rewarding individual performance.

When performance goes awry in vertical organizations, managers can turn to familiar considerations for help:

1. Whether to organize by product, customer, or geography
2. Which functional resources to centralize or decentralize
3. What committees and/or forums to use to integrate across functions or units
4. How to optimize the roles of line versus staff

5. How many levels and what spans of control to use to coordinate tasks and departments

6. How to align individual roles, responsibilities, and accountabilities with functional and/or organization-wide performance objectives

7. How best to plan, budget, review, measure, and reward individual, department, function, and business unit performance

Unfortunately, the vertical organization structure carries a lot of behavioral baggage, including the tendency to ignore the customer. And it bears the highest risk of focusing on decision-making authority instead of work. Many executives have inverted the implied pyramid in vertical organization to communicate their vision of leaders who serve people at the front lines who serve customers (see the inverted pyramid illustration). Otherwise, the inverted pyramid adds little. The work of middle managers and a focus on function remain unchanged. So does the assumption that the individual working in a department is the primary building block of performance.

The team-based organization's circles also suggest that leaders should serve. That structure stresses open communications and collaboration, and it humanizes the organization by eliminating the number and pictorial importance of levels. The team-based organization introduces team performance as an alternative to the individual within a traditional working group. The customer, however, does not appear in the illustration. Moreover, it remains unclear whether functional or process excellence matters most.

The illustration of the horizontal organization presents the richest contrast to that of the vertical. It stresses external and internal customers over bosses, suggests that only work that adds value to customers is critical, demands that everyone think and do, and emphasizes whole process performance, communications, and collaboration. In it, teams as opposed to working groups constitute the primary unit of performance.

Taken as a set, the most critical performance-driven distinctions that emerge from the illustrations operate at two levels. First, the big picture turns on whether your performance challenge requires people

Basic Design Choices

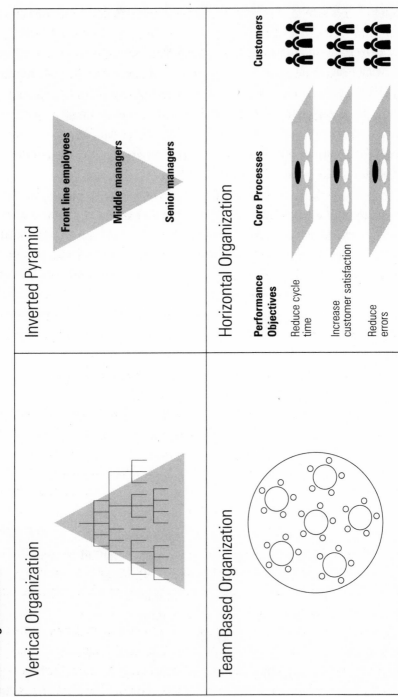

to learn more from the multiple repetition of tasks (function) or the multiple repetition of *coordination* across tasks (process). With the boundaries drawn around that choice, you can, of course, use visionary words and actions (e.g., "boundarylessness") to adjust against inflexibility. And you can use nonstructural design elements (planning, budgeting, reviewing, compensation, and so on) to the same purpose. But your big picture must answer this: *Does performance depend more on getting continuously better at functional excellence or process excellence?*

Second, at the small-picture level, the central question is, when does the primary unit of performance require the individual accountability of traditional working groups versus the individual and mutual accountability of teams? By combining the performance agenda behind the big and the small pictures, your design choices become clear (see the diagram on page 268). For any major challenge and its constituent parts, when and why should you use working groups versus teams to become continuously better at functional versus process excellence?

Three implications should guide how you respond:

♦ *Both/and mix.* Because most organizations face a variety of performance challenges, they should use hybrid designs that reflect *both* function *and* process, *both* working groups *and* teams. The need to become continuously better at customer satisfaction, for example, caused Ford Motor Company's Customer Service Division to organize most of its people around process. But the division's need to continuously improve functional excellence in employee relations and control left the people doing those jobs in a functional arrangement. Moreover, depending on the specific small group performance goal at hand, people within Ford's Customer Service Division might be part of working groups or teams.

The both/and character of design also varies at different levels of organizations, much like a layer cake. Kodak, for example, chose to organize worldwide manufacturing functionally both at the top level and the level below (e.g., black-and-white versus color film). Yet, at the next level down, the leaders of the Black & White manufacturing unit believed their fifteen hundred people needed to become continuously better at coordinating across process. They organized Black & White into a horizontal "flow" with subsidiary "streams."

▶ *Reengineering versus reorganization.* Your organization design choices must reflect the source of *continuous* improvement to performance. BAI, for example, achieved significant performance gains by fundamentally reengineering its retail banking processes. Once those were in place, however, the bank chose to organize around function instead of process. Wireboard, by contrast, chose both to reengineer its manufacturing plants and to reorganize around process.

Big Picture/Small Picture Choices

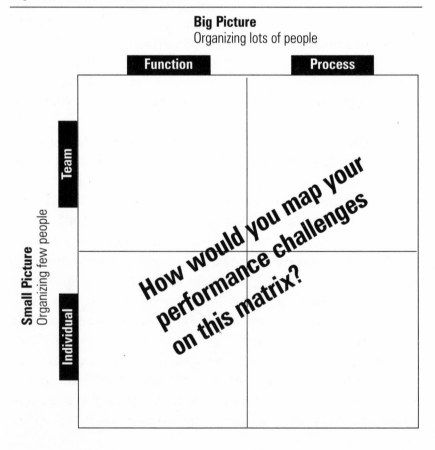

Reengineering, then, helps you fundamentally reconfigure work, whereas reorganizing helps you decide how best to array people so that they become continuously better at that work.

▸ *Behavior change implications.* Organizing around process and teams is more likely than using functions and working groups to require new behaviors and skills from existing employees. Indeed, that explains the increasing use of the horizontal organization and teams as visions for how organizations can meet challenging new performance aspirations. Such new designs, however, represent behavior-driven change initiatives. If you choose them, you must develop a set of strategies for ensuring that people take responsibility for making them work.

TEAMS AND WORKING GROUPS

How should individuals in small groups organize to deliver performance? Part of the command-and-control legacy includes our deep-seated belief that there is only one answer. Regardless of level or function, most of us assume that the primary unit of organization performance is the individual contributing to a hierarchically structured working group. Today, however, there is an alternative: the team (see the graph on page 270). As always, performance should guide your choice.

If a group can achieve its goals through the sum of individual contributions, then the traditional working group makes sense. As the team performance curve indicates, working groups have a range of effectiveness. The discipline that determines the difference in performance, however, is well known. No significant skill or behavior change is needed.

Effective working groups benefit from clear purposes and goals. People share information and insights to ensure that good decisions are made; practice teamwork to help each other do their jobs; and work hard to reinforce each other's performance ethic. Moreover, whether they are CEOs, executive directors, senior vice presidents, middle managers, or supervisors, effective working group leaders manage people in time-honored fashion. The boss sets direction, purpose, and goals; delegates individual responsibilities; and monitors performance. Good working group leaders listen carefully, of course. They seek opportunities for people to grow and encourage teamwork values. But effective working group leaders ensure that they as the boss are in control. And their primary focus for control is always individual performance and accountability.

If, however, a performance goal requires more than the sum of individual contributions, the working group approach falls short. A team is needed to deliver collective work products and real-time integration of multiple skills, perspectives, and experiences. "Collective work products" include any important contribution of two or more people working together. "Real time" means beyond and between meetings where things are reviewed, discussed, decided, and delegated.

At the heart of the team choice lies the need for mutual accountability in addition to individual accountability. With mutual accountability, however, comes risk. To deliver team performance, people

The Team Performance Curve

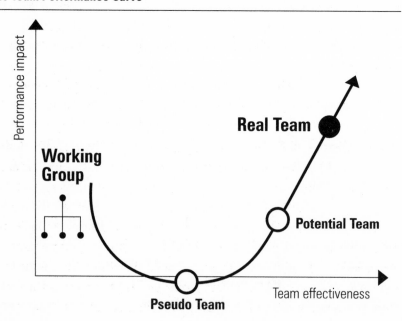

must take chances on constructive conflict, hard work, interd
dence, and trust. As discussed in the Magma Metals story in Chapter
Seven, that demands much more than initial feelings of respect and
promises. It calls for applying the discipline that determines real
team levels of performance: a small number of people with complementary skills who are mutually committed to a common purpose, a
common set of performance goals, and a commonly agreed upon working approach.

For many existing employees, the skills, behaviors, and working
relationships required by this discipline are new. How well they learn
them determines whether they deliver real team performance or
make less effective contributions. For example, as the team performance curve illustrates, small groups that choose the team approach
and are trying to apply the discipline but have yet to succeed are
potential teams. Those that are not even trying, notwithstanding a
declared choice for "team," are pseudoteams that should be disbanded.

Unlike most working group leaders, many team leaders must learn
new skills and behaviors. Their challenge is to ensure that the team, not
the leader, is ultimately in control. This demands balancing action and
patience in moving teams up the performance curve. Team leaders who
succeed believe in the team's purpose and people; continually build
the commitment, confidence, and skills of the team; keep the team's
purpose, goals, and approach fresh and relevant; manage key relationships with people beyond the team; and—like everyone else on the
team—do real work. When a team is in control, leadership is inevitably
shared—something that effective working groups never require.

Any small group of people can apply the team discipline to deliver
performance regardless of the organizational culture and arrangements that surround them. Indeed, the power of the discipline
explains why teams are the best single vehicle to deliver both performance and change as well as why a single team can often drive change
without the overhead associated with a major reorganization.
However, you need to distinguish between the case of the single team
versus many teams. If your organization vision requires the latter,
then you need to develop a strategy for change that will continually

increase the number of small groups of people who are taking responsibility for learning the discipline of team performance. Don't leave it to chance.

THE HORIZONTAL ORGANIZATION

If the illustration of the horizontal organization on page 266 best captures your particular performance challenge, then you must apply design considerations that differ from those of the vertical organization. In recent years, a dozen rules have emerged as most useful:

1. *Organize people primarily around process, not function.* First, you must use formal organization structure and boundaries to shift the focus of continuous performance improvement to processes and work flows instead of functions, departments, and tasks. You must truly *organize* around process. As described in Chapter Nine, some processes such as new product development and order generation through fulfillment might span all or nearly all of the enterprise. Or, as with Kodak's Black & White flow, the choice to organize around process might lie below a higher-order functional challenge. But if you make this choice, remember it is process, not function, that marks the boundaries in your big picture.

Many organizations have taken reengineering's cue to emphasize process performance and process ownership while remaining functionally organized. They appoint individuals or teams to be process owners, but do not reorganize to make those owners the bosses of the people doing the work of the assigned process. Instead, the people doing the work of the new process continue to report formally to functional bosses even while they are asked to take on additional process responsibilities. By failing to formally redesign organization structure, such organizations fall short if their performance really does depend more on those people getting continuously better at process than function.

2. *Use hierarchy to link work flows.* Hierarchy emerges from the division of labor. In vertical organizations, hierarchy connects business units, functions, departments, and tasks. In horizontal orga-

nizations, it links processes and work flows. If a single team can perform an entire process, no formal hierarchy is required. For example, Modicon Inc., a Daimler Benz subsidiary that makes automation-control equipment, has assigned its new product development process to a single team of fifteen people from engineering, manufacturing, marketing, sales, and finance.

The team discipline, however, usually breaks down within groups larger than fifteen to twenty people. If your process encompasses more people than that, you probably need to break up their efforts into subprocesses and tie them together through hierarchy. At Karolinska Hospital in Stockholm, for example, nurse coordinators have the hierarchical authority needed to ensure smooth handoffs across the range of work activities—both administrative and medical—that define the patient flow process.

You can keep hierarchy to a minimum by reducing the number of activity areas, or subprocesses, into which any process is divided. As a rule, the broader and more integrated the work flow assigned to a team, the greater the scope within which that team can problem-solve and innovate. The greater the scope, the fewer the number of teams needed to perform the entire process. The fewer the number of teams, the less hierarchy needed to link them together.

3. *Set and evaluate end-of-process performance goals that benefit customers, shareholders, and employees.* Typically, processes do a better job than functions of delivering results that benefit all the constituencies who matter to an enterprise: customers/beneficiaries, shareholders/funders, and employees. In setting appropriate end-of-process goals, remember that you want explicit both/and tensions that force people to continuously improve at delivering a combination of such things as yield (e.g., volume of sales, number of new products that succeed, contribution to profits), cost (e.g., unit cost or total process cost), time (e.g., cycle time or timeliness of deliveries), and quality (e.g., rate or absolute number of errors). By selecting such both/and goals, for example, the Ford Customer Service Division hoped to improve both speed and quality. By contrast, according to one senior executive, the previous functional organization did not have "a single quantifiable goal for 'fixing it right the first time.'"

Once you have set the end-of-process objectives, you can break them down into a series of specific goals that make sense for sub-processes. In this way, each subprocess team becomes an internal customer for the team before it and all teams simultaneously pay attention to the ultimate needs of the external customer.

4. *Assign ownership of processes and process performance.* Ask an individual or a team to hold themselves responsible for overall process performance. Process owners establish the overriding purpose of their process organizations as well as the tough but doable end-of-process goals that translate purpose into reality. They create processwide forums to review, revise, and syndicate purpose and performance objectives. They make sure there are explicit agreements on the handoff requirements between upstream and downstream activities. They build commitment and skills, evaluate team contributions, give people the resources and opportunities needed for success, and resolve disputes or problems that impede progress. They worry much more about their span of coordination than about their span of control. At General Electric's Medical Systems X-ray plant, for example, only one person stands between the plant manager and the 170 people on the factory floor.

Leading a process is demanding. For example, Kodak's Black & White flow leaders established the whole process purpose of becoming "Kodak's premier job shop" and "delighting customers." They set specific objectives regarding cycle time, work in process inventory, total production costs, on-time deliveries, and customer satisfaction. They endlessly communicated and celebrated process performance. And they tried anything they could think of to give people the resources and opportunities needed for success.

5. *Make teams the principal building block of performance.* More often than not, teams—not working groups of individuals—are the primary unit of performance in process organizations. Because they hold themselves mutually accountable for performance, teams are more likely to deliver the coordination required for excellent process performance. Teams also can tackle larger challenges because they bring more skills, perspectives, and direct control over tasks to on-going problem solving. Moreover, for most people, working in teams is more rewarding than working alone.

Consider, for example, General Electric's plant in Salisbury, North Carolina, which manufactures electrical products. Its people fall into two groups: self-managing teams and technical advisors. Team members are cross-trained to perform the tasks necessary to the entire manufacturing process. They measure themselves against the plant's overall goals regarding cost, quality, speed, and flexibility. They set their own performance targets and production and work schedules; make hiring and separation decisions; and hold themselves responsible for plantwide concerns such as housekeeping, safety, and communications. They *are* the plant.

6. *Push ambiguity up, not down.* The horizontal organization is not the matrix in disguise. The matrix is the vertical organization's response to complexity on its own functional terms. People are formally assigned to pay attention to more than one goal, but boundaries remain functional. By contrast, the horizontal organization concentrates on delivering continuous process improvement against externally defined objectives. The most critical difference has to do with ambiguity.

The matrix requires individuals in the middle of the enterprise to respond to multiple bosses. A mid-level marketing manager, for example, must meet the demands of a geographic general manager and a national marketing head at the same time. Direct (solid) and indirect (dotted) lines of authority are used to help, but ambiguity remains. *The subordinate—not the bosses—has the integrating responsibility.* Indeed, the performance goals of the bosses typically remain very clear—and very much in conflict. In this case, for example, the geographic head worries about geographic results and the marketing head worries about marketing results. Moreover, the matrix is focused on decision making instead of work flows. For example, that no one in Ford's functionally organized Customer Service Division had "a single quantifiable goal for 'fixing it right the first time'" is not surprising—such goals demand an orientation toward work instead of decisions.

In the horizontal organization, responsibility for resolving ambiguities rests with the process owners. For example, when American Express Financial Advisors abolished the job of sales general manager in favor of a seven-person process owner team, the company pushed the tough choices up, not down. This characteristic helps distinguish whether you are serious about setting boundaries around process. As mentioned earlier, many enterprises have assigned ad hoc responsibility for process performance to managers who otherwise do not have authority over the people doing the work. Such efforts fall short because they perpetuate the matrix's bad habit of pushing ambiguity toward the middle instead of keeping it with those having the hierarchical authority to clarify performance challenges on an ongoing basis.

7. Combine managerial and nonmanagerial activities as often as possible. Teams should aspire to be self-managing. This makes particularly good sense when teams are organized horizontally around work flows. The people who do a certain kind of work know best how to improve it. Through their experience, they have seen it all before; through their proximity, they are positioned to experiment with seeing it in new ways. As problems appear, self-managing teams can take action in real time, without interrupting critical work flows.

Self-management ranges across a wide spectrum of activities. Teams at Johnsonville Foods, for example, do their own job design, scheduling, budgeting, hiring, peer evaluation, firing, goal setting, measurement and cross-training. Indeed, the full range of possibilities explains why teams should aspire to self-management. Like any other skill and behavior challenge, learning how to do all the things listed for the Johnsonville teams takes time. But the better teams become at managing themselves, the more powerfully they contribute to the whole process.

8. Treat multiple competencies as the rule, not the exception. The greater the number of skills or competencies a person brings to a team or process, the richer the contribution to performance. By contrast, vertical organizations stress task specialization. Choosing to organize horizontally, of course, does not mean ignoring special exper-

tise. Rule 11 below suggests ways to ensure it. But in setting boundaries around process, you *are* choosing coordination over task.
Therefore, you should help people learn the multiple competencies
they need to deliver superior process performance.

The GE Salisbury plant provides an excellent illustration. To make
and deliver seventy thousand product variations, every worker on
every team in the plant knows how to operate every machine in the
plant. They also understand the purpose of each machine, the profit-
and-loss implications of its successful operation, and the interpersonal skills needed for effective plant performance. These multiple
competencies help them solve problems in real time, keep the tightly
integrated operations up and running, and respond smoothly to changing customer needs.

9. *Inform and train people on a just-in-time-to-perform basis,
not on a need-to-know basis.* Vertical organizations have traditionally used information to make decisions, not to enable people to do
their work. Concern for control caused information to be kept on a
need-to-know basis. Many of today's performance challenges, however, require leaders to give people information and support on a
need-to-perform basis. American Express Financial Advisors, for
example, give frontline sales people the continuing stream of client
satisfaction survey results needed to reach their overall process goal
of 95 percent client retention.

Similarly, Sealed Air Corporation, a maker of packaging materials,
ensures that frontline teams have the information needed to improve performance against machine downtime, zero defect, plant
safety, and other key performance measures. In addition, teams
routinely review the sources of customer satisfaction, how total
costs are determined, and how the company's strategy relates to
both. Finally, employees receive ongoing instruction in the problem-
solving techniques necessary for continuous improvement and
innovation.

10. *Maximize supplier and customer contact.* Encourage direct,
regular contact among suppliers, customers, and the people working
any process you choose to organize around. Such firsthand exposure

enhances the quality of insight and sense of participation that sustain continuous improvement. People understand their work better when they see, talk with, and get to know the people who use the products and services they create.

There are many ways to nurture such contact. Employees at one Sealed Air plant, for example, meet regularly with their major customer to discuss each other's needs. The plastics mold maker Nypro Inc. uses technology to provide its shop floor teams direct, real-time information about how teams at its customer's facility are doing on jointly agreed upon productivity, quality, and waste goals for both companies. Some parts of Motorola include supplier or customer representatives as full working members of in-house teams.

11. *Employ ad hoc forums and technology to maintain functional excellence.* Horizontal organizations are not the death knell for functional specialization and expertise. No pharmaceutical company, for example, can flourish without leading biochemists. The choice to draw boundaries around process implies emphasis, not exclusion. It also demands that you find ways to meet ongoing needs for specialization. Start by distinguishing between functional excellence and functional bias. For example, the concern among Tandem sales people that the company not abandon sales expertise in going to solution selling teams said more about reluctance than about required core competencies.

Once you have identified areas of performance-mandated specialization, you can use ad hoc forums and technology to maintain cutting-edge skills. Hallmark, for example, operates "centers of excellence" to which people return to keep up their functional skills between process assignments. McKinsey's Rapid Response Network provides a model switching mechanism that keeps dispersed specialists in touch with the most current techniques. Indeed, computer network bulletin-board technology permits specialists to leapfrog the switch and stay in direct contact with their colleagues about critical issues at all times.

12. *Reward individual skill development and team performance, not just individual performance.* Configure reward systems and career paths to reinforce the skills, values, and behaviors necessary to process performance. Pay-for-knowledge approaches compensate people for learning multiple competencies. For example, workers at General Electic's Bayamon, Puerto Rico, plant are rewarded for the number of different jobs they master as well as the communications skills and business understanding they develop. Career paths should follow a track of ever broadening roles in work flows and core processes instead of the more familiar chimney-like paths that characterize vertical organizations. Finally, as discussed above, the team discipline requires that the team, not any individual boss, be in control. Real teams inevitably learn that only the team can succeed or fail. Reward systems, then, ought to worry about team performance while leaving individual differentiation up to the team itself.

MOTOROLA GOVERNMENT ELECTRONICS GROUP: MAKING A HORIZONTAL ORGANIZATION WORK

In 1989, David Wolfe and his fellow leaders at Motorola's Government Electronics Group (GEG) confronted a familiar organization performance and design dilemma: whether to centralize or decentralize its management of purchased supplies. Such materials account for more than half of GEG's cost of doing business and determine its ability to produce hundreds of electronic products and systems for NASA, the U.S. Department of Defense, and other government and commercial customers.

At the time, GEG used a decentralized, functional, and hierarchical approach to supply management. Each of the four key departments—purchasing, supply quality assurance, reliability/components engineering, and bidding/estimating—existed at both the group and divisional levels. Seven organization levels separated the head of supply management from frontline employees. Department objectives stressed getting the lowest price and no bad parts. To meet those objectives, seven hundred people were assigned to—and measured on—a variety of individual tasks ranging from purchasing to inspection to recordkeeping.

This decentralized organization gave each GEG division what seemed like better service than they had received from previous centralized approaches. Some people became continuously better at understanding the range of materials and supplies available, others at getting the best price, and still others at policing suppliers. At the same time, however, decentralization had generated a familiar set of problems: excessive redundancy costs, poor coordination, narrow skill and career development, adversarial relations with suppliers, a lack of a shared perspective on quality, and lost opportunities for better pricing.

GEG's leaders feared that merely swinging the pendulum back to centralization would help in some areas (e.g., volume purchasing), but hurt in others (such as responsiveness to the needs of the divisions). They needed a different solution. "Everyone knew that what was happening to the defense budget would continue and even accelerate," says David Wolfe. "We had to get dramatically, not just marginally, better. But we were confusing our suppliers. One division might have a supplier on their blacklist and another handing the same supplier gold stars. And our talent was spread pretty thin. We didn't have enough technical, engineering, and quality talent to really get our suppliers up to speed on quality."

David and his colleagues expressed their vision of *what* and *why* for GEG supply management as giving all customers what they needed when they needed it at the lowest total cost. But in choosing a horizontal design, they also painted a visionary picture for how teams of people could transform the contributions of suppliers into the satisfaction of customers.

To make this picture come alive, GEG's leaders set end-of-process performance objectives that included percentage of rejects, number of corrective actions, late deliveries, and cycle time in addition to orders and price. They demanded that suppliers become partners in delivering quality, and then regularly asked suppliers a detailed series of questions to find out how good a partner and customer GEG was. Where possible, they added suppliers and customers to their teams. They eliminated four levels of hierarchy and provided the information, cross-training, and other help teams needed to develop multiple competencies and become self-managing. All the efforts paid off. In the first two years, GEG's horizontal supply organization reduced cycle times by a factor of four, increased supplier quality tenfold, and dropped head count more than 30 percent.

CONCLUSION

Visions for transforming whole organizations can include pictures as well as words. As discussed in Chapter Nine, one such picture displays a vision of how the various initiatives under way harmonize with one another to create and focus the energy needed for change. Organization designs can form yet another helpful picture—if they make boundary-setting choices, focus on work instead of decisions, avoid the illusion of alignment first, and encompass all of the people who must contribute to performance results.

Designs that favor process over function and team over working group also may require many existing people to learn new skills, behaviors, and working relationships. That certainly was the case with Motorola GEG. Accordingly, David Wolfe and his colleagues used the new management principles to shape a strategy for making their new horizontal design stick. In their case, they turned to a team (mutuality) of senior leaders who, because of complexities associated with the one-time switchover to the new approach, worked hard to come up with the new design before implementing it. Once the design was ready, the leadership team employed both mutuality and hierarchy to gain specific and personal performance commitments from an increasing number of people and teams who mattered. Most critically, as always, the leaders of the new design initiative lived the change they wished to bring about.

New organization designs are typically the unique province of those at the top. In deciding, therefore, whether to use design to paint a vision for how to transform your organization, remember that performance must be your guide. If, for example, your challenge requires new behaviors and skills from existing people, then you probably must seriously consider team- and process-based organizations. But the true test of whether you need teams and the horizontal organization is performance, not faddishness. Whatever performance requires you do in the way of design, remember that you must avoid slipping into endless debates over decision-making authority. If that is happening, you have dropped the ball. Yes, a picture can provide new vision. But only if its brush strokes—as intended and as being painted during the period of debate—reveal the future instead of the past.

Chapter Eleven

Personalizing Your Vision of Change

If you are a leader, you *will* personalize your vision of how people can get through a period of behavior-driven change. Your actions will put a subjective stamp on the organization's future. There is no escaping that. When people contemplate you as a leader, they look at every aspect of your vision. They attend to your words. They look at the pictures you draw. They listen to your strategies and initiatives. All those matter a lot. But any adult considering whether to follow you also looks closely at your personal actions. More than your words, pictures, and initiatives, your *actions* convey what you—as a person—believe and are most likely to do.

That actions speak loudest is not new. That actions are unavoidable is not discussed or reflected on as much. Everything you do or say, or don't do or don't say, constitutes action. Speeches, memos, hiring, firing, meeting agendas, interviews, customer visits, decisions, body language, dominating conversations, not dominating conversations—everything. Even inaction is action when perceived in leaders. You should not mistakenly assume, as many leaders do, that you can stand above it all and remain the objective, omniscient lawgiver that mythology and mechanistic views of organizations have ensconced as one archetype of leader. It does not work that way. Arm's-length distancing, lack of involvement, cautious action, impartiality, judiciousness, cool emotions—these and a thousand other descriptions only characterize choices that you as leader make, conscious or otherwise, about how you will act. But act you will. So, get used to this: the people in your organization will find *you* out.

All the more reason, then, to take the responsibility—and the opportunity—to find yourself out. Leaders who stop learning about themselves disappoint in all circumstances, but especially during periods of behavior-driven change. When performance depends on many people from top to bottom and all across your organization learning new skills, behaviors, and working relationships, how can you hope to lead unless you too take personal responsibility for living the change?

Given the nature of today's performance challenges, there are plenty of skills, behaviors, and working relationships that you as leader must learn to transform your organization. There are, for example, the philosophy, discipline, and techniques of total quality. Have you mastered them? Reengineering might profoundly reshape performance for those who understand what it means and how to do it. Do you? Through strategic alliances, you can avoid relentless and mutually destructive price wars from overcapacity in globalizing markets. Do you know how to make them work? When information technology is coupled with new ways of working, all key players—suppliers, customers, and employees alike—can collaborate to ensure the mass customization of speed, service, and specificity. Do you know how to lead in that world?

Do you understand the different managerial disciplines required to deliver process performance versus function performance? Team performance versus individual/working group performance? Do you understand the principles and strategies for leading behavior-driven performance and change versus performance-only challenges?

I suggest that *you* have the opportunity to grow. Do not, however, confuse taking responsibility for your own change with awkward-sounding dictates to "model leadership behaviors." People emulate leaders. They look for consistency between walk and talk. Therefore, the posture you assume at every moment will be closely scrutinized. By behaving in ways you deem important—adhering to principles and purpose, seeking innovation, active listening, investing yourself in people, remaining performance focused—you give others the courage to practice new behaviors and skills.

But you cannot be an effective role model without being yourself. You cannot wear conviction like clothes, donning costumes for different audiences and situations. Leaders who do so fool no one but themselves. Their behavioral "suits" look all too empty. That kind of modeling is an intellectually driven put-up job, a not quite human act easily perceived as false and manipulative by people who are paying attention. When people look at your actions to define vision, they peer into the whole of you: mind, heart, and gut. They are looking at your character. They are looking at whether your personal vision of how to get through a period of change includes the courage to change yourself.

THE CONSEQUENCES OF YOUR CHOICE

Whether or not you as top leader take responsibility for your own change has consequences. Before articulating them, however, let me repeat once again: too many people use the excuse of "no top management commitment" to avoid taking responsibility for their own behavior change and performance. Armed with the new principles and strategies, any individual can get through a period of change regardless of whether top management chooses to join them. Do people face constraints in the absence of top management commitment? Yes. Would the odds and rewards increase if you, as top leader, actively joined the "we" making change happen? Yes, again. But adults who wait for top management commitment reveal more about reluctance than about the full range of possibilities before them.

If you report in to top management, therefore, do not read this last chapter as an out. You have too much to gain in seizing the responsibility to perform and change. Consider the stories of Kodak's Black & White, Dun & Bradstreet, Tandem, and McKinsey. Top managers who were senior to the change leaders in those stories were not fully committed to the changes at hand. Yet in each story hundreds of people successfully navigated through a period of performance and change. Moreover, think about the story of Educational Alternatives. That company's leadership *is* entirely committed to transforming performance in public schools. They also have much to learn about managing behavior-driven change. Their commitment suggests they have the chance to do so. But top management commitment alone is not enough to ensure change.

The quality of your commitment as top leader, then, neither precludes nor guarantees that other people will take responsibility for their own best future. But all of your actions—everything you do and do not do—confront people with a choice. If your personal vision of *how* includes the conviction and courage to take charge of your own change, people have a both/and choice. They can choose *both* to follow you *and* to lead themselves and others through change. However, if your actions betray no responsibility for your own change and an indifferent commitment to living the new vision, you force people to the harsh edge of an either/or dilemma. *Either* they can take responsibility for their own change and chart a course through the inconsistencies and obstacles your actions generate, *or* they can follow you down the path of the status quo.

Taking Responsibility Through Actions That Matter to Performance

The principles for managing behavior change in others apply to you as top leader as well. Only you can take responsibility for your own behavior change. Your direct reports cannot do it for you. Nor can middle managers or people at the front lines. Or consultants, advisors, customers, suppliers, or members of your board of directors or trustees. You can ask for help and reinforcement from others. But only you can identify and work through your own readiness and reluctance related to understanding, desire, planning, action, and performance-based reinforcement.

To construct a from/to job description for yourself would take little time, for example. Or, if you prefer, you could list the skills, behaviors, and working relationships you believe most critical to learn. You could perform those or similar exercises alone or with your top management colleagues. Remember, you will do a better job if you place your personal challenge in the context of the overall vision for the organization. The list below is an agenda that you and your senior colleagues can use at an offsite session to help you discuss how and why your own behavior and skill change matters to the purpose and performance of the whole organization.

Articulating your personal from/to challenge will help, but it is not enough. You cannot take charge of your own change without risking the experience of change in a performance context that matters. Whatever offsite exercises you use—private or group reflection, from/to workshops, vision development sessions, Outward Bound bonding experiences, leadership training—your actions can build courage in yourself and others only when you take charge of change onsite.

Like anyone else, you are most likely to take responsibility for your own change if specific, personal performance consequences depend on it. Otherwise, you too can fall victim to change for the sake of change. Top leaders, however, often find it difficult to identify specific opportunities to make measurable contributions to performance. This is not

---

OFFSITE AGENDA

Day One: Morning
- ▶ Vision of What/Why

Day One: Afternoon
- ▶ Organization's "From/To" Challenge
- ▶ Change Board

Day Two: Morning
- ▶ Leadership Group's Own "From/To" Change Challenge

Day Two: Afternoon
- ▶ Vision of How

because of laziness or self-interest. Quite the contrary. Rather, the long-range and ambiguous nature of the results to which top leaders must hold themselves accountable are not easily parsed into specific, measurable, near-term, and personal contributions.

This is truer of behavior-driven challenges than traditional performance-only matters. As a top leader, for example, you are familiar with setting, measuring, and holding yourself accountable for decisions to add capacity, acquire or sell a business, modify pricing, introduce new products, alter advertising, and downsize the organization. Indeed, the power of such decisions to dramatically shift organization performance seduces many leaders into acting as if their most critical personal challenge is to make sweeping decisions. That certainly simplifies leading. But it does not get the job done when implementing any major decision depends on many existing employees learning new skills, behaviors, and working relationships.

When decisions alone are not enough, leaders have trouble linking their non-decision-making actions to performance. What personal contribution can and should you as leader make, for example, to a new strategy that depends on broad-based behavior-driven change? Once the decision is over, what can you do to make performance and change happen? Your first obligation is to understand when decisions are not enough. Beyond that, however, you must use three personal performance contexts—setting direction, communicating, and managing other leaders and the leadership agenda—to experience and live the change you hope to bring about.

TAKING RISKS IN HOW YOU SHAPE VISION AND STRATEGY

Perhaps your organization does not yet have a vision of what, why, and how. Or perhaps your current vision or strategy needs revitalizing. Your actions and choices in how to develop a new or different vision will put a personal stamp on the vision itself. Consider, for example, the three steps contained in the following popular approach:

1. You ask a small task force of senior people to recommend a vision and/or strategy (usually of what and why alone). The task force might

be your top management group, a group of high-potential employees, or a blend of the two. The task force might include consultants. The group works hard for a period of months to develop a fact-based understanding of the challenge ahead and concludes by recommending a vision and strategy.

2. You and your direct reports discuss and debate the recommended vision. You work hard to understand the reasoning and facts that lie behind the recommendations and whether you agree that they make sense. After some period, and with the approval of corporate if needed, you adopt a modified version of the vision that reflects your thinking.

3. You and your direct reports communicate the vision to the organization. If broad-based behavior change is implied by the vision, people throughout the organization take time—perhaps several months, perhaps longer—to understand the implications and to decide whether to take responsibility for making them happen.

Those actions evidence a vision of leadership that gathers advice from critical people, grounds decisions in facts, invests the time and effort commensurate with the important decision at hand, affords senior leaders the chance to understand new directions, and attends to organizationwide communications. There is nothing wrong here. Such efforts, for example, can and have produced visions of what and why that are rationally credible, emotionally purposeful, simple, meaningful, inclusive, and performance driven. Still, the approach characterizes leaders who are sequential, hierarchical, decision driven, and acting well within their comfort zone. Such leaders have not yet seized the opportunity to live the change their visions may ask others to embrace.

By contrast, consider taking more personal risk. Use visioning as a behavior-driven change initiative itself. Instead of shaping a process with the single objective of identifying the best vision and strategy for the organization, craft an approach that has two goals: *both* identifying the best vision *and* maximizing the number of people, including yourself, who emerge from the visioning process having taken responsibility for change. The following actions can help you accomplish that:

▶ *Enlist the contributions of many, not just a few.* A vision big enough to inspire a whole organization is big enough to be created by the whole organization. Therefore, instead of building vision from the contributions of a small task force followed by the senior management group, divide the challenge into several subtopics and ask multiple teams of people from throughout the organization to participate in shaping the vision from the beginning.

Work with those teams to continually increase the number of other people participating. In addition to people on the teams, for example, others might use emerging ideas even before any final vision is established. Or they might give input and reaction to the teams. Or you may discover additional opportunities for participation.

This approach demands that you and the teams work hard to develop both the best vision and the number of people participating in shaping the vision. Leaders who have followed this approach have gotten hundreds of people to take responsibility for vision even before a final vision emerges.

▶ *Ask how, not just why and what.* If the emergent vision will be behavior driven, do not wait until the conclusion of why and what to begin to shape the *how.* Specifically include the construction of a vision of *how* in the charter of the teams you enlist. Ask them to identify the words and concepts that they hope will create and focus energy and meaning. If organization design shifts appear important, ask the teams how to avoid the trap of descriptions, decisions, and alignment. Ask them to distinguish between behavior-driven initiatives and performance-only initiatives. Ask them to craft initial strategies for building the experience-based trial and repurchase curves of successful behavior-driven initiatives.

▶ *Demand that people wear two hats, not just one.* Make sure that every person in the visioning process wears at least two hats: their own and yours. In wearing their own hat, everyone benefits from the wide variety of perspectives represented. In asking each person to wear the top leader's hat, people benefit from the whole-organization perspective so critical to linking purpose, performance, and change. Make the wearing of your hat more than a mere notion.

Do not, for example, let teams avoid choosing a direction or fully exploring implications because of narrow perspective or timidity. Force them to make hard choices if they are required, or to find both/and solutions if hard choices can be deferred or avoided. Help them to help you—both during and beyond the visioning phase—by experiencing the kind of leadership that will carry the organization toward its best future.

▶ *Treat vision as something people live now, not just in the future.* The traditional sequential approach keeps vision in the future. Vision remains something "we talk about now, but only make happen later." You want to bring vision into the present tense. You want people to shape vision by experiencing vision. You want people to define their path ahead by walking the path itself. You can do this by asking people, "What can we do *now* to both further and better understand the aspirations we should pursue?"

The answers to this question should include performance-based actions and experimentation that go beyond customer surveys, "what if" scenarios, and other analytical exercises. If, for example, the vision will include speed, demand speed from specific people now and ask them to contribute their learning to the vision. If the vision will seek trust and partnership between your organization and certain suppliers or customers, demand that that partnering begin now. If the vision will shift working relationships within the organization from command to collaboration, then demand that shift in the very teams who are contributing to the vision, including your own. In those and other ways, you can get your organization to develop vision by living vision and to deliver visionary performance today instead of only in a tomorrow that might never arrive.

COMMUNICATING HOW TO USE THE NEW PRINCIPLES AND DISCIPLINES

Anytime you as top leader communicate with other people—whether in person or through various media, whether formally or informally—they want to understand what you see. They pay attention to whether you persistently link the issue at hand with the broader purpose and performance aspirations of the organization. They assess how well you appreciate the gap between the organization's current reality (the "from") and its best future (the "to"). And they expect you to articulate—to see—their role in helping you get from the "from" to the "to." For all these reasons, you should never stray far from the central themes and objectives in your vision of what and why. You must repeat yourself constantly. You must seize the unique circumstances in each context—who is there, what issues are in question, what progress has been made, what is left to be done—to keep the meanings within the vision fresh and vital.

People also use your communications to observe your personal vision of *how*. They hope to learn *how* you expect the organization to get through the period of change. Here you lead best by practicing the new management principles. Start by keeping performance as the primary objective. Guide people through all four levels of performance: purpose (e.g., quality), conceptual performance (e.g., no defects); metrics (e.g., defect rate), and specific goal (e.g., "reduce defect rate from 3 percent to 1 percent"). Enlist others to help you explore the both/and performance challenges ahead: periodic and continuous, money and time, qualitative and quantitative, individual and team, function and process. Demonstrate your own understanding of how all key constituencies—employees, customers/beneficiaries, shareholders/funders, and perhaps others (e.g., key suppliers or partners)—can contribute to and benefit from your vision.

Your central message ought to be "We will make the future happen today by *performing* our way through the period of change." You should always leave people—individuals, small groups, large groups, the whole organization—with a better understanding of how their specific and current performance contributions matter to the whole organization's purpose.

With performance and purpose as your constant reference, you also need to say, "We can get through the period of change by mastering many different performance disciplines because one size no longer fits every challenge." You can show them how to do this by help-

ing specific people—individuals or small or large groups—choose
among and practice the following:

1. *The discipline of individual performance and change*

▶ Does performance require this person to learn new skills,
behaviors, or working relationships?

▶ Can this person articulate to your satisfaction the from/to
changes in job objectives, use of time, key relationships, skills,
and purpose? Can you articulate the same to the person's
satisfaction?

▶ Has this person taken responsibility for his or her change?

▶ To the extent not, what explains his or her reluctance? Understanding? Desire? Minimum capability? Planning? Action?
Reinforcement?

▶ What can you do to help the person address the sources of
reluctance? How can you help the person experience the
change at hand in a performance context that matters?

▶ To the extent the person has seized change, how can you reinforce the effort? How can you help the person and yourself
learn what has worked and what has not? How can you provide
the "thank you" that will motivate further effort, learning, and
performance?

2. *The discipline of team and working group*

▶ Has this group of people used their performance goals to
choose between the working group and team disciplines?

▶ If so, have they made the best choice? Have they pursued the
working group discipline for goals they can achieve through
the sum of individual best contributions? Have they chosen
the team discipline when performance demands collective contributions from the real-time integration of multiple skills and
perspectives?

▶ If they have not made a choice, how can you help?

▶ If they have picked the working group discipline, are they performing well? Is the leader in control? Does he or she gather

input, make timely decisions, delegate individual responsibilities, monitor performance, and make adjustments? Does the leader keep people informed of the group's purpose and each individual's expected contribution? Does he or she encourage cooperation, information sharing, and the reinforcement of a strong performance ethic? What can you do to help?

▶ If they have picked the team discipline, are they performing well? Do they have a common purpose? Common goals? Commonly agreed upon working approach? The needed blend of skills? Are they small enough in number? Are they holding themselves mutually accountable? Is the team in control? What can you do to help?

3. *The discipline of process and function*

▶ Are these people doing the work of function and/or process needed to deliver performance?

▶ Can people articulate performance-driven distinctions between function and process? Do they understand the sources of functional excellence most critical to performance? The sources of process excellence? Can they distinguish bias and habit from value added?

▶ Are they delivering the functional excellence needed for performance? Process excellence? If not, why? If so, why? How can you help?

▶ Are they applying total quality disciplines to continuously improve processes and tasks that span relatively small numbers of jobs and departments?

▶ Are they applying the reengineering discipline to reconfigure work that spans an entire function, multiple functions, the organization as a whole, or suppliers, the organization, and customers?

▶ Can they distinguish the reengineering of work from the reorganization of people around work? In making organization boundary and design choices, are they looking to become continuously better at function or at process? Does their choice make sense? How can you help?

4. *The discipline of recognizing behavior-driven change*

▶ Does the group of people understand whether they face a performance-only challenge versus a behavior-driven performance-and-change challenge?

▶ Can they succeed through managing assets and policies quite apart from people?

▶ Can they deliver performance through redirecting the efforts of already capable people?

▶ Can they selectively add new people instead of getting many existing employees to learn specific new skills and behaviors?

▶ Or will implementing new decisions and directions require many existing people to learn new capabilities?

▶ Do they know whether the people who matter to performance understand the implications of the change for their own behaviors and urgently believe the time to act is now?

▶ Can they minimize the number of the existing employees who must change; the number of new skills, behaviors, and working relationships they need to master; and the extent to which they need to master such skills by collaborating in real time across functions, processes, and other organization boundaries?

▶ How can you help?

5. *The discipline of improvising strategies for behavior-driven initiatives*

▶ Has the group of people embraced the ten new management principles? Do they, for example, understand that they cannot take responsibility for another person's behavior change?

▶ Have they adopted the perspective of managers of a behavior change business like Weight Watchers?

▶ Have they used a Change Board or equivalent analysis to segment their market and understand readiness and reluctance?

▶ What strategy have they devised to build an ever increasing experience-based trial and repurchase curve? What role will awareness-building play in their strategy? Have they set specific performance goals for their initiative?

- How will they employ hierarchy ("tell") to influence the personal performance commitments of people who matter? Exchange ("trade")? Mutuality ("team")?
- What level of coordination and control, if any, does performance require?
- How will they provide just-in-time help and reinforcement?
- Are they living the change they hope to bring about?
- How can you help?

All these are phrased as questions. But you know you must blend a variety of styles in communicating. Depending on your audience and objective, you must make demands, ask questions, facilitate discussions, explain and answer, review progress, make decisions and promises, encourage and reward, identify shortfalls, and demonstrate understanding. Above all, you must tell the truth and listen. By keeping purpose, performance, and the disciplines people can use to deliver them both as your constant companions, you will help everyone see your personal vision of how to get through the period of change.

USING THE LEADERSHIP AGENDA TO CONTRIBUTE PERSONAL PERFORMANCE AND CHANGE

Organization performance now requires that everyone—including you and other top leaders—both think and do, perform and change. The choices you make for what goes on the leadership agenda, and what does not, will put your personal stamp on vision. So will your choices of who will lead, and whether and how you hold them and yourself accountable for delivering purpose, performance, and change. Through such choices, you and your colleagues must demonstrate the will to manage yourselves to the people you hope to lead through a period of behavior-driven change.

You must also use such choices to seize your own opportunities to experience the skills, behaviors, and working relationships that otherwise might remain abstractions. If you are at the top of an enterprise today, you probably suffer an unprecedented disadvantage.

Unlike top executives of ten or twenty years ago, you cannot assume that your rise to the top has given you the full array of managerial experiences needed to guide yourself and others. You cannot assume that you "have been there before." Indeed, if you do, you are likely to re-create a past that no longer works instead of a present and future that do.

Consider the traditional path to the top of the pyramid. You or your colleagues started by learning how to make the individual contributions demanded from the boss and moved on to being the boss who got things done through direct command of others. Next, you learned to get things done within areas of your functional and technical expertise indirectly through others. Having mastered that step, you then learned how to get multiple things—not all within your functional expertise—done indirectly through others. And, finally, you rose to a position that demanded attention to abstractions like vision, strategy, and organization design in addition to people. Because your managerial experiences were mostly individual, working group, function, and business unit ones, you could rightly claim to "have been there before" so long as "there" involved anyone below you in the pyramid.

The pyramid you rose through no longer exists. It may lie upside down or on its side. It is certainly squatter and flatter. It may not even be a pyramid. Where performance challenges continue to be pyramidlike—individual, working group, function—you "have been there before." But when performance itself has shifted footings, you must find new ground to stand on.

Of all the new disciplines reviewed in this book, the most critical for you to experience are those of team and process performance, behavior-driven initiatives, and individual change. If you do not, you are at great risk of confusing yourself and others. You will continue to equate team and teamwork. You will call everything a process. You will assume that a clear articulation of the what and the why of vision are enough to get people to change. Therefore, in addition to how you shape a visioning process and communicate, you can take the following steps to apply the new management principles and disciplines to yourself and your senior colleagues:

▶ *Take responsibility for behavior-driven initiatives and process ownership.* The best way to experience using the new principles and strategies is by taking direct responsibility for using them. Start by distinguishing behavior-driven from non-behavior-driven initiatives. Then give each top manager—alone or as part of a team—the opportunity to lead a single, behavior-driven initiative. Recognize the significant time and attention required and make adjustments. But also recognize the benefits of this *experience.* By directly using the new principles to shape and improvise a strategy for continually increasing the number of people taking responsibility for their own performance and change, each of you will learn how to manage change instead of only describe it.

As a top management group, take the responsibility to distinguish between reengineering a major business process and reorganizing around it. If you believe you will need to reorganize, discuss how you will avoid the trap of decision-only power struggles. Also, consider whether you will reengineer first or reorganize first. Some major business processes like integrated logistics or order generation through delivery are so complex that you should reengineer first. Others, such as the new product development process, can often be reengineered best by assigning organization ownership first. Regardless of the sequence, if you decide a significant aspect of the organization's performance depends on people becoming continuously better at process instead of function, then ask the appropriate top leaders—not middle managers or staff people—to take responsibility for process performance.

▶ *Grow leadership skill and capacity through increasing team performance at the top.* Do not either implicitly or explicitly set as your objective "becoming a team." Get beyond that motherhood trap by disciplining yourselves to deliver team performance at the top *when it is needed.* Look at the items on your leadership agenda—key customer, supplier or alliance relationships, shareholder and financial community relations, vision and strategy, developing high-potential people, leading behavior-driven and non-behavior-driven initiatives, managing and monitoring performance of businesses, functions and processes—and force yourselves to choose when the team or working group disciplines will work best.

When individual contributions make the best sense, demand them. Most top leadership groups have plenty of opportunity to deliver far more effective working group performance than they currently do. When team performance is demanded, however, then insist on using the discipline of team.

Do not, for example, equate the whole enterprise's purpose with the team's purpose. Instead, make certain the team has a concrete purpose and set of goals that it must deliver as a team. Select team members based on skill instead of assuming the whole top management group must be members of every team. If skills are needed beyond the top management group, get them. And choose team leaders based on their attitudes and beliefs instead of hierarchy or status. Even the best chief executives can learn a tremendous amount about team, leadership, and behavior change by being a team member as well as a team leader.

By holding yourselves accountable for delivering both working group and team performance, you will significantly expand the leadership capacity in the organization. First, by reaching out to others beyond the formal top management group, you increase the number of people who lead. Second, by learning that not everyone in top management must be on every team, you increase the number of team performance opportunities the top group can tackle. Third, by experiencing the team performance discipline yourselves, each of you will become more effective leaders in the eyes of other people who also are learning when and why to use the team versus working group disciplines.

▶ *Hold individual leaders accountable for their own performance and behavior change.* If you are the top leader, only you (or the board of directors or trustees) can hold yourself accountable for your own performance and change. Unless you do, you have not fully taken responsibility for living the change you wish to bring about. In addition, however, you must hold other top leaders accountable for delivering both performance and change.

No one is as dangerous to an organization going through a period of change as a high-placed, pure resistor. Indeed, one of the most common laments of chief executives who have failed or are struggling with change is that they did not act soon enough to replace top people who would not change. As you reflect on this sobering reality, remember that most senior executives, like most people, only reluctantly take responsibility for their own performance and change. You must, therefore, afford each senior person the opportunity to use performance challenges to work through understanding, desire, planning, action, and reinforcement. And you must give them the personal reinforcement they need to succeed, including joining them in a self-conscious effort to learn what works, what does not, and how to keep moving forward. Most senior executives have the minimum capability needed to learn new skills, behaviors, and working relationships. Many will succeed if they are given performance-and-experience-based opportunities to do so. But if they do not succeed, you must get them out of the way.

In holding yourself and others accountable, you demonstrate that *performance-based opportunities* for personal growth are central to your personal vision of *how* the organization can get through a period of change. By sticking with or changing top leaders, you also demonstrate that only those who take responsibility for their own change can contribute to and benefit from the organization's best future.

CONCLUSION: LEAD THE HUMAN ENTERPRISE

Leading an entire organization of people through a period of behavior-driven change is a different, more complex challenge than any of you may have expected when you aspired to reach the top rung of enterprise. Yet, as you know well, broad forces at work now confront you with the blunt reality: change or lose. Find a way to lead your people and yourself through the period of change or remain forever, unsustainably stretched between the world of the "from" and the world of the "to."

As you move forward, however, remember just how fortunate you are. The past forces at work—scale-driven mass markets, high-volume and standardized manufacturing, capital intensive plant, machinery and equipment, unskilled labor, scientific management through command and control—that condemned your grandparents and parents to toil within mechanistic organizations have died. Only the habits remain.

New powers now demand organizations to become human enterprises. And you—yes, *you*—can choose to lead that transformation. You can invite everyone in your organization to share in shaping the vision for the future. You can work every day to help people see how their own performance and change matter to the whole enterprise's purpose—to their customers, beneficiaries, funders, shareholders, alliance partners, and themselves. You can help them learn the disciplines that will sustain personal performance and change. And you can experience the same disciplines in pursuit of your own performance and change. You can give people the courage to change, grow, and perform by having the courage to live the change yourself. And yes, you too can join the "we" who are making the organization's best future happen today.

Notes

Chapter Three

Page 75.   My favorite example . . .: Ben Hamper, *Rivethead* (New York: Time Warner, 1986).

Pages 76-80. Minnesota Department of Administration: Michael Barzelay with Babak Armajani, *Breaking Through Bureaucracy* (Berkeley: University of California, 1992).

Page 81.   "By establishing our original goal . . .": Jan Carlzon, *Moments of Truth* (Cambridge: Ballinger Publishing, 1987), p. 125.

Page 82.   "If somebody can't tell me . . .": Robert Slater, *The New GE* (Homewood, Ill.: Richard D. Irwin, 1993), pp. 215–216.

Page 84.   Consider the experience of Dorothy Jacobson . . .: Robert H. Schaffer, *The Breakthrough Strategy* (Cambridge: Ballinger Publishing, 1988), pp. 157–158.

Page 99.   "By treating the line agencies as customers . . .": Barzelay with Armajani, *Breaking Through Bureaucracy*.

Chapter Four

Page 110.   "I made it a personal goal . . .": Stephen J. Frangos with Steven J. Bennett, *Team Zebra* (Vermont, Oliver Wight, 1993), p. 64.

Page 111.   "Turnaround? . . .": Frangos with Bennett, *Team Zebra*, p. 69.

Chapter Seven

Page 183.   "We were hundreds of millions . . .": unedited transcript, *The Discipline of Teams,* Harvard Business School Management Productions, 1994.

Page 184.   "Management's stated intention . . .": unedited transcript, *The Discipline of Teams.*

Page 184.   "There was guerrilla warfare . . .": unedited transcript, *The Discipline of Teams.*

Page 184.   "There was no dialogue at all . . .": unedited transcript, *The Discipline of Teams.*

Page 193.   "Each night I think about . . .": unedited transcript, *The Discipline of Teams.*

Pages 194-197.   Coordinating the Reengineering of Banca d'Italia: Hall, Rosenthal, Wade, "How to Make Reengineering Really Work," *Harvard Business Review,* November–December 1993.

Chapter Nine

Page 235.   "EAI will not have the luxury . . .": Thomas Waldron, "Every Child Is So Special," *The Baltimore Sun,* June 14, 1992.

Page 236.   "The project is in peril.": Gary Gately and Mike Bowler, "Tesseract's Tough Test," *The Baltimore Sun,* June 4, 1995.

Page 249.   "By the way . . .": Madeleine L'Engle, *A Wrinkle in Time* (New York: Dell, 1962), p. 21.

Chapter Ten

Pages 272-282.   The Horizontal Organization: adapted from Ostroff and Smith, "The Horizontal Organization," *The McKinsey Quarterly,* No. 1, 1992.

Page 274.   "a single quantifiable goal . . .": Rahul Jacob, "The Struggle to Create an Organization for the 21st Century," *Fortune,* April 3, 1995, p. 94.

Index